The
TRACKER'S
HANDBOOK

T0040114

The

TRACKER'S
HANDBOOK

How to Identify and Trail Any Animal, Anywhere

Len McDougall

Skyhorse Publishing

Skyhorse Publishing books may be purchased in bulk at special discounts for sales promotion, corporate gifts, fund-raising, or educational purposes. Special editions can also be created to specifications. For details, contact the Special Sales Department, Skyhorse Publishing, 307 West 36th Street, 11th Floor, New York, NY 10018 or info@ skyhorsepublishing.com.

www.skyhorsepublishing.com

10 9 8 7 6 5 4

Library of Congress Cataloging-in-Publication Date is available on file.

Cover design by Jane Sheppard

Print ISBN: 978-1-62914-406-1
Ebook ISBN: 978-1-63220-151-5

Printed in China

Contents

Hooved Animals

Family Cervidae

The cervids, members of the deer family, are ungulates (hooved animals) of the order Artiodactyla (hooved animals with an even number of toes). All cervids have a split hoof, which is actually a pair of modified, heavily nailed toes in front and a pair of smaller toes, called dewclaws, located slightly above them at the rear of the foot. All species leave a split, heart-shaped track, and dewclaws may print behind the hooves in softer terrain. All species are herbivores, and none have upper incisors, only a hard upper palate that enables them to tear away food plants by pinning them between incisors and the palate.

NEW WORLD MOOSE
(*Alces alces*)

The largest member of the deer family, the moose, is also native to northern Europe and Russia, where it was once known as elk. It was misnamed after explorers to the New World applied that name to the first giant deer they encountered, the wapiti. The wapiti was thereafter known as the American elk, while the true American elk became moose.

Geographic Range

Moose are found throughout the northern United States, in states bordering Canada, throughout southern Canada and into Alaska, and downward along the Rocky Mountains into Colorado.

Habitat

Moose prefer forests with plenty of water. Pines offer protection from driving winds and snow, while willows, elkslip, and aquatic browse along shorelines provide summer browse. Biting fly and mosquito hatches of spring and early summer cause moose to migrate to higher elevations where rivers and ponds are swollen with melting snow, and strong breezes keep biting insects from landing on them.

Winter browsing includes poplar, aspen, and cottonwood bark, which scars trees with identifiable sign. Moose domains typically encompass just a few square miles, and the animals move only as needed to find a location that offers protection from weather, ample food until spring, and water. Mountain moose move to protected valleys, and forest moose go to secluded beaver ponds and floodings where spring-fed inlets never freeze entirely.

Physical Characteristics

Mass: Bulls are 1,400 pounds or more at maturity; cows are roughly 10 percent smaller than bulls.

Body: Shoulder height is 5 to 6 feet; body length is 8 to 10 feet from tip of nose to tail. Moose have long legs, a thick rump, and a broad back. Bulls carry palmated antlers from spring to early winter, when old antlers that can span 4 feet across are shed and new ones begin to grow.

The moose's face is distinctive, with a long, thick muzzle, a big nose, and a large, drooping lower lip. A fold of loose skin, or dewlap, hangs beneath the jaws of mature males, growing longer as its owner ages. Large, erect ears are prominent and pointed. Moose have excellent senses of smell and hearing but nearsighted vision.

Tail: It is similar to the domestic cow, but shorter, about 8 inches long.

Tracks: Being heavy, moose leave clear tracks in all but the hardest soil. Split-heart hoof prints are similar to

This 3-year-old bull moose, with budding antlers still "in velvet," is feeding on grasses, horsetails, and asters in a damp ditch.

This healthy young bull carries several harmless cysts, like human warts, that are likely to freeze and fall off in the coming winter.

the whitetail's but more than twice the size, measuring 4 to 7 inches long, 7 to 9 inches with dewclaws, and they are unlike the more circular and concave wapiti track. On hardpacked trails only the foremost portions of hooves leave an impression, resulting in shorter tracks that can be mistaken for those of a whitetail.

Scat: Normal moose scat is typical of deer, consisting of packed brown pellets that are egg or acorn shaped, 1 to almost 2 inches long, about twice the size of whitetail or mule deer scats. Variations in shape occur with changes in diet, with soft masses that resemble cow pies occurring when an animal is making the transition between bark and woody shrubs to succulents and fruits. A scat unique to moose is the mushroom-shaped dropping that appears most commonly in moose that have fed on long, green grasses.

Coloration: The fur is short and dark brown, becoming interspersed with gray (grizzled) as the animal ages.

Sign: Moose leave identifiable marks. The paths they plow through browsing thickets are obvious. Shrubs at the side of the trail are broken and uprooted when bulls practice with their antlers in late summer and autumn, and there may be scraps of discarded antler velvet at these places. Moose beds and wallows are identifiable as horse-size impressions of plants and soil that have been compressed under massive weight. Moose entry and exit points into mucky bogs are marked by wide troughs.

Winter signs of moose (and elk) include gnawings in the smooth bark of poplar and other softwood trees that serve as winter foods. These trees are scabbed over with rough, black bark as the wound heals.

Vocalizations: Moose are generally silent. A cow calling for a calf emits a soft lowing, like the mooing of a domestic

This bull moose in full autumn antlers is preparing to take one or more mates. (Photo courtesy USFWS.)

A very protective moose mother in spring with two week-old nursing calves. (Photo courtesy of USFWS.)

cow. A mother may also issue a huffing grunt to warn off intruders. During the autumn mating season, moose become more vocal, especially amorous bulls. Rutting males are boisterous and fearless and have been known to charge people, livestock, and even automobiles. Bull moose in heat may grunt like hogs and bellow like domestic bulls. The more vulnerable cows and calves communicate more quietly.

Life span: Moose live to 10 years in the wild, up to 27 years in captivity.

Diet

An adult moose requires 10 pounds of vegetation per day. Like all ruminants, moose have an efficient digestive system for processing rough vegetable fiber. Foods browsed from

The left front hoofprint of a large bull moose in a muddy grass marsh. Note how grass stems have been cut cleanly by the hoof edge under massive weight.

shorelines include pond lily, water lily, marsh marigold, horse-tail, and rough grasses. Moose in Michigan's Upper Peninsula have been observed eating quantities of jewelweed (in the *Impatiens genus*). a plant known best as a remedy for poison ivy. Moose swim well, and their long legs permit them to wade through deep muck, where water plants grow thickest. Wintering moose eat a rougher diet of mostly willow twigs and bark, wading through snows too deep to be negotiated by shorter deer.

The right front track of a moose with the left rear track on top of it; quadrupeds learn to place the hind foot, which they cannot see, onto the same spot the forefoot had been, thus avoiding tripping hazards.

Mating Habits

Moose are sexually mature at 2 years. Mating occurs from September through October, with cows remaining in heat for thirty days. Cows initiate rutting with sexual pheromones in their urine and from tarsal glands inside the knees of the hind legs. Male moose become territorial during the rut, and their behavior toward intruders can be hostile.

Cow moose undergo an eight-month gestation period before giving birth to one or two unspotted calves in April or May. Newborn calves can outrun a human at two days old

These formless masses, large in comparison to the darker whitetail scat pellets around them, are the aging scats of a large bull moose whose diet has consisted of succulent aquatic plants, and a little mud.

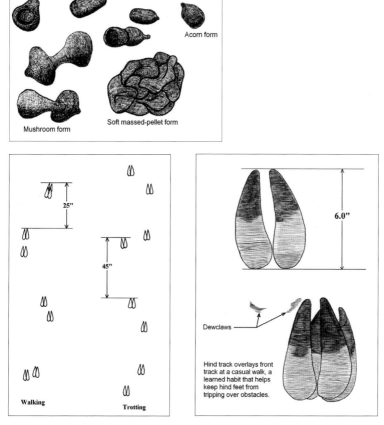

Various forms of moose scats.

Pellet form

Acorn form

Mushroom form

Soft massed-pellet form

25"

45"

Walking

Trotting

6.0"

Dewclaws

Hind track overlays front track at a casual walk, a learned habit that helps keep hind feet from tripping over obstacles.

As a moose's gait changes, so does its track pattern.

Moose tracks.

and can keep up with their mother by three weeks. Weaning occurs at five months, in September or October. Moose calves stay with their mother for at least a year after birth, until the next calves are born.

Behavior

Moose are primarily nocturnal and most active at dawn and dusk. Preferred bedding areas are places that have concealing vegetation and a plethora of scents to confuse

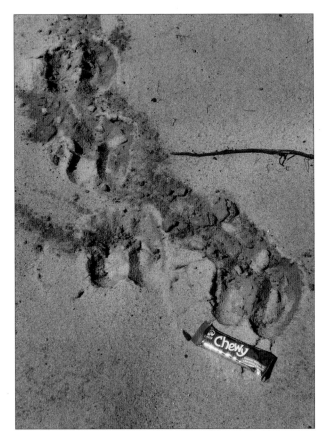

This moose stopped, looked about, and took a short, tentative step in riverbank sand that that been rained on, dried, and crusted over, with finer loose sand below.

predator noses. Adult moose are solitary, but two or more may feed in a particularly lush spot.

Moose are generally not migratory, but in Russia, moose are known to journey 200 miles between summer and winter habitats. Strong swimmers, they can cross swollen rivers and traverse deep snow.

Moose mothers are protective of calves, and, with a running speed of 35 miles per hour, they are dangerous to all predators. Sharp front hooves are the primary weapons of either sex, although antlered bulls may also use their heads.

WAPITI, OR AMERICAN ELK
(Cervus canadensis)

Cousin of the European red deer, the wapiti is second in size only to the moose. This large ungulate once roamed across what is now the United States, but, with little fear of predators, human or otherwise, elk made easy targets, and native populations were hunted to extinction in Indiana (1830), Ohio (1838), New York (1847), and Pennsylvania (1867). Protection came too late to save the eastern subspecies of forest-dwelling elk, *Cervus elaphus canadensis*, which is now extinct. Efforts to transplant elk to the eastern United States from the West have been attempted on three occasions, with limited success.

A bull elk with half-grown, velvet-covered antlers cools itself in a river on a hot July day.

Geographic Range

Wapiti were once common throughout the Northern Hemisphere, but today large populations are found only in western North America, from Canada down through the Rocky Mountains to New Mexico. Small populations are also found in Kentucky, Michigan, and Pennsylvania. Asia and Europe are home to a subspecies of elk known as red deer, or roebuck.

Essentially a mass of soft pel lets, this elk scat denotes a succulent diet of fresh green plants.

Habitat

Elk prefer open prairies where their good vision and sense of smell enables them to detect threats by sight and scent, but the species has learned to become comfortable in forests. Elk have a greater tendency to migrate than white-tailed or mule deer.

Physical Characteristics

Mass: Elk are 900 to 1,100 pounds. Males are generally 20 percent larger than females.

Body: Shoulder height is 4.5 to 5 feet; length is 6 to 9 feet. Elk are stocky and barrel shaped, with muscular humps at the shoulders and flank. Hindquarters are higher than the shoulders, creating a jacked-up silhouette.

Tail: The tail is short and surrounded by a dark-bordered blond patch that covers most of the rump in an inverted tear-drop shape.

Tracks: Tracks are 4 to 4.5 inches long (discounting dewclaws), cloven, and much rounder than those of moose or deer. Hooves are concave, resulting in track impressions that are deepest around their outer perimeters.

Scat: Scat is dark brown pellets, egg or acorn shaped, 0.75 to 1 inch long.

Coloration: Known as the "ghost of the forest," the wapiti has a dark-brown head, neck, and legs, with a blond body that lends a ghostly appearance in twilight. A blond rump patch provides a visual beacon for herd members to follow.

Sign: Sign includes mud wallows, which are bathtub-size depressions created by rolling in wet earth to dislodge fur and parasites or to scent bulls with their own urine in rutting season. Wapiti feed on the smooth bark of poplar, aspen, and cottonwood trees in winter, leaving trunks scarred with bottom-teeth-only scrapes that heal as rough, black bark scabs.

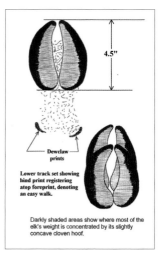

Lower track set showing hind print registering atop foreprint, denoting an easy walk.

Darkly shaded areas show where most of the elk's weight is concentrated by its slightly concave cloven hoof.

4.5"

Dewclaw prints

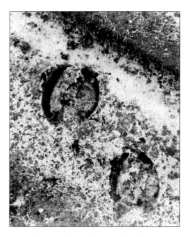

Note how these elk tracks (front left at top, hind left at bottom) are impre ssed most heavily around the outer edges, denoting the wapiti's concave cloven hooves, which make tracks similar to those of the caribou.

A track pattern of an elk walking on a damp sandy road.

Vocalizations: Best known is the bugle call of a mature rutting bull. This loud, high-pitched call, intended to be heard by receptive cows over long distances, begins as a low grunt, then abruptly becomes a hollow squeal that spans several seconds and repeats two or three times. Breeding males make coarse grunting and growling sounds, reminiscent of domestic cattle. The alarm call used by

Outside of the October–November mating season (rut), bull and cow elk live separately in same-sex herds, but in any herd a dominant cow is the alpha leader.

either sex is a piercing squeal. Cowlike mooing between mothers and calves keeps them close to one another.

Life span: Elk live 10 years in the wild, longer in captivity.

Diet

The elk's diet is herbivorous but varied. They eat many types of grasses and forbs, marshland plants (such as marsh marigold), and their namesake elkslip. In winter the diet includes bark,

This handsome bull in December will be shedding its polished antlers in a few days, and another set will begin growing almost immediately.

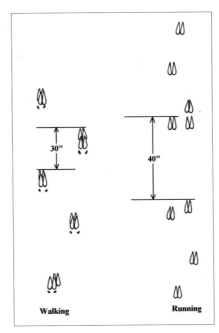

Elk track patterns.

twigs, and buds of aspen, poplar, beech, basswood, and evergreens. Elk are ruminants, feeding and then retiring to a resting place, where the partially digested cud in their primary stomach is regurgitated to be rechewed and broken down further into usable nutrients.

Mating Habits

Both genders reach sexual maturity at 16 months, but bulls under

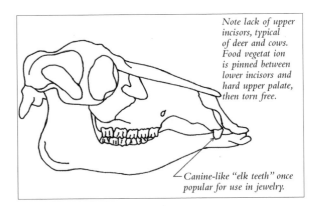

Note lack of upper incisors, typical of deer and cows. Food vegetation is pinned between lower incisors and hard upper palate, then torn free.

Canine-like "elk teeth" once popular for use in jewelry.

Note that the wapiti, like all deer, lacks upper incisors, and must tear food plants free, rather than biting them off cleanly—trackers should be alert for raggedly torn grasses and plant stems.

2 years will probably not mate because of competition from stronger males. Mating season begins in late August and goes through September, with a gathering of mature bulls and cows, peaking in October and November, when actual mating oc-curs. Cows initiate the mating period by emitting pheromonal scents. Bull elk are known for the harems they gather, but harems are usually maternal families consisting of a dominant female and her offspring. A typical harem consists of one bull, six adult cows, and four calves.

Courtship battles between rutting bulls are shoving matches in which competitors lock antlers and attempt to shove one another's head to the ground, whereupon the weaker animal withdraws. The objective isn't to harm an opponent, although injuries sometimes result.

Bull elk mate as many cows as possible before the rut ends. Gestation is eight to nine months, with a single, 35-pound spotted calf being born in April or May. If food is abundant, cows might have twins, but this is abnormal. Newborn calves and mothers live separately from the herd for about two weeks, and calves are weaned at about sixty days. Male calves leave their mothers at 2 years, often by banishment. Females may stay with the family herd for their entire lives.

Behavior

The most social of deer, wapiti spend their lives in herds. Except for mating season, adults run in same-sex herds of males and females that may number several dozen. The dominant animal in every mixed-sex herd is always a cow. Within bachelor herds, males get along well with each other and commonly accept strangers into their company. Cows are less accepting of strangers. Cow and bachelor herds may share the same feeding areas, but the sexes do not socialize outside of the rut. If alarmed, a mixed gathering of elk will flee in two same-sex herds.

Dominant cows are more territorial than bulls at all times of year. Territorial battles aren't common, but matriarchs protect territories against usurpers, and fights between cows are more violent than mating contests among bulls.

WHITE-TAILED DEER
(*Odocoileus virginianus*)

Known alternately as the Virginia or flagtail deer, the whitetail is a popular game animal whose financial value has spawned an entire hunting industry. No animal has been more researched, because no other game is so commercially valuable. Threatened by unrestricted hunting until the 1940s, whitetails have

The tracks of a doe and her fawn going to a river to drink, then returning to the forest.

made a strong comeback, with some estimates ranging as high as 26 million animals in the United States alone.

Geographic Range

Common throughout the United States, whitetails inhabit all but the most arid regions, extending northward to southern Canada and southward to Mexico, Central America, and northern South America.

Habitat

This newborn fawn's mother was killed by a car just a few yards away; unable to survive on its own, the fawn was spared a lingering death by hungry coyotes with their own young to feed.

Whitetails can live in any habitat with sufficient browse, water, and concealment. They often graze in groups in open places. The species' efficient digestive system can metabolize rough vegetable fibers, even bark and twigs. The least migratory deer, a typical whitetail spends its entire life in an area of about one square mile, moving only between open feeding and concealed bedding places. The animals are intimately familiar with every facet of their habitat.

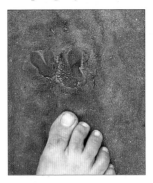

These small, rounded hoofprints are typical of newborn whitetail fawns.

Physical Characteristics

Mass: *Whiteails are* generally 150 to 200 pounds, with some exceeding 300 pounds in the far north. Subspecies, such as the Key deer of Florida and the Coues deer of Arizona, average 50 pounds and 75 pounds, respectively.

Body: These deer are muscular and less barrel shaped than other deer species, measuring 4 to 7 feet from chest to rump. Shoulder height is 3 to 4 feet. Their powerful hindquarters and strong, slender legs propel them at speeds in excess of 30 miles per hour. Whitetail antlers have a single main tine, or beam, from which single-point tines extend. Antlers are usually shed in January and begin to grow again in April. Interdigital scent glands between hoof halves carry signature and alarm scents. At 2 years, bucks grow mature, tined antlers. Metatarsal glands on the outside of each hind leg and a larger tarsal gland on the inside of each hind knee are used for olfactory communication, with musk from them becoming especially pungent during mating season.

Tail: The tail is 4 to 5 inches long and brown on top with white underneath. The tail is held erect when the deer is fleeing, exposing its white underside and giving rise to the common name, flagtail.

Tracks: Cloven hooves leave a split-heart impression when the toes are together, with two dewclaws behind and slightly above. Length is 3 to 3.5 inches without dewclaws.

Scat: Scat is typically oval-shaped pellets, sometimes acorn shaped, 0.5 to 0.75 inches long, dark-brown color, lightening with age.

Coloration: The coat is reddish in summer, gray in winter. The chest and belly are white. The nose is black with a white band running around the muzzle, the chin is white, and white circles are around the eyes.

This fresh whitetail scat deposit shows the variety of shapes the normal pellet form can have.

Whitetail track in soft mud showing dewclaw imprints as round holes to the rear.

Sign: Sign includes raggedly torn grasses. Saplings with bark scraped from them by a buck's antlers (rubs) are seen, especially in early autumn. Patches of urine-scented, pawed-up earth, called scrapes, are seen during the mating season. Lower

This left front whitetail track was made in wet sand during a rainstorm.

branches of cedars and pines are stripped of foliage.

Vocalizations: Whitetails are normally silent. The alarm call is a forceful exhalation, like a sudden release of pressurized air. Does bleat softly to fawns, but the sound carries only a few yards. Mortally wounded deer bleat with goatlike sounds.

An adult whitetail buck with mature antlers in November. (Photo courtesy USFWS.)

Life span: Whitetails live 8 years in the wild, up to 20 years in captivity.

Diet

Whitetails are generally nocturnal, with crepuscular (dusk and dawn) feeding patterns. They tend to visit water sources in early morning, after feeding. Summer foods include grasses, alfalfa, clover, elkslip, and aquatic plants. Winter browse consists of buds and tender twigs of evergreen trees, especially cedars, as well as the bark and buds of staghorn sumac, river willow, beech, and dead grasses found in hummocks along the banks of streams and rivers. In more arid country they can subsist on prickly pear, yucca, and tough, fibrous shrubs.

Mating Habits

Mating season begins in September and October with a proestrus rutting, during which bucks polish their antlers against trees and advertise sexual availability with urine-scented scrapes of pawed-up earth. During this period bucks spar with one another, usually far back in the woods, in elimination rounds that determine which is strongest. Battles are shoving matches in which contenders lock antlers and push until one withdraws. Occasional injuries result, and, in rare instances, both bucks have died because their antlers became inextricably locked, but the intent is never to injure an opponent, just to drive it away.

When mating begins in mid-October, bucks will have established their territories. Until the rut ends in late November (December in warmer southern regions), breeding males are fixated on mating and may be active anytime. Does, which may mate in their first year, play a passive role, depositing pheromone-laden urine onto a buck's scrape as they travel between feeding and bedding areas. Pregnant does need to gain body fat to survive a winter of pregnancy, so bucks check their scrapes frequently, pursuing does that leave messages.

Whitetails are the most widespread and adaptable American deer.

Whitetail bucks are polygamous, mating as many does as possible during the 30- to 45-day rut. Bucks may remain with one female for several days, until she comes into estrus, but after mating, the male moves on. Does are in heat for a single day; if a

Newborn whitetail fawns are surprisingly well camouflaged in their spotted coats.

doe goes unmated during her day of fertility, she comes into heat again approximately twenty-eight days later. Should this second heat pass with a doe still not becoming pregnant, she will not come into heat again until the following October.

Gestation lasts through winter, with a duration of six to seven months. Does bred for the first time normally give birth to a single spotted fawn in April or May, with twins being the norm

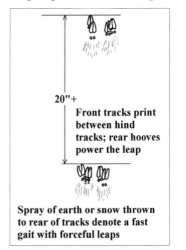

20"+

Front tracks print between hind tracks; rear hooves power the leap

Spray of earth or snow thrown to rear of tracks denote a fast gait with forceful leaps

Track pattern of leaping whitetail deer.

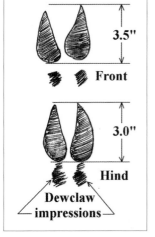

3.5"

Front

3.0"

Hind

Dewclaw impressions

Whitetail tracks.

Whitetail walking track pattern showing that the hind hoof (right) sometimes registers ahead of the front foot.

thereafter, sometimes triplets if food is abundant. Fawns walk within hours of being born and within a week begin nibbling on vegetation. Mothers leave fawns hidden in grasses or underbrush while they graze nearby, checking on them frequently, and eating their feces to prevent predators from scenting them.

If a carnivore approaches a hidden fawn, the mother tries to distract it and lead it away, even feigning injury to keep the predator's interest. Weaning occurs at six weeks, but fawns remain with their mothers for the rest of the summer and sometimes through the winter, even though mothers are likely to become pregnant again.

Behavior

Whitetails are nocturnal, traveling from secluded bedding areas to feeding places at dusk, then returning to the safety of dense forest at dawn. They may move about within the seclusion of bedding areas during the day, and especially in spring, groups might graze in the open during daylight hours.

When winter snows cover ground plants, whitetails move into protected yards where pines and especially cedars provide windbreak and browse. In most places, winter yards are also summer bedding areas, enabling deer to use established trails year-round.

Whitetail does are the most dominant deer, and they are more territorial than bucks because survival demands securing a domain with food, water, and shelter. Territorial disputes between does are settled with flailing hooves and are often violent.

Whitetail deer are mostly solitary, but an abundance of food, especially crops, can cause them to herd in large numbers. Agriculture causes whitetail populations to explode in farming regions where predatory species are unwelcome, sometimes resulting in overpopulation, disease, and an increase in car–deer accidents.

This form of whitetail scat is actually a mass of soft pellets, caused by eating rich succulents.

MULE DEER
(*Odocoileus hemionus*)

Mule deer are close cousins of the whitetail but inhabit only the western part of the United States, where migrating whitetails have begun to overlap their territories in recent years. Subspecies include the black-tailed deer of America's northwest coast.

Geographic Range

Mule deer are found from southwestern Saskatchewan through central North and South Dakota, Nebraska, Kansas, and western Texas, with sightings in Minnesota, Iowa, and Missouri. Gaps in population occur in arid regions of Nevada, California, Arizona, and the Great Salt Lake Desert.

Habitat

O. hemionus occupies a range of habitats, including the California chaparral, the Mojave Desert, semidesert shrub regions, the Great Plains, the Colorado Plateau shrubland and forest, the Great Basin, and the Canadian boreal forest. Mulies prefer open grassland for grazing and are seldom found in deep woods.

Physical Characteristics

Mass: Mulies range from 110 to more than 400 pounds. Males are 25 percent larger than females.

Body: Mule deer are stocky, barrel shaped, and 4 to 6 feet long; shoulder height is 3 feet; ears are large and mulelike, 4 to 6 inches long. Antler spread is up to 4 feet, with the main beam forking into points, rather than individual tines growing from the main beam. Adapted to open country, *O. hemionus* has good distance vision.

This all-doe herd of mule deer, composed mostly of related offspring and siblings, is an example of how males and females in the deer family tend to remain segregated except during the autumn mating season.

Tail: The tail is 5 to 9 inches long, dark brown or black above, white below, tipped with a black or sometimes white tuft (depending on subspecies).

Tracks: Tracks are nearly identical to the split-heart print of the whitetail but usually larger in adults, measuring about 3.5 inches long, discounting dewclaws.

Scat: Scat is typically deerlike, pellet or acorn shaped, with individual pellets averaging about 0.5 to 0.75 inches long. Sometimes pellets will be massed together when browse has been succulent.

Coloration: Fur is dark brown to red during summer, becoming more gray in winter. The rump patch is white in younger individuals and yellows as the animal ages. The throat patch is white. A dark, V-shaped mark that is more conspicuous in males than females extends from between the eyes upward to the top of the head.

Sign: Sign includes saplings with bark scraped by bucks rubbing their antlers. Bucks make urine-scented scrapes during the rut. Both sexes wallow in mud like elk, but depressions are smaller.

Vocalizations: The alarm is similar to the blowing of a

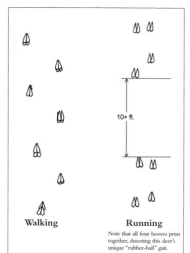

10+ ft.

Walking

Running

Note that all four hooves print together, denoting this deer's unique "rubber-ball" gait.

Mule deer track patterns. Note this species' feet-together "rubberball" bounding run, which is unique among North American deer.

whitetail but more prolonged, ending with a high-pitched whistle. Mule deer are vocal when grazing together, communicating softly with grunts, snorts, mooing sounds, and low squeals.

Life span: Mule deer live about 10 years in the wild.

Diet

Cud-chewing ruminants, like other deer, mule deer have a slightly less efficient digestive system than their cousins, requiring more easily digestible green plants in their diet. To counter a lack of green browse in winter, mule deer feed with more urgency than other deer throughout summer to put on enough fat to sustain them through winter.

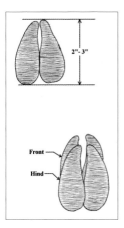

Mule deer tracks showing the split-heart clove n hoof common to all deer species, and the placing of hind feet into front tracks during a normal casual walk.

Green grasses, acorns, legume seeds, berries, and fleshy fruits are among the preferred foods.

Mating Habits

Mule deer breed slightly later than whitetails, beginning in October and peaking from November through December. Like whitetails, bucks create urine-scented scrapes of pawed-up earth that receptive does urinate onto as they pass between feeding and bedding areas. Males are polygamous, having more than one mate per breeding season, and there is no bond between mates.

Fresh mule deer scat shows the same pellet form exhibited by all deer species, from moose to whitetails. The ball of compressed pellets on the right indicates a rich diet of succulent greens.

Bucks competing for mates lock antlers and shove hard against one another until the weaker opponent withdraws. Injuries sometimes occur, but the objective is to establish which is the stronger, not to harm one another.

Mule deer does are less likely to mate in their first year than whitetail does. First and second births usually produce a single fawn, with twins being the norm thereafter. Gestation lasts 29 weeks, with most fawns born mid-June to early July. Fawns weigh 6 to 10 pounds at birth, with twins typically weighing less than singles and

Mule deer are the whitetail's western cousin, identifiable from a distance by their large, mule-like ears.

males being slightly heavier than females. Fawns can walk within a few hours of birth and begin nibbling vegetation within weeks. Fawns are weaned by 16 weeks and attain full skeletal development at 3 years for females, 4 years for males; both continue to grow until the ages of 8 and 10 years, respectively.

Behavior

Mule deer prefer a small home range but migrate when conditions demand. Two-year-old bucks are driven off by mothers to prevent inbreeding. Seasonal travel may be prompted by biting flies, deep snow, and drought.

Mule deer bed down during daylight in concealing thickets but are less shy about napping in the open than whitetails. Predators include cougars and wolves, with bears and coyotes preying on fawns. Mulies can see predators from as far away as 400 yards, and their bounding, feet-together, "rubber-ball" run of more than 30 miles per hour makes them hard to get hold of.

In winter, mule deer browse on commercially important trees, such as the Douglas-fir and ponderosa pine. This has prompted state governments to buy tracts of land that provide suitable winter habitat.

O. hemionus is susceptible to numerous viral, bacterial, and parasitic diseases. Gastrointestinal worms are common, and infection by parasitic meningeal worms causes permanent neurological harm. Free-range livestock may infect mule deer that graze the same pastures with hoof-and-mouth disease or bovine tuberculosis.

CARIBOU
(*Rangifer tarandus*)

Best known as reindeer, caribou have been domesticated to pull sleighs and wagons, as well as for their milk, and are still an important source of food in arctic cultures.

Geographic Range

Caribou were once native to all northern latitudes, but extensive hunting drove this most northern deer from much of its original range. Large herds are still found in Alaska, Canada, Scandinavia, and Russia; unrestricted hunting of them is no longer allowed anywhere.

Habitat

Caribou are most at home in arctic tundra, where they migrate long distances as seasons and availability of food change. They can adapt to temperate forest but require cold winters.

Physical Characteristics

Mass: Bulls weigh from 275 to 600 pounds; females weigh from 150 to 300 pounds.

Body: Shoulder height is 3 to 3.5 feet; length is 4.5 to 7 feet. Caribou are stocky, with thick legs and abnormally large knee joints, and have a large snout and nose pad. Both sexes are antlered, but males carry identifiably larger antlers.

Tail: The tail is 4 to 6 inches long, dark on top, white below.

Adult bull caribou in early autumn; bloody tissue at end of brow tine is a remnant of the "velvet" that nourishes antlers during growth.

Tracks: Large cloven hooves leave round impressions, 4 to 5 inches long; males make larger tracks than females. The feet are slightly broader than they are long and flat with deeply cleft hooves. The pad between hoof halves expands in summer to provide better traction against soft terrain but shrinks in winter to conserve heat.

Scat: Scat is acorn-shaped pellets, about 0.5 inch long, sometimes clumped together in a mass when the animal has fed on succulent browse.

Like all cervids, caribou shed their antlers in early winter, after the rut; unlike other deer, both males and females grow antlers.

Coloration: The coat is heavy, with dense, woolly underfur. Coat color is brown to olive, with whitish chest, buttocks, and legs. Coloration varies with geography; animals in Greenland and northeastern Canada are nearly white.

Sign: Browsed reindeer moss (*Cladina rangiferina*) lichens are a staple in the caribou diet. Shed antlers are found on open tundra.

Vocalizations: Caribou make grunts, squeals, and whistles, especially during migrations. Cows moo softly to young calves. Caribou have thick tendons that snap across a bone in the foot when they walk, producing a clicking sound (alluded to in the Christmas carol lyrics, "Up on the housetop, click, click, click").

Life span: Caribou live 5 years in the wild, up to 13 years in captivity.

Diet

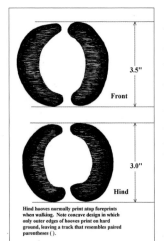

Hind hooves normally print atop foreprints when walking. Note concave design in which only outer edges of hooves print on hard ground, leaving a track that resembles paired parentheses ( ).

Caribou are herbivores and ruminants that can digest most types of vegetation, including green leaves, evergreen buds and foliage, and small twigs. When other browse is unavailable, caribou may feed predominantly on their namesake reindeer moss, a hardy lichen that grows in carpet-like masses and is common to open, barren places around the globe.

Caribou hoofprints as they might appear on firm ground. (Dewclaws do not register.) Note rounded form.

Mating Habits

Mating season occurs throughout October, with northern-most herds rutting earliest. Both sexes can breed at 2 years, but competition normally prevents males from mating until age 3.

Cows are seasonally polyestrous; those not impregnated during the first 10-day period of estrus will come into heat again 10 to 15 days later. Caribou bulls gather harems whose size may exceed twelve cows.

In May or June, after a gestation of 8 months, a single calf is born. Twins may occur if food is abundant, but they are not common. Calves weigh 12 to 19 pounds at birth; they can follow the herd within an hour and can outrun a human within a day.

Behavior

Caribou are diurnal (active during daylight) and gregarious, forming herds that can number from 10 to more than 1,000 individuals—as many as 200,000 animals during seasonal migrations. Caribou are the most migratory deer, traveling up to 1,000 miles between northern summer habitats to southern winter pastures. Migrations happen abruptly, with smaller

Caribou migrate in sometimes vast herds in spring and in autumn.

Unique among deer, caribou hooves are extra large and rounded to max-imize weight displacement (like snowshoes) and traction on snow.

Caribou bull in late summer, with grown antlers still covered by velvet.

Caribou scat resembles that of other deer, being pellet shaped with a normal diet, sometimes massed or soft when the diet has been rich in succulents.

groups coalescing into vast herds that can number 20,000 animals per square mile and travel 30 miles per day.

Caribou are the fastest-running deer, able to sprint at 50 miles per hour for short distances, and healthy adults can quickly outdistance their greatest predator, the arctic wolf. They cannot so easily escape rifles, and by the 1600s, they had been hunted to extinction over most of their European range; by the 20th century, they had become scarce over much of

Caribou track pattern, trotting.

their Canadian range. Presently there are thirty wild herds in North America, the smallest in Idaho and Washington, numbering about thirty animals each. The largest herds, in Canada and Alaska, number more than 50,000. Hunting laws have been enacted to protect existing populations.

Family Suidae

Family Suidae is composed of sixteen species of hogs in eight genera. Suids originated in southern Eurasia, on large, remote islands, such as those in the Philippines, and throughout Africa. Humans introduced *Sus scrofa*, the wild boar from which domesticated pigs were bred, into nonnative habitats around the globe, including North America, New Zealand, Australia, and New Guinea. Fossilized evidence of suids has been discovered from the Oligocene period (30 million years BC) in Europe and Asia and from the Miocene period (15 million years BC) in Africa.

WILD PIG
(*Sus scrofa*)

The true wild boar of Eurasia is the ancestor of all domestic swine. They share most behavioral and physical characteristics and have been transplanted as game and farm animals around the world since before the Middle Ages. Wild boars and domestic pigs interbreed freely, and where both exist, they have hybridized into a third type of swine that shares the traits of both.

Geographic Range

Wild pigs are very adaptable, and in many regions domestic hogs have escaped captivity to become part of local ecosystems, often with severe negative impact on native species. *Sus scrofa*, the wild boar from which all domestic pigs were spawned in approximately 3000 BC, occupies the largest range.

Originally there were no pigs in the Americas. Peccaries were found in South America, Mexico, and the southwestern United States but are not considered true swine. The first domestic pigs arrived with European immigrants but were unable to survive in the vast wilderness of the New World. In 1893, fifty wild boars were transplanted from Germany's Black Forest to a hunting preserve in New Hampshire's Blue Mountains. These were followed in 1910 by a release of Russian wild boars in North Carolina, another in 1925 near Monterey, California, with a few released on California's Santa Cruz Island.

Habitat

Sus scrofa is found in a variety of habitats, most typically where acorns, grasses, and roots are abundant. Short legs make swine poorly suited to deep snow, and none are sufficiently furred to endure prolonged sub-freezing temperatures. Temperatures below 50

degrees Fahrenheit are uncomfortably cold to wild pigs, although many survive in places where there is mild snowfall. Conversely, swine cannot tolerate hot climates, where lack of a protective coat makes them prone to sunburn and heatstroke. During hot weather, pigs seek shade during the day and wallow in mud to cool themselves.

Physical Characteristics

Mass: Wild pigs weigh from 160 to 450 pounds, occasionally weighing more than 1,000 pounds. Females are about 20 percent smaller.

Body: The body is barrel shaped and very stout, with short, thick legs. Body length is 4.5 to 6 feet; shoulder height is up to 3 feet. The head is large, with a short, massive neck and long muzzle ending in a flat, disk-shaped snout with large nostrils. Eyes are small and close set, relative to head size.

Sus scrofa has an advanced sense of taste and a very good sense of smell. Long-range eyesight is poor. Interbreeding between feral and true wild pigs has led to a variety of ear shapes, ranging from small and erect to large and folded over at their fronts. Most prominent is the flat, disk-shaped snout of tough cartilage, used for rooting in soil.

Although considered an omnivore, pigs have canines similar to carnivores. The upper canines grow out to curve backward into large, arced tusks that function as tools for digging and as weapons. Tusk lengths range from 3 to 9 inches, with longer tusks indicating older animals. Upper and lower canines grow throughout the animal's life but are so closely set that jaw movements keep them honed to sharp points. (Canines are sometimes removed from farm piglets, but second-generation feral hogs have all of their natural teeth and tusks.)

Tail: The average length of the tail is about 8 inches. True wild boars have straight tails with tufted ends, while domestic swine tend to have coiled tails; hybrids may have a combination of both.

Tracks: Pigs are cloven hooved, with dewclaws usually printing to the rear of hoof prints. Tracks are equally sized, 2 to 4 inches long, shaped like deep U's. Dewclaws in the front track are longer and more prominent than hind dewclaws.

Scat: Scat is usually large pellets, similar to those of a deer, but ranging from 3 to more than 6 inches long, sometimes massed together. When the animals have been feeding on succulent vegetation or rich meat, scats may become soft and disk shaped, like small cow pies. Recognizable content includes undigested plant fibers, insect legs and carapaces, seeds, and small bones.

Coloration: True wild boars possess a grizzled, dark-brown coat with whitish guard hairs that are typically longer and shaggier than those of hybridized feral pigs. Feral pigs often exhibit the splotched skin pigmentation of domestic hogs.

Sign: Well-traveled trails are made by herds of foraging pigs. Rooted-up soil with grasses and roots neatly clipped free are made by the animals' sharply mated incisors.

Vocalizations: Pigs make grunting, oinking, and squealing noises when excited or threatened. Some researchers believe that *Sus scrofa* speaks a rudimentary language, but a scientific analysis still needs to be performed.

Life span: Pigs live about 20 years.

Diet

Swine, a primitive ungulate, have a simple digestive system with a two-chambered stomach that processes tough plant fibers less efficiently than the stomachs of deer or cows. Pigs are omnivorous, with a diet that includes fungi, leaves, roots, bulbs, fruit, snails, insects, snakes, earthworms, rodents, eggs, and carrion. They use their tough snout, tusks, and forefeet to unearth food plants.

Sus scrofa's broad diet has enabled the species to survive in a variety of environments, from deserts to mountainous terrain, so long as winter snows are shallow enough to permit the short, heavy pigs to travel without foundering. Their omnivorous diet brings swine into direct competition with black bears, and both species have killed one another in territorial disputes. Wild pigs aren't the gluttons they are purported to be and are typically much leaner than farm-raised hogs.

Being self-sufficient, they are more active than domestic pigs and subsist on a less-fatty diet. Like domestic swine, wild pigs are host to parasitic infections (trichinosis, cysticercosis, brucellosis) that are transmittable to humans who eat undercooked meat and who make contact with suid scats.

Mating Habits

Swine become sexually mature at eighteen months but grow until 5 or 6 years old. They are herd animals, and only one dominant male (boar) is permitted to breed, so males are driven from the herd and run in bachelor herds or establish their own domains at 2 or 3 years of age.

Mating season runs from mid-November to early January, peaking in December. The rut can be unnaturally violent, and large boars frequently inflict serious, even mortal wounds on one another while battling for possession of a harem that may

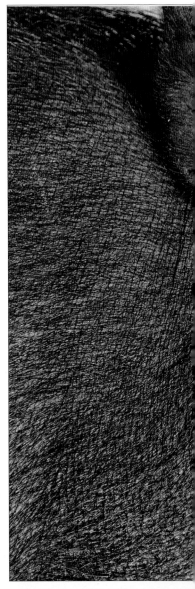

number up to eight sows. Extra-thick skin covering the chest, shoulders, and underbelly offers some protection against stab wounds, but fights are usually bloody. Sows are in estrus for 3 weeks and are willing to copulate for 3 days during that period. Females not impregnated then will probably come into estrus again before the mating season ends. In northern regions, where snows are deeper and winters longer, sows birth one litter per year; in warmer climates breeding may take place year-round.

Gestation lasts about 4 months, with litters of three to sixteen (five is average) piglets being born in April. Newborns are 6 to 8 inches long and have brown fur patterned with nine or ten paler longitudinal stripes on the back. Sows withdraw from their herds to a secluded, defendable grass- or leaf-lined nest a day prior to giving birth. Few predators challenge a ferociously protective mother sow, but boars have been known to kill and eat their own newborns, while coyotes and birds of prey are quick to snatch piglets if they can. On average, only about half a litter can expect to reach maturity.

Sows rejoin their herd 1 to 2 days after giving birth, and by 1 week the small herd of mother and suckling young are able to travel with the larger, extended-family herd. The young begin feeding on solid foods almost immediately but suckle from their mothers for 3 months. The piglets' stripes disappear entirely at about 6 months, and they take on the color and pattern that will mark them for life.

Behavior

Wild *Sus scrofa* in Europe congregate in herds that may number 100 individuals, although twenty or fewer is normal.

Sometimes two or more dominant females join their herds when food is abundant, finding greater safety in large numbers. Both sexes coexist peacefully, but in a defined hierarchy, at all times of year. Males 18 months and older band together in bachelor herds or sometimes live alone during the non-breeding months. Outsiders are challenged by dominant animals of either gender, particularly if food is scarce, but herd members are tolerant of one another.

Feral pigs are no more migratory than is necessary to find suitable habitat, but they can easily cover 10 miles a day. The normal gait is a trot of roughly 6 miles per hour, and pigs seldom walk except when feeding. At a fast run, the average adult can reach speeds in excess of 20 miles per hour.

In ancient times pigs served not only as food but also as farming tools: A plot of rough land could be made ready for arable crops just by turning a herd of pigs loose there, where the animals' natural rooting and pawing would loosen the soil as well as a drawn plow. Early Egyptians are said to have used deep swine hoofprints as planting holes for their seed, and pig dung is among the best fertilizers.

Sus scrofa's extremely acute sense of smell may be superior to that of a tracking dog, and it has long been exploited by humans to find truffles and other mushrooms of which pigs are fond. Pigs have been used experimentally for tracking people lost in a wilderness and for cadaver recovery, but the swine's temperament and lack of agility make this animal more difficult to work with than a dog. In medieval times pigs were trained to run down and kill game.

COLLARED PECCARY
(*Tayassu tajacu*)

Peccaries are distant cousins of the African warthog and Eurasian wild boar but are smaller than true swine. Peccaries have fewer teeth than true swine and a two-chambered stomach that appears to be in transition between ruminants (cud chewers) and omnivores. There are two major species: the collared peccary and the white-lipped peccary, with fourteen recognized subspecies in North and South America.

Geographic Range

Collared peccaries are found in warmer latitudes, from northern Argentina throughout Central America and northward to Arizona, New Mexico, and Texas.

Habitat

In South and Central America, collared peccaries inhabit tropical rainforests and low mountain forests. In the southwestern United States and northern Mexico, the preferred habitat includes rocky deserts of saguaro, mesquite, and prickly pear cactus, which the pigs ingest, spines and all, with impunity. Collared peccaries are sometimes pests in residential areas, where they've become accustomed to rooting through human garbage.

Physical Characteristics

Mass: Collared peccaries weigh from 30 to 65 pounds.

True swine are not native to the Americas, but peccaries are found from southern North America to South America. (Photo courtesy Arizona Game and Fish Department.)

The cloven hooves of a peccary more closely resemble those of a deer than the more closely related wild boar.

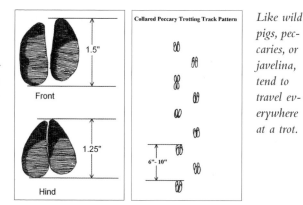

1.5"

Front

1.25"

Hind

Collared Peccary Trotting Track Pattern

6"- 10"

Like wild pigs, peccaries, or javelina, tend to travel everywhere at a trot.

Body: The body is piglike, but much smaller than true swine, and stout and barrel shaped, with short legs. Shoulder height is 20 to 22 inches; body length is 35 to 40 inches. The large head has a long, tapered muzzle, ending in a disk-shaped snout designed for rooting. Collared peccaries have short, straight tusks that fit together tightly enough to hone one another with every jaw movement, giving the species its common name, javelina (javelin-like). Javelinas have a distinct dorsal, or "precaudal," gland on the rump that secretes hormonal scents used in communication. Peccaries have poor eyesight, good hearing, and a rudimentary language.

Tail: The tail is about 3 inches long and straight, as a wild boar's.

Tracks: Peccaries have cloven hooves on all four feet, and tracks are 1 to 1.5 inches long. Stride is 6 to 10 inches; hind hooves usually register in front tracks. Peccaries have two

Long, spear-like canines show why early Spanish settlers called the peccary "javelina." (Photo courtesy Arizona Game and Fish Department.)

An icon of the American southwest, the peccary, or javalina, has been an important source of meat, of tough hides for shoes, and a source of revenue from sport hunters. (Photo courtesy Arizona Game and Fish Department.)

Peccary scat showing the little pig's fondness for eating prickly pear cactus—spines and all.

dewclaws on the forefeet, one on the hind feet; true swine have two dewclaws on all four feet.

Scat: Scat is usually pellet-shaped segments, like those of deer, but much longer (2 to 3 inches). When peccaries are feeding on succulents, scats may be a flattened disk (cow-pie) shape. Scat may contain bones of rodents or birds, eggshells, and insect carapaces.

Coloration: The peccary's coarse hair is grizzled gray to nearly black, with white guard hairs that give it a salt-and-pepper appearance. There is a yellowish patch on the cheeks and a collar of yellowish hair encircling the neck just ahead of the shoulders. Both genders are nearly identical in size and color, but male genitalia may be obvious.

Sign: Easily followed trails are made by a number of hooves and rooting noses. Chewed cactus, especially prickly pear leaves (spines and all are eaten), is a sure sign of peccaries. From downwind at closer ranges, there may be a scent of musk from the animals' urine and precaudal scent glands.

Vocalizations: Peccaries grunt, squeal, and growl. They are very vocal, possibly because they possess poor long-distance vision and need to communicate vocally to keep contact with other herd members in sagebrush country, where visibility might be limited to a few feet. The alarm call is a coughing sound, almost a bark. Peccaries can squeal like pigs and do so when in mortal danger.

Life span: They can live 15 to 20 years, up to 24 years in captivity.

Diet

Collared peccaries are herbivorous, with two stomachs for digesting coarse plant material, but they aren't picky eaters. Prickly pear cactus leaves are a legendary peccary food in arid regions, and peccaries will eat carrion given an opportunity. The species also eats frogs, snakes, lizards, the eggs of ground-nesting birds, roots, fungi, and fruits.

Mating Habits

Male collared peccaries reach sexual maturity at 11 months, females at 8 months. There is no set mating season; rutting is triggered by changes in climate, particularly rain, to ensure that pregnancy and rearing of young occur during a plentiful season. Rain brings abundant food, which helps to guarantee that pregnant mothers are well fed, so most young are born in rainy months. Conversely, years of drought retard population growth.

As herd animals, peccaries live by a rigid social hierarchy. The dominant boar is the only male permitted to breed. Nonbreeding males may remain with the herd when rutting begins but are not allowed to approach females in estrus. Bachelor herds don't exist as they do in most herd species.

After a 4-month gestation, mothers give birth to two to four piglets, with twins being the norm. In contrast to other social species that are predominantly female, the ratio between genders is approximately equal. Prior to giving birth, peccary mothers-to-be seek out a protected cave or other shelter in which to have their litters. Newborns are sometimes killed,

Protective mothers, female javelina with young travel in small family herds called "sounders." (Photo courtesy Arizona Game and Fish Department.)

possibly eaten, by more dominant herd members, especially if food is scarce. But that risk passes quickly, and after 1 day, the mother and litter rejoin the herd, where she provides fierce protection for her offspring.

Peccary young are light brown with five wide black stripes running longitudinally down the back. They follow their mother everywhere but may be nursed by grown sisters from previous litters. Females have four nipples, but only the rear pair produce milk, forcing mothers to nurse while standing and the piglets to suckle from behind her, rather than from the side like true swine. Piglets begin feeding on vegetation within a week but are not weaned until 2 to 3 months.

Behavior

Collared peccaries live in groups of five to fifteen individuals of all ages and both genders that eat, sleep, and forage together. A dominant boar leads, with subordinates ranked according to social prominence. Exceptions are the old, ill, and seriously injured, which are left behind when they can no longer keep pace.

Peccary herds avoid contact with groups outside their own territory and defend their territories against intruders. Feeding subgroups of males, females, and young form from within large herds, and these may break away to become the nucleus of new group herds. Territory size depends on herd numbers and the availability of food and water. Territorial boundaries are established by herd leaders, who employ urine, scats, and powerful-smelling oily musk glands to leave their scent on trees and other landmarks. Scats mark trail intersections and are refreshed periodically (usually daily). Herd members that meet after having been apart rub against one another head-to-rump, sharing spoor from scent glands.

Both peccary genders vigorously defend their young and their territory. Warning behaviors include laying back the ears, raising hair (hackles) along the spine, and releasing odorous musk from the rump (precaudal) gland. Next comes a pawing of the ground and an audible chattering of teeth. Finally, a peccary will charge, attempting to knock the adversary down, biting with canines, and sometimes locking jaws with an opponent. Fights may be bloody but are seldom more than superficially injurious before the weaker animal withdraws.

Collared peccaries are responsive to environmental changes, including precipitation, ambient temperatures, and length of day. Even feeding behavior changes with the seasons. When winter makes the desert cooler and the nights longer, foraging begins earlier in the evening and ends later in the morning. In summer, when days are hotter and longer, herds seek shade to sleep through the heat of the day, foraging only at night.

Considered a game animal, especially in Arizona, peccaries become nuisances by rooting up gardens or raiding trash cans. Their major predators—coyotes, pumas, jaguars, and bobcats—avoid human habitation, helping to explain the peccary's attraction to civilization. The species is not in danger, although about 20,000 are killed in Texas each year by sport hunters. Subspecies living in South America are threatened by rainforest destruction and loss of habitat.

Pawed Animals

Family Canidae

Members of the dog family are characterized by having four toes on each paw (discounting a dewclaw that doesn't show in tracks), and each toe tipped with a fixed claw. A long tail is universal, as are long canine teeth designed for inflicting mortal wounds to prey. All are digitigrade, normally walking weight forward on the toes and prepared to instantly spring into pursuit or flight, so the heaviest impressions will be from toes and claws, with heel pads printing more faintly. All eat meat but also require vegetation in their diets. Every species has erect, pointed ears that rotate to hone in on sounds, and all have an acute sense of smell.

Wolves and coyotes are social, living in family packs that might comprise several generations of offspring, with a dominant alpha (parent) pair who are the only members permitted to mate. Foxes are solitary except for mating. Adult males universally cock a leg to urinate against a usually stationary object to mark territory. Females squat to urinate, as do males in the presence of a dominant male, but ruling females may lift one foot slightly off the ground. Urine carries odors that identify individuals, territorial boundaries, gender, sexual readiness, size, and age.

Urine posts are refreshed, usually daily, and trackers should be mindful that scent posts often mark the boundaries between two territories.

GRAY WOLF
(*Canis lupus*)

The gray (or timber) wolf is the largest of forty-one species of wild canids worldwide. Gray wolves are the ancestors of all domestic dogs, including feral breeds, such as Australian dingos (*Canis lupus dingo*) and New Guinea singing dogs (*Canis lupus halstromi*). Genetic evidence indicates that gray wolves were domesticated by humans at least twice, possibly as many as five times. All wolves in North America—except the red wolf (*Canis rufus*)—are *Canis lupus*, although some biologists split these into as many as thirty-two regional subspecies.

Long, strong legs, big feet for running more than 35 mph on snow and uneven terrain, sharp vision in daylight and darkness, keen hearing and sense of smell, the most massive and powerful jaws in the canid world, and a tail that never curls—all of these help to explain why tribes of old knew the gray wolf as "God's Knife."

Geographic Range

Gray wolves once occupied the northern hemisphere from the Arctic through central Mexico, North Africa, Europe, and Asia. Today there are an estimated 5,700 wolves living in the lower forty-eight states, with approximately 4,000 of those in the Great Lakes region and about 1,500 in the northern Rocky Mountains. Canada claims an estimated 50,000 wolves,

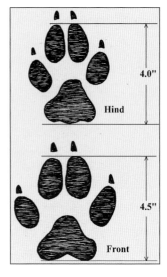

Gray wolf tracks.

4.0"

Hind

4.5"

Front

while Alaska estimates about 10,000; both classify wolves as game animals. In 2009, wolves in the Eastern Management Region of Michigan, Wisconsin, and Minnesota were removed from the endangered species list.

Once common throughout Europe, wolves are now scattered in Russia, Poland, Scandinavia, Spain, Portugal, and Italy, with small populations in Japan and Mexico. Wolves were exterminated from Great Britain in the 16th century and nearly so in Greenland during the 20th century. Today Greenland's wolves have recovered. The species has also shown resilience against advancing civilization in the United States, even expanding their range across Michigan's Mackinac Straits in 1997 to become established in the state's Lower Peninsula.

Biologists claim that each wolf accounts for twenty-seven deer kills per year, but that estimate doesn't take into account that a lone wolf can rarely catch a deer and can subsist entirely on small rodents and other animals—even fish.

Habitat

Gray wolves are highly adaptable, able to live in most environments. A pack's territory may encompass hundreds of square miles, but wolves range only as far as environmental factors demand. If an area provides prey and water without competition from other large predators, a territory may be only a few square miles. Where a pack's food supply is migratory, as with caribou herds on the Arctic tundra, packs may travel hundreds of miles. Studies show that road development has little effect on gray wolf migrations.

Physical Characteristics

Mass: Wolves weigh from 60 to 135 pounds; females are about 10 percent smaller.

Body: Wolves are doglike but with a more massive head and muzzle and heavier, longer legs. Body length is 40 to 50 inches; shoulder height is 26 to 38 inches. The normal gait is a trot of about 6 miles per hour that keeps the spine very straight, making an opportunistic wolf less noticeable than a dog, which has a typical rocking gait.

Tail: The tail is 14 to 20 inches long, bushy, darker on top than below, with a black or white tip. A gray wolf's tail never curls but is held

An almost common occurrence; this adult blue heron was grabbed at night while it roosted in a marsh—note the outline of punctures in the shape of a wolf's jaw—but the young wolf that killed it hadn't yet learned that herons (unlike the tastier sandhill cranes) have a foul, fishy taste.

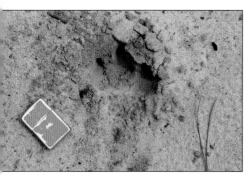

This wolf was alert—or "on its toes"— when it made this track. The heaviest toe impression on the right side indicates that this is a right-side paw print.

straight down when relaxed, straight back when running, or straight up when agitated. All dogs, including wolf hybrids, curl their tails.

Tracks: Wolves have the largest tracks of all canids. The front is 4 to 5 inches long; the hind is 3.5 to more than 4 inches long. Tracks always show claws. Straddle is 4 to 6 inches; stride is 26 to 30 inches. Tracks are notably different from a coyote's and distinguishable from domestic dog tracks by their larger size and configuration. Hind heel pads have three distinct lobes to the rear—typical of canines—but front heel pads show only two lobes in tracks, leaving a chevron imprint that is unlike the three-lobed front tracks of a coyote or fox. Some dogs, like Siberian and malamute huskies, display a chevron-shaped fore track, but the tracks are smaller. Large feet distribute body weight over a wider area, like a snowshoe; the front track of a 90-pound yearling measures 4 inches long, while a dog of the same weight will have a front paw that measures 3.5 inches or less. Coyotes are sometimes mistaken for gray wolves, especially in their thick winter pelage, but a wolf is at least twice the size of its cousin, with a broader, less-pointed muzzle and shorter, less-pointed ears.

Scat: Scat is irregularly cylindrical, segmented, normally tapered at both ends, typically 1.5 to 2 inches in diameter, 6 to 8 inches long. Fur is wrapped in a spiral around the outside, encasing sharp bones that could harm the digestive tract. Fresher scats are dark brown or black, becoming gray as organic matter decomposes. Except for size, gray wolf scat is identical to other wild canids that share similar diets. One difference is that an adult wolf has bite pressure exceeding a half-ton per square inch, and it can crush larger bones to obtain fat-rich marrow, making large shards of bone a hallmark of wolf scat.

Coloration: Gray wolves tend to exhibit three color phases: The common gray phase is typified by combinations of coarser white guard hairs, with black, gray, red, and brown on the upper body and head. The back has a black saddle; the belly is lighter gray to white, with a black spot above the tail (precaudal) gland. Pups are normally born black,

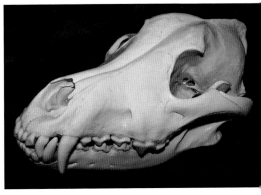

The skull of this 2-year-old female wolf shows the powerfully constructed jaw, heavy canines, and massive carnassial (cutting) molars that make the species such capable carnivores.

becoming grayer with age; black and darkly marked wolves are younger than lighter wolves. Completely white coats are most often seen on Arctic subspecies in the far north.

Sign: Gray wolves excavate burrows to capture marmots, but look for tracks, as bears, coyotes, and badgers also dig up marmots. Dominant males urinate on trees as territorial

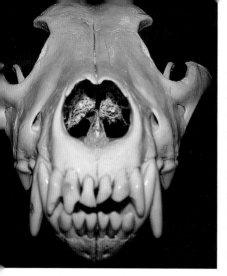

The chipped and worn incisors on this four-year-old gray wolf skull are an indication of how tough it is to live in the wild.

claims and an indication of social status. They urinate as high up on a tree as possible to demonstrate their size. Females may also urinate at scent posts, usually squatting, sometimes raising one leg. Wolves habitually transport large prey in pieces to a safe, often elevated, location before feeding. Regular feeding spots will be littered with bones.

Vocalizations: Wolves are normally silent, but a social lifestyle demands communication. Howling, heard most often at dusk when packs gather to hunt, is usually initiated by the alpha male. Gathering howls warn other packs that a territory is claimed and serves to get pack members psyched up for the hunt. Howls are mostly monotonal, occasionally wavering, but never with the yipping or prolonged barking of coyotes and dogs. Wolves issue a single, deep bark when alarmed but seem incapable of barking repeatedly.

Life span: Wolves live about 10 years in the wild; up to 15 years in captivity.

Diet

Gray wolves are meat eaters but require some vegetables to obtain minerals and vitamins not provided by prey. Wolves in captivity are usually fond of green beans; wild wolves eat blueberries, fruits, young grasses, and pine buds.

Renowned for the drill-team precision with which hunting packs bring down large quarry, wolves avoid prey that could injure one of them. The ideal prey is a weak, sickly individual, but deer that are weak from starvation are not eaten, because toxins accumulate in muscle mass when it cannibalizes itself.

In midwinter, when the alpha pair leaves to mate and seek out a den, packs may regroup at night to hunt larger prey. Mature pack members may strike out to find their own mates and territories. Lone wolves can rarely bring down deer, so much of their diet is mice, squirrels, rabbits, raccoons, and other small animals.

The left front track of a 140-pound gray, or "timber," wolf. Like nearly all quadrupeds, the largest, most heavily imprinted toe is the outermost, opposite the human design.

Mating Habits

Gray wolves mate between January and March, with those in the southern latitudes breeding first, because spring comes to them earlier. Only the parent, or alpha, pair mate within a pack, which is itself a family unit. Adult offspring naturally leave to establish their own territories at 2 to 4 years of age, but weaker omega (lowest-ranking) wolves may remain with the parents indefinitely.

Like other canids, a female wolf's breeding cycle has four stages: anestrus, proestrus, estrus, and diestrus. Estrus (when the female can copulate) lasts 5 to 14 days, half that of a dog. Males are brought into heat by females; their testicles, which are normally retracted, unlike dogs', descend only during this period.

Two weeks prior to mating, the alpha pair leaves the pack to dig a den, always near a source of freshwater. Dens begin with a tunnel that is roughly 18 inches in diameter and 10 feet long. The tunnel opens into a chamber about 4 feet high by 6 feet long and 6 feet wide, with an elevated floor to prevent flooding. Small caves and natural shelters may be used, so long as these offer protection from the elements and bears, which will prey on pups. The same den may be used every year if it is left unmolested.

As the pregnant alpha female becomes more vulnerable, she will spend more time in the den, and her mate will bring her food. Gestation lasts 60 days, with pups born between March and May, depending on how long winter lasts in that region. Litter size is typically six, with newborn pups weighing 8 ounces.

Born blind and deaf, newborn pups are completely dependent on their mother for eight weeks; she will stay with them constantly, except to drink and expel waste, for their first 3 weeks. During this time she will also make sure that the den's interior is fastidiously cleaned of anything that might bring disease to her young. Pups gain about 3 pounds per week, feeding on rich milk and regurgitated meat. Predigested meat is easier for the young pups to metabolize, and adults can carry more of it in their stomachs than in their mouths.

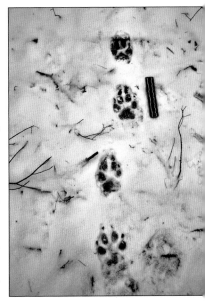

Pups are weaned at 9 weeks, freeing the mother to join pack mates on hunts. Pups leave the den to play fight, watched over by a babysitter (usually the weakest member of the pack). By 10 months, the pups have grown to 65 pounds and hunt with the pack. Female pups are sexually mature at 2 years and may leave to find their own mates. Males reach full maturity at 3 years.

Gray wolf track pattern in fresh snow. Bottom to top: Left front, left hind, right front, right hind.

Behavior

Gray wolves are exceptionally social, with pack sizes ranging from two recently mated animals to more than thirty. A pack is actually a family, usually the alpha pair and their offspring and sometimes a brother or sister of the alphas. Unrelated adults are rarely accepted into an existing pack, but orphaned pups are always adopted.

Wolf packs must have a hierarchy: Alpha males lead, but packs have been ruled by a widowed alpha female. Pack members are subordinate to the alphas. If an alpha male is killed, the female may leave to seek out a new mate, leaving the beta, or second-strongest male, to lead. Newly paired alpha mates seeking their own domains may travel with a third female, usually a sister of the alpha female. This ensures that a mated pair has the strength to take large prey and provides a backup mate should the original alpha female be killed. The second female also serves as a babysitter for the first litter of pups.

Packs virtually never fight among themselves, because harming a member of the team weakens its ability to hunt. The pack hierarchy is strictly adhered to: Alphas and pups eat first, followed by betas, subordinates, down to the omega wolf. Pack members are brought food if they become incapacitated, but they often leave the pack voluntarily.

Wolf packs have two annual phases: The stationary phase occurs during spring and summer, when pups are too small to travel with the pack. The nomadic phase spans from autumn to late winter, when packs follow migratory or yarded deer herds. A pack may travel more than 75 miles in a day, most of it at night, at a lope of about 15 miles per hour.

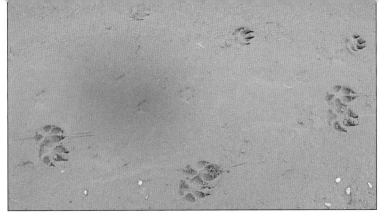

The track pattern of a walking coyote (bottom) contrasts with the red fox track pattern above. The coyote front track is 3 inches, while the fox tracks are 1.5 inches. Note the "mustache" at rear of the coyote's front heel pad, and that the hind foot registers on top of the front track.

COYOTE
(*Canis latrans*)

This miniature wolf takes its name from the Nahuatl tribe, who called it *coyotl* (the "trickster"). All tribes within its range respected the species for its intelligence. With the extermination of large predators, coyotes became the dominant carnivore in North America, and the species has thrived in every environment, from desert and forest to prairie and suburb.

Geographic Range

Native to the Americas, coyotes are found from Central America throughout Mexico and the lower forty-eight states, northward into central Canada and Alaska.

Habitat

Coyotes have proved very adaptable to a broad range of environments and climates. They thrive in the southern Mexico jungles, the deserts of the Southwest, and in bitter-cold northern forests. Coyotes in many areas have learned to recognize people as a food source, and in suburban areas they have made themselves pests by raiding garbage cans.

Physical Characteristics

Mass: Coyotes weigh from 30 to more than 60 pounds in the far north.

Body: Coyotes are lanky and more slender than the gray wolf. Body length is 40 to 50 inches; shoulder height is 23 to 26 inches. They have large, pointed ears and a narrow, tapered muzzle with a small black nose pad. The coyote is about half the size of a gray wolf and much larger than any fox. The eyes have a yellow iris and round pupil. Molars are structured for crushing small bones, and canines are long and narrow.

Tail: The tail is roughly half the body length, 20 to 25 inches long, bushy with a black tip. A coyote's tail droops normally and is held below the back when running, while a gray wolf's tail is nearly always held straight back, in line with the spine.

Tracks: Tracks are about 2.5 inches long for the forepaws, and hind paws are roughly 10 percent smaller. Tracks as long as 3.5 inches have been reported in northern forests. Heel pads of all four feet have three rearward lobes. Walking stride is 14 inches; straddle is 4 inches.

Scat: Scat is black to brown, growing lighter and grayer with age; length is 3 to more than 4 inches, cylindrical, segmented, about 1 inch in diameter. It may be a purplish color in blueberry season but is usually wrapped in a sheath of fur that encases small bones and indigestible objects.

Coloration: Fur is gray-brown to yellow-gray, often with rust-colored patches around the neck, shoulders, and flanks, and usually grizzled black on the back. Belly and throat are lighter, even cream colored. Forelegs, sides of the head, muzzle, and feet are reddish brown. There is one molt per year, beginning with profuse shedding in May and ending in July. Winter coats grow in late August or in September in more southerly ranges.

Arguably the most successful and adaptable carnivore in the Americas, Canis latrans ranges from the Arctic Circle to Central America.

A coyote that scratches with all four feet after urinating is advertising its claim to the surrounding territory.

Sign: Sign includes urine-scented tree trunks and stumps, marked by males about 8 inches above the ground, or half as high up as a gray wolf, and gnawed rib ends and cartilaginous joints on deer carcasses. Large leg bones are left intact, not crushed as they would be by a wolf or bear.

Vocalizations: Coyotes make shrill howling, barking, and yapping noises, almost screeching at times, especially when family members congregate at dusk or dawn. The scientific name, *Canis latrans*, is Latin for "barking dog."

Life span: They live 8 to 10 years.

Diet

Coyotes are mostly carnivorous, eating almost any type of meat: lizards, snakes, grasshoppers, birds, eggs, even fish. An average diet consists of squirrels, rabbits, and especially mice. One of nature's best mousers, coyotes stand motionless in the middle of a meadow, cocking their heads and ears from one position to another as they pinpoint the location of scurrying rodents under grass or snow. When a mouse has been located, the coyote leaps into the air, often clearing the ground with all four feet, and pounces onto its prey with the forefeet. This technique is effective in winter, when rodents travel under snow through tunnels that a coyote can collapse by jumping onto them, trapping prey inside. Once caught, rodents are swallowed whole.

Coyotes are often seen by hunters who bait deer, because the little wolves have learned to associate hunters with both vegetables and fresh meat. In winter, coyote families may form a pack to hunt small, weakened deer, but they prefer safer prey, such as rabbits and voles. Deer are large and dangerous to even a pack of coyotes, whose members are one-third the size of an adult whitetail. A sharp-hooved kick to the ribs or jaw could be fatal if it prevents a coyote from eating or running fast, so deer are low on the coyote's list of preferred prey, and those they do hunt will be weak or wounded.

Coyotes are fond of fruits, including blueberries, wild grapes, elderberries, and other sugar-rich fruits that help to put on precious fat against the cold of winter. In blueberry country the scat of coyotes, and all canids, will frequently be purple between the months of August and October.

Mating Habits

Both genders reach sexual maturity at twelve months but, to prevent inbreeding, must leave their parents' territory to find mates. Mated pairs are monogamous but infrequently "divorce" to take other mates, even after being together for several years.

Coyote pairs retire to a secluded den in January, using the same site year after year if it remains unmolested. Dens are excavated near water, sometimes under the roots of a large tree, and always in a place where good drainage keeps the den from flooding during wet weather. Each den is a smaller version of a wolf den, consisting of a narrow tunnel about 12 inches in diameter that extends up to 10 feet, terminating at a nursing chamber that measures 3 feet high, 3 feet wide, and 4 feet long.

Mating season is late January through March. Copulation is usually initiated by the female, who paws at the male's flanks to indicate her estrus. Females are monoestrous, remaining in heat for just 5 days, so there is urgency to become pregnant. Like those of a wolf, a male coyote's testicles remain retracted until mating season prompts them to descend.

Typical coyote scat at a trail intersection serves as a territorial marker. Note feather quill between 3- and 4-inch marks, and an abundance of fine rodent hairs.

Actual coitus between coyote pairs occurs between February and March. Gestation is 60 days, with a litter of one to as many as nineteen pups born in April or May. Pups weigh 7 ounces at birth. At 10 days pups will have doubled in size, and their eyes will have opened. At 3 to 4 weeks, the pups emerge from the den to play while parents protect them from predators, particularly birds of prey. The male brings food to his family, feeding pups regurgitated meat and occasionally babysitting while the mother leaves to drink or relieve herself. At 35 days, the pups weigh 3 to 4 pounds and are weaned.

Coyote pups mature quickly; by 6 months, they weigh nearly 30 pounds and can fend for themselves. By 9 months, male pups typically strike out on their own, while female pups may remain—babysitters for future generations—for about 2 years.

The coyote is a genetically unique species but shows a penchant for interbreeding with similar canids. The red wolf (*Canis rufus*) is thought to be disappearing as a species partly because it breeds readily with coyotes. Dogs, particularly those with coyote-like characteristics, have also mated with coyotes, producing a hard-to-identify "coydog." Most recently, DNA testing has revealed that probably most of the gray wolves in Minnesota have some coyote genes in their bloodlines.

This well-worn trail along the sloping bank of a river enables coyotes to patrol silently while looking for prey below, yet able to see into the surrounding forest without revealing more than its own head.

Behavior

Because coyotes are so well equipped to catch small prey, they seldom form packs. Packs that do exist form up at dusk, gathered by prolonged howls from the alpha male, who is greeted by high-pitched yaps and barks from those (mostly offspring) that join him. Pack members may split up while hunting, communicating the finding of meals large enough to be shared with long, broken howls that are much higher pitched than the monotonal howls of the gray wolf. Nightly hunts encompass roughly 3 square miles.

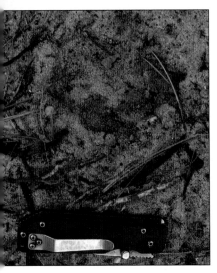

Right front foot of a 50-pound coyote on packed early-spring sand; smallest innermost toes failed to print clearly, while larger innermost toes pressed hard into the sand.

Coyote territories are only as large as required but generally encompass less than 12 square miles. Territories are bounded by olfactory scent posts consisting of urine and scat deposits left on trails, especially at intersections. Most scent marking is done by males, but alpha females may also scent territories.

One ancient myth claims that coyotes and badgers (*Taxidea taxus*) sometimes hunt together cooperatively, the coyote using its acute nose to locate burrowed rodents, which the badger digs out. Badger and coyote do double-team burrowed prey,

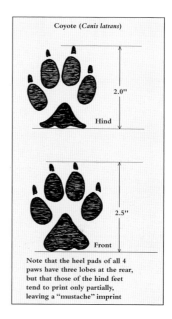

Coyote (*Canis latrans*)

2.0"

Hind

2.5"

Front

Note that the heel pads of all 4 paws have three lobes at the rear, but that those of the hind feet tend to print only partially, leaving a "mustache" imprint

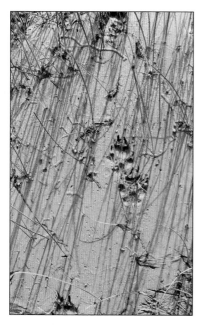

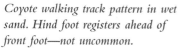

Coyote walking track pattern in wet sand. Hind foot registers ahead of front foot—not uncommon.

but the badger's keen nose needs no assistance, and the two do not share meals. The intelligent coyote knows to position itself near the escape tunnels common to burrowing species, waiting while the single-minded badger digs toward its prey. The cornered prey can wait for certain death from the badger, or it can try popping out of an escape tunnel, risking the coyote's lightning-fast jaws.

GRAY FOX
(*Urocyon cinereoargenteus*)

North America's largest native fox, the gray has never been as visible as its imported European cousin, the red fox. (Photo courtesy National Park Service.)

Gray foxes are native to North America and were in fact the reason that red foxes *(Vulpes vulpes)* were imported to the New World from Europe. When early settlers attempted to practice the nobleman's sport of fox hunting from horseback, they learned that this continent's largest native fox has a unique ability to extend its semi-retractable claws and climb trees like a cat. In the vast forests of America, this made for a short chase, so the nonclimbing red fox was imported for sporting purposes.

Geographic Range

Gray foxes range from southern Canada to northern Venezuela and Colombia. This species does not inhabit the more-mountainous areas of the northwestern United States, the Great Plains, deserts, or eastern Central America.

Habitat

Gray foxes inhabit forests, where their unique ability to climb trees enables them to escape predators. They may be seen in adjoining fields, where they forage for grasshoppers and rodents, but they are never very far from tall trees.

The gray fox's semiretractable claws give it a unique ability to scale trees. (Photo courtesy Illinois Dept. of Natural Resources.)

Physical Characteristics

Mass: Gray foxes weigh 7 to 13 pounds.

Body: They have a long bushy tail, short legs, and elongated body; body length is 31 to 44 inches; shoulder height is about 14 inches. The broad skull with widely spaced temporal ridges distinguishes it from other North American canids. The muzzle is narrow and tapered, ending in a small black nose pad. Ears are shorter and less pointed than those of the red fox. Males are only slightly larger than females.

Tail: The tail is bushy, black-tipped, 8 to 17 inches long, and typically shorter than the red fox's.

Tracks: Tracks are about 1.5 inches long for all four feet, hind foot slightly narrower than front. Semi-retractable claws usually show in tracks. Heel pads of front and hind feet have three rearward-pointed lobes, but usually only the outer edges of the outermost lobes show in hind tracks.

Scat: Scat is segmented, tapered at one or both ends, 2.5 inches long, 0.5 inch in diameter, and often encased in a spiral of fine rodent fur. It is indistinguishable from red fox scat, except that gray foxes normally eat a more-vegetarian diet of berries and fruits, and their scats contain more seeds and vegetable matter.

Coloration: It is easily confused with a red fox, especially when the latter is a "cross" phase of mottled red, gray, and black fur. The gray fox is grizzled gray and black along its back, neck, and upper tail. The upper head and muzzle are grizzled, with patches of white at the tip of the muzzle, on the cheeks, and on the underbelly. Sides of the neck, legs, body, and tail are rust colored.

Sign: Sign includes food caches buried in shallow holes or holes left by removing cached foods, trees that have been marked with urine at a

Gray fox scat in early autumn, showing a predominance of blueberries, a vital prewinter staple for most carnivores.

Although classed as a carnivore, the gray fox diet is comprised largely of berries and insects, with a few rodents, crayfish, and other small animals. (Photo courtesy Berkely University.)

height of about 8 inches, and yellow stains on snow. Gray foxes are unusual among wild canids in that they tend to den throughout the year, typically under tree roots, in rock crevices, or in hollow trees, and individuals often have several dens within their territories. Den entrances are much smaller than those of coyotes, largely because coyotes prey on gray foxes.

Vocalizations: Gray foxes make high-pitched barks, yaps, and growls, like those of a small dog. They are less vocal than red foxes.

Life span: They live 8 to 10 years.

Similar in size and general outline to the red fox, a gray fox's heel pads can often reveal its species through its tracks.

Gray Fox track pattern

Walking

Diet

Gray foxes are good hunters, able to pounce on mice in fields or catch rabbits in brushy swamps, but this canid's diet has an added dimension because it can climb trees to snatch roosting birds at night or to rob nests of their eggs. They prey on frogs, grasshoppers, and locusts; eat carrion; and catch small fish.

Gray foxes also eat vegetation, probably more than any other wild canid. Blueberries are a favorite, but the gray fox can climb into the upper branches of fruiting trees, such as wild cherries, to get fruits that are beyond the reach of its non-climbing cousins.

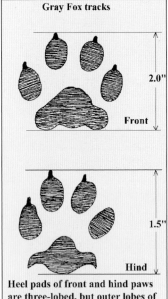

Gray Fox tracks

2.0"

Front

1.5"

Hind

Heel pads of front and hind paws are three-lobed, but outer lobes of hind feet tend to print only partially, with a mustache pattern.

Mating Habits

Gray foxes become sexually mature at 10 months. Mating occurs in late winter—March in the north, February in the south. (A rule of thumb is that gray foxes mate about 1 month after red foxes.) Mated pairs are believed to be monogamous.

Gestation is 50 days, with up to seven pups born in a secluded woodland den in April or May. Pups nurse for 3 months. The father brings food to the nursing mother and stands guard while she leaves to drink or relieve herself, but he takes no active role in parenting during the suckling stage and doesn't enter the den.

Gray fox pups are the most precocious of North American canids: immediately after wean-ing they leave the den and begin hunting with their parents. At 4 months, the pups have all of their permanent teeth and weigh about 7 pounds. By 5 months, the pups have left to fend for themselves, and the mates separate to resume a normally solitary lifestyle. Radio telemetry data indicate that separated family members remain within their own established territories, so inbreeding is unlikely.

Behavior

Gray foxes are solitary, deep-forest dwellers, and a tracker who sees one should count himself or herself lucky. The species is reclusive and seldom vocal, keeping to secluded dens in shadowed woods by day and hunting at night. This secretive behavior is explained by the fact that so many species, including raptors, coyotes, and bears, consider them prey.

But gray foxes are not easy prey; their light weight enables them to run across snow and boggy areas that are too soft to support larger carnivores. Sharp, semiretract-able claws enable them to climb trees in pursuit of sleeping squirrels and to escape enemies that they can't outrun. Gray foxes have been labeled as chicken killers, but instances where they have been guilty are rare. Most often the culprit is a raccoon, but such leaps of logic are made believable by adages like "a fox in the henhouse" and "sly as a fox."

RED FOX
(*Vulpes vulpes*)

Native to Europe, the red fox was transplanted into North America so that early noblemen could enjoy the gentleman's sport of fox hunting from horseback with hounds. The native gray fox, with its ability to climb trees, was unacceptable prey, so the red fox (which cannot climb trees) was brought to the New World. Soon after, the red fox, with its phenomenal adaptability to the most hostile environments, escaped captivity to become permanently established as part of the American ecosystem.

Geographic Range

Red foxes have thrived in every location. Today the species is common throughout the continental United States; in all but the most frigid regions of Canada and Alaska, where it overlaps the range of the arctic fox; and in Australia, Japan, and across Asia.

Habitat

Red foxes occupy an extraordinary range of habitats that includes deciduous and pine forests, arctic tundra, open prairies, and farmland. The species has become common in suburban areas, where it preys on rodents more adroitly than a house cat. Preferred habitats have a diversity of plant life, particularly fruits and berries. Unlike the reclusive gray fox, red foxes are frequently seen in open places.

Physical Characteristics

Mass: Red foxes weigh 7 to 15 pounds.

Body: They have a slender, elongated body and short legs; body length is 35 to 40 inches; shoulder height is 15 inches. Ears are long and pointed, with black backside; muzzle is long and slender, tipped with a prominent black button nose. Eyes are yellow, denoting good night vision.

Tail: The tail is bushy, rust colored, and 13 to 17 inches long, with a white (sometimes black) tip. A precaudal scent gland is located on the dorsal base of the tail, identifiable by a patch of dark fur.

Tracks: Tracks are larger than those of the gray fox but with smaller toe pads. About 2.5 inches long, the hind foot slightly smaller and narrower. There are four toes on each foot, with claws showing. Feet are heavily furred in winter. Heel pads of all four feet leave a chevron-shaped print. A noticeable ridge runs across the front heel pad, also in a chevron shape, that prints more deeply than the rest of the pad.

Scat: Scat is similar to that of other canids—cylindrical, segmented, and tapered at the ends but with a predominance of berry seeds and vegetable matter when available. It often has a spiral of fur wrapped around small bones and is 0.5 inch in diameter by 4 inches long.

A nonnative immigrant that was purposely brought to America by settlers from the Old World, the red fox is a marvel of adaptability whose range extends from the Arctic Circle to Central America.

An adept hunter, the red fox is the marathon runner of foxes, able to chase down tree squirrels (shown above) before they can climb to safety, and even to snatch flushed birds out of the air.

Coloration: Fur is rust colored to deep reddish brown on the upper parts, whitish on the underside. The lower part of the legs is usually black. There are two cross phases that sometimes occur: One, the "cross fox," is a grizzled coat of intermingled rust and black fur with a usually reddish belly; the other is the "silver fox" phase, with a silver-gray upper body and black mask around eyes, and dark-gray to black legs. Too common to be mutations, cross foxes make up about 25 percent of a given population, and silver foxes make up about 10 percent.

Sign: Spring birthing dens are excavated in the sides of hills, marked by a fan of loose soil around a main entrance that may measure 12 inches across. Escape tunnels branch from the underground chamber, usually within 10 feet of the main entrance. Small mounds or holes where food was cached nearby indicate an active den.

Vocalizations: They are more vocal than the gray fox, with high-pitched yapping and barking, reminiscent of a small dog. The alarm call is a single sharp, high-pitched bark, almost a shriek.

Life span: Red foxes live 10 years.

Typical red fox scat, 0.75 inches in diameter, with segments joined together by a sheath of rodent fur, reveals a more carnivorous diet than the gray fox.

Diet

Classified as a carnivore, this fox is almost omnivorous, eating rodents, rabbits, fish, and insects, as well as fruits. Blueberries are a favorite, but grapes, pears, apples, and most fruits are favored.

Red foxes are skilled rodent hunters. Like the coyote, a fox stands motionless in a meadow, cocking its head from one side to another, swiveling its acutely directional ears to pinpoint a mouse scurrying under grass or snow. When a mouse is located, the fox springs high into the air, all four feet leaving the ground, and comes down hard onto the rodent with both forefeet, stunning the prey.

Bolder than most wild canids, red foxes in autumn have learned to associate humans and gunshots with the rich venison liver, kidneys, and heart that some deer hunters leave behind.

Mating Habits

Mating season is timed with the arrival of warm weather, varying up to 4 months from one region to another. In the deep south, mating occurs in December and January; in central states, from January to February; in the far north, between late February and April.

Vixen (female) red foxes are in estrus for 6 days. Females signal their readiness to prospective mates through pheromonal scents several days prior to coming into heat. During the preheat period, males fight almost bloodlessly to compete for breeding status. Males have an annual cycle of "fecundity"

Red foxes lack the grizzled black saddle of the gray fox and have black legs. Bright yellow eyes denote good night vision.

Red Fox track patterns

LR
RR

Walk   Trot   Run

(sperm production) and are sterile the rest of the year.

Copulation lasts about 15 minutes, punctuated by barking and yapping from the male. Females may mate with more than one male to help ensure impregnation. Delayed implantation prevents fertilized eggs from attaching to the uterine wall for 10 to 14 days and helps to guarantee that a female is physically fit for pregnancy; if she isn't, the fertilized egg spontaneously aborts.

Pregnant females pair off with their strongest mate, retiring to a secluded location to excavate a birthing den. The male doesn't enter the den after its completion. Gestation lasts 49 to 56 days, with shorter periods indicating healthier mothers.

Between February and May, depending on latitude, the female births five to thirteen kits (pups). Kits are born blind and weigh 3 ounces. By 14 days their eyes are open, and at 5 weeks, pups are playing outside, running back into the den when the mother barks an alarm. Kits are weaned at 10 weeks, and the father, who has provided food to mother and kits, leaves to resume a solitary life.

Kits remain with the mother, learning to hunt and forage, until the following autumn, when the young adults disperse, sometimes traveling more than 100 miles before taking a mate at 10 months of age.

Behavior

Red foxes are solitary hunters of small animals. The prolific nature of rodents keeps the average territory small, as does an omnivorous diet of berries and fruits, but there will always be a source of water somewhere within a typical range of 3 to 9 square miles. Territorial battles are rare and are seldom more than a nip-and-chase, with the resident fox having the home advantage.

More nomadic than the gray fox, a red fox has several dens throughout its territorial range;

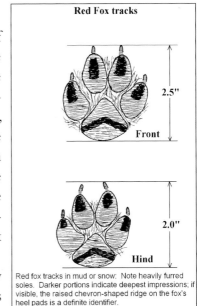

Red Fox tracks

2.5"

Front

2.0"

Hind

Red fox tracks in mud or snow: Note heavily furred soles. Darker portions indicate deepest impressions; if visible, the raised chevron-shaped ridge on the fox's heel pads is a definite identifier.

these dens are linked to each other, and to buried food caches, by trails that are patrolled daily. One of these is a maternal den that will be used year after year, so long as it remains undisturbed. The others provide owners with a place to escape if chased by larger predators. With a remarkably fast running speed of 30 miles per hour, a healthy, alert fox can usually reach safety before being overtaken by a faster carnivore.

Red foxes are known to take an occasional chicken, but predation is limited to small animals, and very often foxes take the blame for the marauding of skunks and raccoons.

Family Felidae

Cats are a family of hunters that split off from other mammals during the Eocene Period, 40 million years ago. All are endowed with acute senses of smell, hearing, and vision, and with sensitive whiskers that can detect changes in air currents. All species are armed with very sharp, retractable claws on all four of their toes, as well as a front dewclaw that functions like an opposable thumb to grip prey. Cats possess uncanny stealth, lightning-fast reflexes, daggerlike canines that kill quickly with a brain-piercing bite to the base of a victim's skull, and unmatched agility. Most hunt at night, when extraordinary night vision and binocular eyesight gives them an advantage over their prey. Cats may eat fresh carrion, but they don't normally eat animals that have been dead long enough to decay, the way scavenging coyotes and bears do.

JAGUAR
(*Panthera onca*)

Revered as a forest god by pre-Columbian civilizations in southern Mexico, Guatemala, and Peru, the jaguar's name means "kills in a single bound." There are eight subspecies, all threatened, and some are extinct except in zoos. The greatest threats to this largest American cat come from buyers of illegal furs, who pay exorbitant prices for the jaguar's spotted pelt, and for clearing old-growth forest, where the cat's dappled coat provides good camouflage. Little is known about how jaguars live in the wild, and most existing data have been gathered from zoo specimens.

Geographic Range

Native to Central America, jaguars once ranged as far north as Arizona, but, by the late 1900s, none were thought to exist north of Mexico. Two independent sightings in 1996 confirmed jaguars still reached as far north as Arizona and New Mexico. In February 2009, the only known free-living jaguar in the United States was euth-

Like several species, including leopards, red foxes, and occasionally a cougar, individual jaguars may have a "black panther" coat. (Photo courtesy US Fish & Wildlife Service.)

Massive head, powerful build, and large feet make America's largest cat a formidable hunter. (Photo courtesy US Fish & Wildlife Service.)

anized in Arizona after suffering kidney failure (common among old cats). Today most jaguars live in Argentina and Brazil and as far south as Patagonia.

Habitat

Typical jaguar habitat provides large prey and plenty of water, preferably in canopied forest where their spotted coats are hard to distinguish among undergrowth and dappled sunlight. Dense jungle and scrub forest, reed thickets along waterways, and shoreline forests are ideal, but the species has also been seen in the rocky desert country favored by cougars.

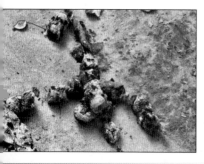

This jaguar scat, about a week old and turning white with age, is similar to that of other large predators but will probably contain remnants of alligators and other aquatic animals. (Photo courtesy Kansas State University.)

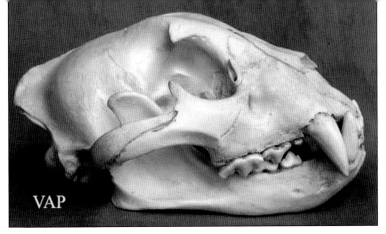

This reproduction jaguar skull shows the powerful jaws and very strong canines that enable it to bring down large prey quickly. (Photo courtesy of The Bone Room.)

Physical Characteristics

Mass: Males weigh 120 to 300 pounds, and females weigh 100 to 200 pounds.

Body: Jaguars are stout and larger and more stocky than a cougar, with a spotted coat, thick limbs, and a massive head. Body length is about 4 feet; shoulder height is 2.5 to 3 feet.

Tail: The tail is 18 to 30 inches long, shorter and thinner than the mountain lion's, and has a black tip.

Tracks: The forefoot is 4 to 4.5 inches, nearly as wide as it is long, leaving a print that is almost round. Hind prints are slightly smaller. Toes are much smaller, and heel pads much larger, than those of the mountain lion. Heel pads of all four feet are three lobed, but the two outermost lobes in a jaguar's front track are larger than the center lobe and extend more rearward, whereas the three lobes in a mountain lion's front track are of nearly equal size. Walking stride is 20 inches but

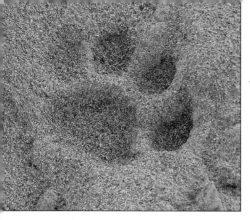

Left hind track of a jaguar in damp sand. (Photo courtesy US Fish & Wildlife Service.)

may vary greatly in the cat's jungle habitat; straddle is 8 to 10 inches.

Scat: Scat is nearly identical to cougar scats; cylindrical, segmented, tapered at one or both ends, usually with fur wrapped around the scat in spiral fashion; about 5 inches long by 1.5 inches in diameter. Differences may be evident from the jaguar's tendency to prey on aquatic animals, including alligators and fish.

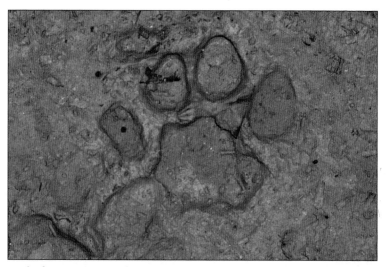

Right front paw print of a jaguar in mud shows why the cat is such a powerful swimmer. (Photo courtesy US Fish & Wildlife Service.)

Coloration: Jaguars are normally yellow and tan with a mottling of black rings, many of which have a single black dot inside—a bull's-eye pattern. Cheeks, throat, underbelly, and insides of the legs are white. It isn't uncommon for a jaguar to be black, a phase in which the cat is known as a black panther. Black panthers are spotted, but mottling is subdued by a coat that's nearly as dark as the spots.

Sign: Sign includes scat deposits at trail intersections, usually near trees that have been clawed and sprayed with urine; alligator remains near water; and large cat tracks on shorelines that enter or exit the water.

Vocalizations: Jaguars are the only New World cats that can roar. Roars differ from those of an African lion, being a series of loud coughs rather than a single unbroken roar.

Life span: Jaguars live up to 22 years in captivity; life span in the wild is unknown but probably 15 years.

Diet

Panthera onca is very much a predator, feeding on terrestrial prey that includes deer, peccaries, and alpacas. The only wild felid that enjoys swimming, jaguars also take aquatic animals, including nutria (a larger cousin to the muskrat), fish, and alligators or caimans up to 5 feet long.

Mating Habits

Jaguars are sexually mature at 3 years. Females breed once every 2 years. Those in tropical regions may breed at any time of year, while those in the north generally mate in December

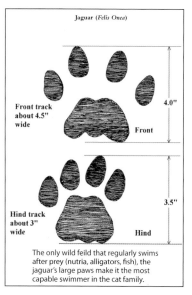

Jaguar *(Felis Onea)*

Front track about 4.5" wide

4.0"

Front

Hind track about 3" wide

3.5"

Hind

The only wild feild that regularly swims after prey (nutria, alligators, fish), the jaguar's large paws make it the most capable swimmer in the cat family.

or January. Females are monogamous, accepting a single mate per pregnancy.

The gestation period for jaguars is 93 to 110 days. Prior to giving birth, the mother, still accompanied by her mate, dens in a small rock cave, a hollow beneath the roots of a tree, or another secure and dry refuge. Jaguars are poor diggers, so dens are natural or appropriated from other animals.

Litter size is one to four cubs, born blind but furred, weighing 1.5 to 2 pounds each. The mother remains with the cubs constantly until weaning them at 40 days, leaving the den only to relieve herself and drink while the father guards the den. While cubs are denned, the father brings food and guards the den but does not enter.

When cubs are 2 months old and able to travel with the mother, the parents separate; fathers take no role in rearing offspring. Cubs will be proficient hunters of small prey at 6 months but remain with the mother for another year before going on their own. Female cubs may remain with the mother for 2 years but must leave before she mates again.

Behavior

Jaguars are solitary, interacting only during the mating period. The cats are known to live within a territorial radius of only

3 miles, but if food is scarce, they may roam 200 miles in search of more-suitable habitat. Jaguars are fast runners but only for short distances. They climb well, are excellent swimmers, and prefer habitats with abundant freshwater. The jaguar's being a keystone species in tropical ecosystems, its predation on herbivorous and granivorous mammals is crucial for controlling prolific species whose overpopulation can negatively affect native flora.

Jaguars have preyed on domestic animals, mostly as the result of humans' clearing forest to move farms into the cats' habitat. Jaguars bear a reputation as man-eaters, but Miskito Indians tell stories of jaguars emerging from the forest to play with village children. Mayan tribes believed that the jaguar was a god who helped the sun to travel beneath the world each night, ensuring that it rose again each morning. Incidents of humans being followed through the jungle by lone jaguars are probably attributable to curiosity.

MOUNTAIN LION
(*Puma concolor*)

Known as cougars, pumas, painters, and catamounts, mountain lions are the New World's second-largest felids. Portrayed as dangerous to people in novels and movies, there have been rare instances where pumas have attacked humans. Usually the cat is an old one, with bad teeth, failing health, and perhaps debilitating arthritis that keeps it from catching its normal prey as well as it used to.

Human victims are typically small statured, alone in rural areas, and engaged in an activity that excites the feline hunting instinct the same way a wriggling string triggers a compulsive instinct in house cats to attack. Breathless joggers and running children are likely victims, but skiers, snowshoers, and backpackers virtually never are because they appear too large to be easy prey; the objective of any predator is not to fight but to subdue prey with as little danger to itself as possible.

Geographic Range

The mountain lion once had a range that spanned the New World from southern Argentina to northern Canada and from one ocean to the other. Conflict between cats and people peaked as a result of increased housing development along the Pacific coast in the early 1990s. This brought the big cats into conflict with homeowners, and state authorities reinstated a hunting season. Animal rights groups responded by illegally livetrapping and transplanting cougars, and by 1994 the animals were being spotted in Pennsylvania, Wisconsin, and Michigan's Lower Peninsula—places where the species had long been extinct.

Habitat

Mountain lions can use a broad range of habitats, from subtropical jungle and northern cedar swamps to alpine forest and desert mountains. Deep snows, craggy rock, and thick undergrowth are not limiting factors. Essentially, the cougars are capable of existing anywhere they can find water, concealing cover, and enough deer-size prey to keep them well fed.

Physical Characteristics

Mass: Mountain lions weigh 75 to 275 pounds.

Body: The body is muscular and lithe, like a domestic cat. Body length is 60 to 108 inches; legs are short and thick, with powerful hindquarters that create a jacked-up appearance. Skull is broad and short, with a high, arched forehead and a broad rostrum (nasal bone). The nose pad is large and triangle-shaped; ears are short and rounded. The mandible is powerfully constructed, carnassial (scissoring) teeth are massive, and long canines enable quick kills of large prey. The upper jaw holds one more premolar on each side than either the bobcat or lynx. Molars have a scissorlike fit, designed not for crushing bone (like scavengers) but for cutting hide and flesh.

Tail: The tail is one-third of total length, 21 to 36 inches long, and tawny brown with a black tip.

Tracks: Prints are more round than the elongated tracks of canids. Front prints are 3 to more than 4 inches long; hind tracks are about 10 percent smaller. Four large toes show in all tracks (front dewclaw doesn't register) but normally with no claws showing, because of retractable claws. The heel pads of front and hind feet have three lobes, but the front pads are more blocky, less rounded. The walking stride is 20 inches; the straddle is 8 inches.

Scat: Scat is similar to that of canids; segmented, cylindrical, tapered at one or both ends; about 5 inches long by 1 to 1.5 inches in diameter. Deer hair wraps around the outer surface in spiral fashion to prevent sharp bones encased within from scratching the intestines.

Coloration: The pelage is short and fairly coarse. Upper body ranges from tan to reddish brown in summer, becoming darker and grayer during winter. The chest, underbelly, and mouth area of the muzzle are white, becoming more yellowed with age. The backs of the ears are black. A dark stripe extends downward around the muzzle at either side of the pinkish nose. The eyes of adults range from bright yellow to grayish yellow.

Sign: Claw marks in trees serve as territorial scratching posts, but the span and thickness of claw marks are much broader than those of a bobcat or lynx. Scats haphazardly covered with soil show claw marks that are usually from the same direction in which the cat was traveling.

Vocalizations: Mountain lions purr when content or when mothers are suckling kittens and can mew like house cats. Other vocalizations include hisses, growls, and the trademark snarl. Kittens mew like domestic kittens but have a loud chirping cry that gets their mother's attention.

Life span: Cougars live about 10 years in the wild, up to 20 years in captivity.

Diet

Like all felids, cougars prefer to hunt rather than to eat carrion. Superbly equipped with stealth, speed, and natural armament, a puma can take down prey larger than itself, typically leaping onto the backs of large animals and dispatching them with a brain-piercing bite to the base of the skull.

Most famed for taking deer-size game, a mountain lion also eats most smaller-size animals and can survive well on a diet that includes no large prey. When the quarry is large, a puma prefers to concentrate on immature or sickly individuals that won't put up a hard fight. Annual food consumption for an adult cat is 600 to 900 pounds.

Mating Habits

Cougars are normally solitary, but when they join to mate, it's a polygamous relationship, with both genders typically breeding with more than one partner. Both sexes mature at 2.5 years, but males won't mate until they have established their own territories, usually at three years. Males remain sexually fertile for up to 20 years, females to about 12 years. Copulation is preceded by several days of courtship that enable a pair to become accustomed to one another. There is no fixed mating season, but breeding generally occurs from December to March. Males respond to pheromonal scents, yowling, and other vocalizations from females with their own eerie caterwauling, sounding much like large alley cats.

Female mountain lions mate every other year, with the mother devoting off years to teaching offspring the skills of survival. The estrus period lasts 9 days, but if the female hasn't achieved pregnancy before a heat passes, she will come into estrus for another 9-day cycle.

Mating battles between males are mostly bloodless, consisting largely of body language. When males do fight, contests are largely of physical strength, without claws or teeth. Injuries do occur, but mountain lions harbor an instinctive revulsion against harming their own kind, and their decidedly lethal weapons are not used with the violence that they could be.

Gestation lasts 82 to 96 days, with mothers giving birth in a secluded cave or den within the father's territory. Litter sizes range from one to six cubs, with three or four being average. Newborns weigh between 1 and 2 pounds and are blind and helpless for their first 10 days of life. The cubs' first teeth erupt immediately thereafter, and they begin to play. The father may bring the female food during the denning period, but he takes no role in rearing offspring. At 40 days the cubs are weaned and accompany their mother on short hunting forays.

Male cubs remain with the mother for 1 year before leaving to establish their own territories; female cubs may remain with her for up to 2 years. Emancipated cubs may remain together for a short time, using the strength of numbers to discourage would-be predators.

Behavior

A mountain lion's solitary lifestyle is interrupted only by breeding and rearing of young. Territorial ranges vary downward from about 60 square miles, depending on the availability of food and water. Residents of either sex mark their territories with urine or fecal deposits, often at the bases of trees that serve as scratching posts.

Cougars are primarily nocturnal, with excellent night and binocular vision. Their main sense is sight, followed by sense of smell, then hearing. Pumas typically have summer and winter ranges in different locations because they follow the migratory habits of deer.

Mountain lions are hunted as sport, and their pelts have considerable value as trophies, rugs, or wall hangings. They can be a threat to domestic animals but tend to avoid human habitation.

BOBCAT
(*Lynx rufus*)

The bobcat is America's most widespread and successful wild cat.

The bobcat is the most dominant wild felid in North America, and this highly adaptable species is comfortable in a broad range of habitats. Having been hunted, trapped, or poisoned to near extinction in some places, bobcats are shy of humans and are rarely seen. That secretiveness may lessen as housing development continues to bring humans into bobcat habitats.

Geographic Range

Bobcats are found throughout North America, from southern Mexico to southern Canada and from the Atlantic to the Pacific coasts. Population densities in the United States are higher in the forested eastern region than they are in western states. The species is rare or nonexistent in the large agricultural regions of southern Michigan, Illinois, Indiana, Ohio, and Pennsylvania.

Habitat

Bobcats can adapt to a wide variety of habitats, including dense forests, wet swamps, semiarid deserts, forested mountains, and brushland. They prefer plenty of cover with trees large enough to climb for the purpose of observation or escape. The species seems well adapted to cold and snow but isn't found in most of Canada.

Physical Characteristics

Mass: Bobcats weigh 14 to more than 68 pounds and are largest in the north.

Body: The body is much like a domestic cat: lithe, well muscled, and built for agility. Cheeks and ear tips are tufted, though not to the extent of the lynx. Body length is 28 to 50 inches; shoulder height is 15 to 20 inches.

Tail: The tail is short, black-tipped, and 3 to 6 inches long—longer than that of the lynx.

Tracks: The tracks are 1 to 2 inches long, some as long as 3.5 inches in the far north. Four toes are on each foot, with no claws showing. All four feet are approximately the same size. Stride is 10 to 14 inches; straddle is 6 to 7 inches. Hind prints may register precisely inside front tracks, leaving an apparently bipedal track pattern. Front of heel pad, toward toes, is concave and distinctly different from any of the canids.

Tufted ears, reddish spotted coat, and pinkish nose pad make the bobcat easy to identify.

Scat: Scat is cylindrical, segmented, and tapered at one or both ends. Length is 2 to 6 inches, diameter is 0.5 to 1 inch, with rodent, rabbit, or deer fur wound in a spiral fashion around small bones encased within. Scats are indistinguishable from those of the lynx and easily confused with those of a coyote or fox, except that canids don't attempt to cover scats with dirt. Unlike cougars, which tend to scratch earth from the direction in which they'll be traveling, bobcats scratch from all directions, leaving raylike patterns of scratch marks all around the scat deposit.

Coloration: The bobcat's summer pelage is darker brown spots against a coat of brown or reddish brown; the winter coat tends to be darker, with spots less obvious, ranging from dark brown to almost gray. In all seasons, the insides of the legs, underbelly, and throat are cream colored to white (darkest in older individuals), and mottled with brown spots.

Sign: Deep scratches in smooth-barked tree trunks, about two feet above the ground, are often scented with the cat's pungent urine. Soft pines seem to be the preferred scratching posts, possibly because the strong-smelling sap helps to conceal the bobcat's own scent.

Vocalizations: The bobcat sounds much like a domestic cat, with noises consisting of soft mews, purring, low growls, and childlike wailing during the breeding season.

Life span: Bobcats live 8 to 10 years in the wild.

Diet

A bobcat's diet includes prey that ranges from small mice to rabbits, to an occasional fawn. The species rarely eats carrion, preferring to kill its own food. Like house cats, bobcats have an uncanny ability to sneak within striking distance of prey. Blue jays, grouse, and other birds are caught before they can fly away from this wildcat's lightning-fast attack. Yearling deer may be taken in deep winter snows, usually by strong cats perched on an overhead tree branch. When a likely victim comes into range, the cat pounces onto its back, anchors itself with hook-like retractable claws, and drives long, sharp canines into the base of the victim's skull. When forced to take prey head-on, the cat may instead clamp its mouth over the windpipe, suffocating the victim.

Officially a carnivore, the bobcat's diet of meat is supplemented with berries and vegetation. Sugar calories from blueberries and other fruits help to put on fat against the approaching winter and provide nutrients that are lacking in meat. Indigestible grasses and sedges are also eaten to help scour intestines and colon.

Mating Habits

Bobcats in the northern range mate in February or March, but those in the South may breed throughout summer; in especially warm areas, females may produce two litters a year. Mating is initiated by the scent of a female coming into heat, which may attract numerous suitors. After a contest that consists mostly of caterwauling, growls, and an occasional scuffle, the strongest male mates with the receptive female, and the pair sets off to find a sheltered birthing den in a rock crevice or hollow log or under the roots of a large standing tree. Poor diggers, bobcats may appropriate existing fox or coyote dens.

This fresh bobcat scat, about 0.5 inches diameter, contains small rodent bones, wrapped in a protective outer sheath of fur.

After a gestation period of 60 to 70 days, the mother gives birth to a litter of two or three blind kittens, each weighing 8 ounces, in late April or May. After 10 days, the young open their eyes and move about the den. The mother stays with the kittens constantly for their first 2 months, leaving only to drink and to relieve herself. During this

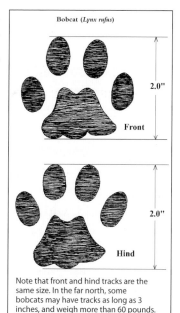

Bobcat (*Lynx rufus*)

2.0"

Front

2.0"

Hind

Note that front and hind tracks are the same size. In the far north, some bobcats may have tracks as long as 3 inches, and weigh more than 60 pounds.

time her mate, who doesn't enter the den, brings food and guards the den when she's away.

Kittens are weaned in June or July, and the parents separate, the male taking no role in rearing the offspring. Kittens hunt with their mother, learning the finer points of catching meals and avoiding danger, until they reach 8 months, usually in December or January. Nearly grown then, males leave first, followed within a month by their sisters. Young adults disperse widely but generally travel no farther than is necessary. Emancipated kittens will likely take—or at least compete for—a mate in their first breeding season.

Behavior

The solitary bobcat interacts only to mate. Females live discreetly, especially if they have kittens, but males blatantly advertise their claim to a territory of about 5 square miles. Partly buried scats left at trail intersections delineate territory. Odorous sprays of urine on tree trunks that may be marked by clawing do the same.

The home range of a dominant male bobcat typically overlaps the domains of several females, giving the resident male a head start at detecting when one of them comes into estrus. The territorial boundaries of two males may overlap, but this seldom leads to conflict except during mating season or if food becomes scarce.

Bobcats don't normally live in dens, but there may be several refuges sited throughout an individual's range. The dens serve as shelter for escaping foul weather that also drives most prey into hiding or for eluding larger predators.

LYNX
(*Lynx canadensis*)

The most northern and most secretive of American wild cats, the lynx is a symbol of wilderness.

This slightly smaller but lankier cousin to the bobcat is one of the most reclusive species in North America. Lynx are supremely adapted to life in the dense timber and deep snows of the far north woods. Lynx pelts—mostly from Canada—have become increasingly valuable since restrictions were placed on the importation of cat pelts in the latter half of the 20th century. Lynx populations have never been in danger.

Geographic Range

The largest populations of lynx are found throughout Canada and in the northernmost regions of Montana and Idaho. There are small populations in New England, northern Wisconsin, and Michigan's Upper Peninsula. With a demonstrated aversion to humans, warming winters, and a continually shrinking habitat, lynx are unlikely to ever be common.

Habitat

Native to North America, lynx are occasionally seen on tundra or in rocky areas in the far north but never far from dense old-growth forests and thick swamps that are its required habitat. Lynx are superbly adapted to life in deep snow but have a pronounced tendency to avoid humans, so anyone who sees one in the wild can count that day lucky.

Physical Characteristics

Mass: *Lynx weigh* 11 to 40 pounds.

Body: Lynx are long legged with very large, furry paws adapted for silent travel atop deep snow. Body length is 29 to 41 inches, and males are about 10 percent larger than females. Pointed ears are tipped with long tufts of fur; cheeks are also tufted, giving the appearance of sideburns. Shoulder height is 15 to more than 20 inches.

Tail: The tail is shorter than the bobcat's, 2 to 5 inches long.

Tracks: Four toes are on each foot, with no claws showing in tracks. Paws are extraordinarily large and well furred, especially in winter, making tracks appear even larger and giving this fast runner an edge when pursuing prey over deep snow. Fore print is 3 to 4.5 inches long, hind prints are about 10 percent smaller. Hind print has three lobes at rear of heel pad, and front print has three lobes on heel pad, but the two outermost lobes extend more to the rear at either side, leaving a chevron-shaped impression unlike the three equal-sized lobes made by the front heel pad of a bobcat. Stride is 14 to 16 inches; straddle is 5 to 7 inches.

Scat: Scat is usually indistinguishable from bobcat scats, being cylindrical, segmented, and tapered at one or both ends. Length is 2 to 6 inches; diameter is 0.5 to 1 inch. Scats are usually only partially buried under soil or snow and typically have an outer covering of fine hare or rabbit fur wrapped spirally around an inner core of small bones.

Coloration: There is some variation, but the usual lynx coat is yellow-brown in summer, becoming grayer in winter, and longer than the fur of a bobcat. Individuals may have dark spots, but lynx generally lack the heavily spotted appearance of a bobcat. The ear tufts and tip of the tail are black, and the throat, belly, and insides of the legs are whitish. Yellow eyes denote good night vision.

Lynx scat, about 1 inch in diameter, encased in a sheath of fine squirrel and hare fur.

Sign: Sign includes scent posts on smooth-barked trees that have been clawed and sprayed with urine and partially covered scats left at trail intersections. Large prey that cannot be eaten immediately will often be cached by burying it beneath debris or snow.

Vocalizations: Lynx are normally silent except during the mating season, when males especially utter a loud shriek or scream that ends with an echoing wail some people have described as eerie, like the wailing of a small child.

Life span: Lynx live 8 to 10 years in the wild.

Diet

A key species in the lynx diet is the snowshoe, or varying, hare (*Lepus americanus*). Being at least as proficient a hunter as its cousin, the bobcat, the lynx is capable of catching rodents, birds, spawning fish, and an occasional yearling deer, but survival of this species relies heavily on snowshoe hare populations. When hare populations rise and then fall in cycles, as they do about every 9.5 years, lynx populations suffer starvation and starvation-related diseases one year later. Lynx may eat carrion if the meat is fresh and not decayed.

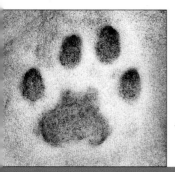

Mating Habits

Like northern bobcats (and unlike southern bobcats), female lynx come

Right front track of a lynx; note that the broad foot—nature's own snowshoe—presses evenly into the snow all around, denoting excellent balance and stealth.

into heat only once a year, in March and April, and raise only one litter per year. Prior to selecting her mate, a receptive female may have several suitors follow her everywhere with wailing, caterwauling, and an occasional fight marked by lots of hissing, spitting, and growling but little bloodshed. After about one week of this competition, the female enters an estrus period of 1 to 2 days and selects a mate. After mating, the pair leaves to find a secluded birthing den in a hollow log or rock crevice.

After a gestation period of 9 weeks, females give birth in May or June to two (and sometimes as many as five) blind kittens, each weighing about 7 ounces. Larger litter sizes are indicative of an especially healthy mother and abundant food. Except for short departures to drink or relieve herself, the mother remains with her young constantly for their first month of life, relying on her mate to bring food and keep watch against enemies. After 1 month the kittens begin eating meat, but continue to nurse for 5 months, and are weaned in October or November.

After weaning, when the kittens have grown enough to travel, the male lynx leaves and takes no part in rearing his offspring. The nearly grown young remain with their mother until January or February before setting

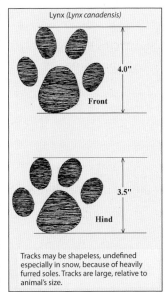

Lynx (*Lynx canadensis*)

4.0"

Front

3.5"

Hind

Tracks may be shapeless, undefined especially in snow, because of heavily furred soles. Tracks are large, relative to animal's size.

off on their own, with males usually leaving first. Freed of her charges, the mother will come into heat again about 1 month later. Her female kittens reach sexual maturity at 22 months, males at 33 months.

Behavior

Lynx are solitary animals, generally avoiding one another except to mate. They are territorial, but a male's domain is likely to infringe upon the territories of several females. Territories vary from 7 to more than 200 square miles, depending on the availability of food and resources.

Lynx are primarily nocturnal, with excellent night vision and keen directional hearing. They lie in wait for hours along game trails, overlooking them from a tree branch or knoll, or they might stalk prey to within a few yards, then pounce onto its back. Long canine teeth deliver a fatal bite to the base of the victim's skull, enabling these cats to swiftly take down animals large enough to be dangerous to them. Hard times prompt females with young to hunt cooperatively for hares, spreading themselves into a skirmish line and moving through brushy areas until one of them jumps prey. This hunting technique appears to be learned rather than instinctual.

Lynx shelter from foul weather in rough dens under rock ledges, in caves, under fallen trees, or in hollow logs. There are likely to be several such refuges scattered throughout an animal's territory.

Family Ursidae

Bears live in North America, northern Europe, Asia, and India. All are large and powerfully built, ranging from up to 600 pounds for a mature black bear to more than 1,700 pounds for the massive Kodiak brown bear. All have five toes on each foot, each toe tipped with a stout, functional claw.

Until the late 20th century, it was believed that bears hibernated, but today we know that bears don't enter the comalike torpor of true hibernators and sometimes leave their dens to wander during midwinter warm spells.

Most interesting to scientists are the bears' physiological attributes. Despite putting on about 25 percent of body weight in fat each year, bears suffer no arterial blockage from cholesterol. Denned bears neither defecate nor urinate for months at a time; they have a remarkable renal system that not only isn't poisoned from a buildup of nitrogen urea but also converts that lethal waste product into usable amino acids, then recycles the water for use in bodily functions. If scientists can learn how a bear reprocesses its own urine, the positive implications for humans suffering from kidney failure could be enormous. NASA, too, is keenly interested in how a bear can remain inactive for several months without experiencing the loss of bone mass suffered by human astronauts.

BLACK BEAR
(*Ursus americanus*)

Smallest of North America's three native bear species, the black bear is the most abundant, adaptable, and widespread. Black bears avoid contact with humans, and people in the midst of black bear country seldom see one. Smokey Bear, fire prevention icon of the U.S. Forest Service, is a black bear.

Geographic Range

Native only to North America, black bears were once common throughout the continent, but today their range is half what it was. The species is found south of the Arctic Circle throughout Canada and Alaska from the Pacific to the Atlantic, from northern California to the Rocky Mountains, southward along the Rockies to central Mexico, and along the eastern seaboard from Maine down to Florida.

Habitat

Black bear habitat is forested, with large trees that can be climbed to escape danger. In the course of a single year, a bear might travel as far as 500 miles, following plants, fish, and other foods as they become available.

Physical Characteristics

Mass: Black bears weigh 200 to more than 600 pounds, and males are about 5 percent larger than females.

Body: They are powerfully muscled, covered by thick fur, and especially large in autumn, when animals carry 25

Ursus americanus is unique to North America, reaching weights in excess of 600 pounds and able to thrive in most environments.

percent of total weight in body fat. Body length is 4 to 6 feet. Head is round, with a short muzzle and erect rounded ears.

Tail: The tail is short, furred, and 3 to 7 inches long.

Tracks: There are five forward-pointing toes on each foot, each tipped with a curved and sharply pointed claw that enables black bears to scale trees. Front tracks are 4 to 5 inches long, 6 to 7 inches if heel pad registers (usually as a large dot).

Hind prints are 7 to 9 inches, long, and 5 inches wide at the toes, resembling a human footprint. Their largest toe is the outermost, opposite our own. The normal walk is a shuffling gait, with a stride of about 1 foot, a straddle of 10 to 12 inches.

The running gait is the quadrupedal "rocking-horse" pattern: forefeet are planted together as the hind feet come forward on either side; when the hind feet hit the ground, the forelegs and back are extended as the animal leaps forward, coming down again on paired forefeet, and the gait repeats.

Scat: Scat is cylindrical, dark brown to black, with flat, untapered ends; insect legs or carapaces may be apparent. When the animal is feeding on meat, scats become carnivore-like, tapered at one or both ends, with small bones and fragments sheathed within a spiral of fur. Length is 2 to 8 inches; diameter is 1 to 2 inches. Rich diets cause cow-pie-like scats.

Coloration: Black bears are usually coal black, brown patches covering either side of the muzzle, bordering a black stripe that extends from top of the muzzle to nose pad. Young bears up to 2 years may have a spot of white on the chest. Black bears west of the Great Lakes are frequently brown and misidentified as brown bears, but they lack the distinctive shoulder hump. A bluish phase occurs near Alaska's Yakutat Peninsula, and those on Gribble Island are almost completely white; all three color phases are found in British Columbia.

Sign: Scat deposits at trail intersections mark territorial boundaries. Trees are used as scratching posts, with five usually deep gouges extending vertically down the trunk from a height of up to 7 feet or as high as the maker could reach.

Scratches are a visual record of a bear's size, but interdigital scents (akin to sweat from human palms) carries information about gender, size, and individual identification. Green trees are sometimes scratched, but standing dead trees seem to be preferred, as well as bridges, fence posts, and power poles. Sows, especially those with cubs, are less obvious, so most of the territorial sign a tracker finds will have been left there by males.

Other sign includes excavations that were dug in pursuit of rodents, rotting logs that have been ripped apart, and fruit trees clawed or split apart at their crotches to reach upper branches.

Vocalizations: Black bears are nor-mally silent. A chomping of teeth accompanied by a froth of saliva at the corners of the mouth indicates anxiety. A loud huffing is another warning to leave, and low bawling sounds are used by mothers to communicate with offspring. Bears bawl loudly during territorial wrestling matches.

Life span: Black bears live up to 30 years in captivity; life span in the wild is about 15 years.

Diet

Black bears are omnivorous, and their digestive system can assimilate

Rich, nutritious blueberries are a much sought-after food source by many species from late summer through autumn, as this purple bear scat shows.

A typical solid bear scat, seen when an animal's diet is omnivorous, consisting of rodent hairs, plant fibers, and insect exoskeletons. Note that ends are nearly squared, not tapered like most carnivore scats.

the rough grass fibers with nearly the same efficiency as a deer. Fat–rich larvae are favored, along with spiders, frogs, and fish. Bears sometimes knock off the tops of anthills and then insert a forefoot into the mass of angered insects; when the paw is covered by attacking ants, the bear licks them off. A black bear's diet varies widely from one season or region to another.

With a running speed of about 30 miles per hour, black bears cannot run down large prey. They appropriate kills from more-skilled hunters if an opportunity presents itself, and they are well equipped for excavating burrowed squirrels. One exception is in late spring, when black bears prowl the thickets in search of newborn fawns.

A black bear's territory may encompass several hundred square miles but seldom more than is necessary to obtain enough nutrition to put on a quarter of its body weight in fat for the coming winter.

One phenomenon that trackers should be alert for in spring is the anal plug of mostly grasses that blocks the colon during the winter sleep. Prior to denning, bears eat a last meal of rough, indigestible sedges and grasses, which mass together in the lower intestine. The plug ensures that no excrement fouls the den during sleep—especially not birthing dens. Expelled anal plugs are cylindrical, two to three inches long, and composed of grass blades, plant fibers, and pine needles, coated with a mucouslike fluid when fresh. Bears remain close to their dens for about a week after waking, so a freshly expelled anal plug indicates that a bear den is nearby.

Black bears leave the feet of squirrel-size and larger prey, biting them free of the carcass as it feeds. The purpose is to remove the sharp climbing claws that could injure the bear's convoluted digestive system, which is unlike the straighter intestines of true carnivores.

Crushed reindeer moss lichens show the left hind and left front tracks of a bear walking toward the right of this photo. Forefoot is behind rear foot; note identifying dot shape pressed into the lichens at far left.

Mating Habits

Males older than 3 years pair with females older than 2 years in June and July for 2 weeks of courtship. After mating, they separate, with males to mate again, if possible. At this time, females with 2-year-old cubs abandon them to mate again.

Bears den in November and December, and only then do fertilized eggs (carried dormant by the sow within her womb) implant in the uterine wall and begin to develop. If a sow is sickly or malnourished, the eggs involuntarily abort. If a pregnant female is healthy and strong, litter size may increase from twins to as many as five cubs.

Black bear dens are inconspicuous and remote, ranging from dugouts under the roots of a large tree to dry culverts under remote two-tracks. Den entrances are just large enough for occupants to squeeze through into a larger sleeping chamber. A small space loses less warmth than a more voluminous area, so den sizes are small and efficient.

Cubs are born in January and February, after a gestation of 10 weeks. Hairless and blind, 8-ounce newborns instinctively make their way to a nipple. Once attached, cubs remain there most of the time until spring, growing

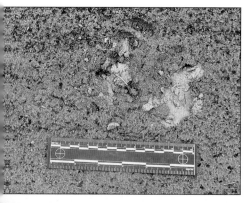

Left front black bear track in rain-dampened sand, identifiable by five forward-pointing toes, and extra-deep impression left by the largest, outermost toe when the animal stepped off.

rapidly. Because black bears are not true hibernators, the mother's body temperature remains almost normal throughout winter, keeping offspring warm while she sleeps.

When mother and newborns leave the den in April or May, youngsters will weigh from 2 to 5 pounds. Cubs travel with the mother on her annual migration, learning the foraging and watering places that they may continue to visit throughout their own lives. By 8 months, the cubs are weaned and weigh 25 pounds or more. They can forage for insects and grasses and catch an occasional rodent or frog, but they are still prey for wolves and larger bears.

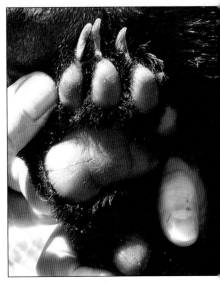

The right forefoot of this bear cub shows the sharp, hooked claws that enable black bears to climb trees and catch fish better than straighter-clawed brown bears. Note distinctive round pad at rear, which prints as a large dot to the rear of foreprints (also seen with brown bears).

By the end of their first summer, cubs weigh about 75 pounds, and the white blaze on their chests has faded to black. The cubs' mother will not mate in their first year, devoting all her time and energy to teaching and protecting her young. When she dens at the onset of winter, the cubs, who have also acquired a thick layer of fat, will den with her. When mother and cubs awaken in spring, she continues their educations until June, when the youngsters, now 18 months old and weighing about 100 pounds, are abandoned or chased off so that the mother may mate again. Female cubs may breed at 2 years, but males probably not until they've established their own territories, usually at 3 or 4 years. Females breed every other year until about age 9; males are sexually active until about 12 years.

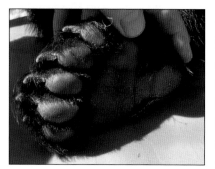

The right hind foot of this yearling black bear shows the humanlike configuration of an animal that walks plantigrade fashion, or flat-footed.

Behavior

Black bears are most active at dawn and dusk (crepuscular), although breeding and feeding activities may alter their patterns. Except for mating season, the overriding purpose in a bear's life is to feed continuously from spring until denning, in early winter. This behavior is an evolved response to sleeping through winter, when normal foods are unavailable. A bear foraging in deep snows would have little chance of survival, but sleeping through winter requires taking enough nutrition into the den with them to survive for 4 or 5 months without eating.

The solitary nature of black bears depends on food availability; well equipped to catch fish with their sharply hooked claws, black bears sometimes come together along stream banks where suckers, trout, and salmon spawn. Similar congregations may be found in large tracts of ripening berries and at landfills.

During the 20th century, it was a favorite pastime for motorists to visit municipal dumps at dusk to watch black bears rummage through human garbage. Dump bears get along well, so long as they respect one another's space, but human observers got into trouble with the bears, so today most garbage dumps are gated and locked after business hours.

Black bears are known to take easily killed livestock, but

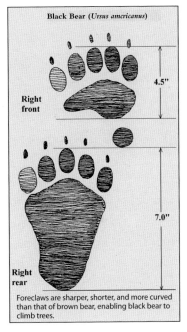

Black Bear (*Ursus americanus*)

Right front

4.5"

Right rear

7.0"

Foreclaws are sharper, shorter, and more curved than that of brown bear, enabling black bear to climb trees.

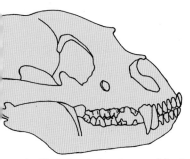

The black bear's jaw is a model of multi-functional design, with canine weapons, camassial cutters, and grinding molars that enable it to eat almost any food.

predations are rare. More real is the damage they can inflict on corn crops, apple and cherry orchards, and bee yards. With their need to feed, bolstered by intelligence, curiosity, and immense physical strength, black bears do considerable damage to crops.

Approximately 30,000 black bears are killed by hunters each year, nationwide, but the species

Despite being equipped with natural weapons that can kill, these bears, like all wild species, fight only until it becomes evident which of them is stronger.

is in no danger from overharvesting. There have been numerous cases of recently emancipated cubs wandering the streets of rural towns, attracted by odors emanating from dumpsters. In a few instances the trespassing animals have been shot dead, but public uproar has caused local authorities to adopt less lethal means of removal.

Black bears normally pose no danger to people; thirty-six humans were killed by black bears in all of the 20th century—fewer than are killed each year by dogs. Mothers with small cubs are most likely to send them up a tree, climbing up after them and waiting for the danger to pass. Few hikers in black bear country will ever see one.

Rarely, bears in the summer rut have stood their ground or even approached a human. The most unbending rule in an encounter is to never run; no human can outrun a bear, and running away excites the animal's predatory instincts, causing it to give chase. Standing fast in the face of a bear charge that nearly always turns out to be a bluff isn't easy, but a person who appears strong is less likely to be mauled.

In rare instances where *Ursus americanus* can legitimately be accused of attacking a person, the intent has been predatory. Few animals eat human flesh, but an old or sickly bear that faces starvation because it can no longer make the long seasonal trek to

The right hind track of a bear in rain-soaked sand. Heel of the humanlike foot did not print because bears and most other species walk with weight forward, on the toes.

follow its food supply might be tempted to prey on a human.

BROWN BEAR
(*Ursus arctos horribilis*—the suffix *horribilis* is sometimes dropped)

The massive and powerful brown bear, President Teddy Roosevelt's personal icon, resides at the top of the food chain throughout the north.

By weight, the brown bear is the largest land carnivore in the world, reaching twice the size of a black bear, and heavier than the taller polar bear. On the basis of the accounts of field researchers, such as Doug Peacock, author of *Grizzly Years*, and anglers who fish with brown bears at Alaska's Denali National Park, the species is neither afraid of nor hungry for humans. Like the normally harmless black bear, there have been instances where an old or sickly individual preyed on a human because it was starving, but in general, brown bears do not regard *Homo sapiens* as edible.

Geographic Range

Brown bears once roamed across the northern hemisphere from the Arctic Circle to Central America. An estimated population of 100,000 can still be found in northern Eurasia, with about 70,000 of those living in Russia. Isolated sightings have been reported from the Atlas Mountains of northernmost Africa and possibly on Japan's Hokkaido Island. In the 20th century, brown bear populations in the lower forty-eight states fell from more than 100,000 animals at the turn of the century to a current low of about 1,000. Brown bear populations

The right front paw of this brown bear dug deeply into the damp sand when the animal changed direction, while its broader hind foot left a much lighter impression.

in Alaska and western Canada remain stable at an estimated 30,000 individuals.

Habitat

Brown bears are at home in most habitats, but the species seems partial to semiopen areas, such as alpine meadows and brushy tundra. Brown bears were a common sight on the Great Plains when the first European immigrants arrived. With a digestive system that can assimilate plants nearly as well as deer, the bears are at home on the plains, but never far from a thicket in which to sleep. In Siberia, brown bears are creatures of the deep forest, while European populations prefer mountain woodlands. So long as a habitat provides food, water, and a secluded place to rest, *Ursus arctos* can live there.

Physical Characteristics

Mass: *Brown bear weigh* 400 to more than 1,700 pounds, and males are 10 percent larger than females.

Body: They are powerfully built, with a distinctive, large hump of muscle between the shoulders. Shoulder height is 4 to 4.5 feet; body length is 6 to more than 7 feet; standing height is 10 feet or more. The head is large and broad, with small, round ears. Facial profile is almost concave, giving the impression of an upturned nose, unlike the rounded muzzle and profile of a black bear.

Tail: The tail is about 3 inches long and well furred.

Tracks: Tracks are similar to those of the black bear but larger; five toes are on all four feet, with almost straight claws extending from the front toes to a length of 3 inches or more.

Brown and black bear scats are often identical in composition when both are feeding in the same areas, and scats of both species can be quite varied, depending on diet. This large, cow-pie-like scat reflects a rich diet of mostly berries and wild cherries.

Forefeet are 5 to 6 inches long, discounting the dot-shaped heel-pad impression that may print 3 or 4 inches to the rear of the forefoot heel pad; forefoot width is 8 to 10 inches. Hind feet are 10 to 16 inches long, 7 to 8 inches wide, elongated, almost human shaped, and tipped with shorter claws.

Scat: Scat is similar to a black bear's but usually larger; cylindrical, segmented, and dark brown to black when fresh, with evidence of seeds, grasses, and berries. Diameter may exceed 2 inches. A single scat may be broken into several segments of 2 to 4 inches in length, or, if the animal is feeding on rich meats, it might be coiled and in a single piece. Rodent and deer hair may be wrapped spiral fashion around the outside.

Coloration: Fur is usually dark brown but varies from blond to nearly black in some individuals. The term "grizzly bear" stems from the white-frosted (or grizzled) appearance of the bear's shoulders and back. The brown bear's muzzle is the same color or darker than its pelage but never lighter colored like the black bear's.

Sign: Sign includes excavations in hillsides and meadows where ground squirrel burrows have been dug out, large rocks and downed logs overturned, bathtub-size depressions in the humus of brushy thickets where a bear slept, and clawed logs and standing trees clawed to a height of 9 feet or more.

Vocalizations: Sounds include grunts, growls, huffing, and bawling. Clacking of teeth, often accompanied by a froth of saliva around the mouth, indicates anxiety, and trackers who witness such behavior should withdraw immediately but slowly, never turning their backs to the bear.

Life span: Brown bears live up to 47 years in captivity but normally less than 35 years in the wild. Potential life span has been estimated to be up to 50 years.

Diet

Brown bears have an efficient digestive system; in spring, before many food plants have sprouted, sedges, roots, and lichens constitute the bulk of a bear's diet. As the warm season progresses and more plants mature, a bear's diet and travels change to match available foods. Calorie-rich berries, pine nuts, and fruits are preferred, and several types of fungi are eaten.

Insects are on the menu, too. Rotting logs and stumps provide larvae whose bodies are composed mostly of fat. Bears eat spiders as they hang in their webs, and ants are gathered when the bear sticks a paw into their hill, licking the attacking insects off with its raspy tongue.

Brown bears will eat carrion they find or can appropriate from other carnivores. The seemingly instinctive hatred between wolves and bears probably stems from the brown bear's practice of stealing carcasses brought down by hunting packs. Brown bears also prey on wolf pups if they can, but even just a pair of wolves is usually sufficient to deter a large brown bear.

In the far north, big Alaskan brown bears frequent fur seal and walrus colonies during their summer mating seasons, seeking out calves, males wounded in mating battles, and individuals weak from age. A brown's 35-mile-per-hour run is too slow to threaten healthy deer, but bears may follow caribou

A bear den excavated into the side of a hill, sometimes under the roots of a large tree, will always have an entrance just large enough for its owner to squeeze through, opening into a large chamber within. (Photo courtesy USFWS.)

Brown bear tracks along a sandy shoreline show this bear's fearless and unhurried disposition.

herds during annual migrations, waiting for weak individuals to fall behind the herd.

Right after the bears emerge from winter dens, but before the summer growing season is under way, most of the meat eaten by a brown bear consists of rodents and ground squirrels dug out of burrows by its massive forepaws. With mice and voles numbering in the thousands per acre, rodents can make up most of a bear's diet in spring. Like badgers, brown bears may be shadowed by a coyote that is there to exploit the bear's work by guarding the prey's escape holes.

Watching grizzlies fish for spawning salmon in spring or fall has become a tourist attraction in places such as Alaska's Denali National Park. Brown bears of all ages, most of whom learned to fish there from their mothers, wait to ambush fish at narrows, rapids, and shallows. Fatty fish flesh is critical to the bears' diet, and they've learned to tolerate one another so that all can share this abundance of rich food. Sows with cubs keep their distance from adult boars, which sometimes kill yearling cubs to force mothers into early estrus.

Mating Habits

Between May and July, sexually mature sows 3 years or older begin advertising through pheromonal scents. Bears 5 or 6 years of age advertise their availability through scat and urine deposits on trails that overlap a female's territory. After a week of courtship, the pair copulate frequently for about 3 days or until the sow knows she is pregnant. Females probably take only one mate per season.

Sows carry fertilized eggs alive but dormant within their wombs until October or November, when the eggs implant in the uterine wall if the female is healthy and fat, or they spontaneously abort to conserve bodily resources for her own needs. In late January to early March, twins (or as many as four cubs) are born. Because brown bears are not true hiberna-

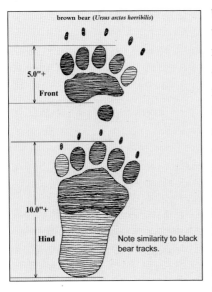

brown bear (*Ursus arctos horribilis*)

5.0"+

Front

10.0"+

Hind

Note similarity to black bear tracks.

tors, the mother bear's body temperature remains near normal and bears awaken easily, but birthing mothers may sleep through delivery. Only 1 pound at birth, blind and naked cubs make their way to a nipple and nestle into their mother's belly fur to nurse continuously until she awakens in April or May. At that point the cubs are fully furred and able to travel with their mother as she begins the same annual foraging trek to seasonal food sources that they will make as adults and teach to their own offspring.

At 5 months, in late June to early August, cubs are weaned and begin to forage for themselves on grasses, forbs, and insects. Mothers share kills with the cubs, but they soon learn to catch rodents, frogs, and other small animals. At the end of their first summer, cubs weigh 50 pounds or more, and most smaller mammals will have become potential prey. Yearling cubs accompany their mothers to rivers to feed on spawning fish but keep their distance from males that might kill them.

Cubs den with their mothers the first winter. When she emerges the following spring, they remain with her until June or July, when she abandons or drives them away so she can mate again. At this time, cubs weigh upward of 150 pounds and aren't easy prey for carnivores. Females are less likely to breed every other year than black bears, and some sows go unmated for up to 4 years. Young brown bears establish their own territories, sometimes traveling more than 100 miles to find suitable unclaimed habitat, and continue to grow until 10 years of age. Male brown bears in Yellowstone National Park have been sexually active until 25 years of age.

Behavior

Ursus arctos may be active at any time of the day, but the species is generally crepuscular. After feeding during the cool night hours, brown bears generally spend the days sleeping in thickets. Be especially careful when hiking in close environments, and be mindful that a surprised grizzly's instinct is to charge, not retreat like a black bear. Carcasses of large animals should be observed only through binoculars, never closer than 100 yards, and from upwind to give warning of your approach. Brown bears camouflage carcasses too large to be eaten at once with a partial covering of leaves and debris. Unfinished carcasses are defended, and you can bet that the owner is nearby.

Territory of a male brown bear may exceed 1,000 square miles, but the average is about 200 square miles, and seldom more than is required to meet the bear's needs. Males' territories are, on average, seven times larger than those of females and normally overlap the territories of several potential mates. Individuals might spend several weeks in one place, but when available foods are gone, so are the bears. A grizzly's omnivorous diet ensures that a number of food sources are available every month of its waking period.

Brown bear adults can't normally climb trees because their claws—sharply curved to give them that ability when they were cubs—have grown out straighter and longer to make them useful as digging tools. This reflects the brown bear's penchant for open habitat, as opposed to the forested environment preferred by black bears, whose sharp, curved claws permit them to climb even smooth-sided trees. This does not mean that climbing a tree is a good way to escape a brown bear, however, because there have been cases in which a bear used the branches of a large pine as ladder rungs.

Brown bears have frequently been observed pushing against dead standing trees until they topple. The objective is to stun animals that might be holed up inside. Once down, the trunk can be torn apart in search of grubs, ants, and wild honeybee hives.

Family Procyonidae

Procyonids include the lesser pandas of Asia, the ringtail and coati of the southwestern United States and Mexico, and the familiar raccoon. Despite the diversity of species within this family, all have five toes on each foot, all are excellent climbers, all have an omnivorous diet, and all are tough, ferocious fighters.

RACCOON
(*Procyon lotor*)

Intelligent, resourceful, and equipped with handlike forepaws that can manipulate objects nearly as well as our own, the raccoon is a real survivor, able to live in most environments. (Photo courtesy USFWS.)

Raccoons (as well as skunks and badgers) are well-known for digging up turtle nests, like this one, in early June, leaving small craters along shorelines that are littered with the remnants of flexible egg shells.

Few animals are better recognized than the raccoon, with its bandit-masked face and striped tail. Considered prey by raptors and larger carnivores when young, a raccoon is ferocious when cornered, and only the largest predators are willing to tackle one. This game nature is a good defense against predators whose objective is to kill food without endangering themselves.

Healthy raccoons are harmless to people unless cornered, but they are also a potential vector for rabies, mostly in March or April, and especially when local populations are high. Raccoons can seriously injure even large dogs and have been known to draw dogs into deep water, where they climb onto the dog's head and drown it. A bearlike drive to

With a similar diet and digestive system, typical raccoon scats resemble miniature bear scats, with a "Tootsie Roll®" shape that is unsegmented and flat on both ends, about 0.5 inches in diameter.

gain fat against the coming lean winter makes the raccoon a nuisance to even suburbanites by being attracted to the odors of human food.

Geographic Range

Excepting the most open and arid places, raccoons are found throughout the United States, from the Pacific to the Atlantic. To the north, their range extends only a little beyond Canada's southern border. To the south, they range deep into Mexico, overlapping more-southern cousins, the coati and ringtail.

Habitat

Raccoons are intelligent and adaptable. Preferred habitat will always have a source of freshwater and include trees large enough to provide for observation or escape. The animals are superb swimmers, able to outdistance most enemies across lakes or rivers, and they require a water source that provides aquatic foods, such as crayfish, clams, and frogs.

Physical Characteristics

Mass: Raccoons weigh 12 to 48 pounds, with individuals reaching 60 pounds in the far north.

Body: Raccoons are stocky, muscular, and thickly furred over a layer of insulating fat. Males are

This soft raccoon scat—whose volume suggests a large raccoon of about 50 pounds—reflects a rich diet of fruits and meat.

generally larger than females, but the largest individuals reported have been old females. Body length is 23 to more than 38 inches; the arched back is 8 to more than 12 inches high. Head is small with a short, pointed muzzle tipped by a black nose. Ears are erect, rounded, and large.

Tail: The tail is striped, with alternating bands of darker fur, 7 to more than 14 inches long.

Tracks: There are five toes on all four feet, each toe tipped with a long, stout claw. Toes are fingerlike, especially on forefeet, with four pointing forward, and a shorter thumblike toe extending to the inside, making front tracks similar to human handprints. Toe tips leave bulbous impressions behind claws. Forefoot length is 2 to 3 inches. Hind feet are flat-soled and elongated, indicating the plantigrade walk of a slow-running, formidable animal. The hind print resembles a human footprint but with features that include four fingerlike toes pointing forward, each terminating in a bulbous tip and claw, and one shorter, thumblike toe well to the rear, pointing inward. Hind foot length is 3 to 4 inches.

Procyon lotor's normal gait is a shuffling walk in which the hind feet often scrape the earth as they travel forward, leaving scuff marks to the rear of the hind tracks. Hind prints generally register separately and beside the front tracks at a relaxed walk, because raccoons are narrower at the shoulder than at the hip. The bushy tail may brush over tracks on dusty soils. Stride is up to 2 feet between paired front and hind prints. Straddle is 3 to 4 inches, and up to 6 inches in larger specimens.

At a fast run of 15 miles per hour on flat ground, the raccoon gait changes to the universal rocking-horse gait of quadrupeds, described in Hooved Animals, in which fore-feet are planted side by side to act as pivots while the hind feet are brought forward on either side. When the hind feet make contact with earth, the coon springs forward, forefeet extended, and the gait repeats anew. At a hard run, the distance between sets of four tracks can exceed 3 feet.

Scat: Scat is cylindrical and usually unsegmented, with the diameter constant throughout its length. Ends are typically flat, as though cut off; scat is 2 to 3 inches long and up to 0.5 inch in diameter.

Coloration: The most obvious characteristics of the raccoon are its black mask around the eyes and a bushy tail with up to ten black rings running circumferentially along its length. The pelage is grizzled, with fur color that varies from gray to reddish.

Sign: Sign includes shells of turtle eggs excavated from buried nests along sandy shorelines and crayfish carapaces and empty clamshells at the water's edge.

Vocalizations: A chirring sound is made when the animal is inquisitive or content. Territorial and mating sounds include a wide variety of screeches, snarls, and growls.

Life span: Raccoons have lived up to 16 years in captivity, but wild raccoons seldom live beyond 4 years.

This track pattern shows that the raccoon was startled into flight, pushing off hardest with its left hind foot.

Diet

Raccoons are omnivorous and opportunistic. Most of their diet is obtained along shorelines, where the majority of sign is found. They are fond of calorie-rich berries, nuts, and fruits of all types, and, in many habitats, vegetation might make up the majority of foods a raccoon eats. Normally solitary, raccoons may descend on cultivated fields in force, decimating an entire crop. Habituated raccoons also damage fruit trees and grape arbors.

Poorly designed for pursuit, raccoons are consummate scavengers. The carnivorous portion of their diets typically includes a wide variety of invertebrates than vertebrates. Crayfish, grasshoppers, beetles, small rodents, frogs, birds, and hatchling turtles are all components of the raccoon's diet. Any animal that a raccoon can take without danger to itself is prey. Carrion will be eaten but only when fresh.

Raccoons are known for their habit of washing foods at the edges of waterways, a practice alluded to by its species name, *lotor*, which translates as "the washer." The purpose behind this practice is thought to be a sorting process in which sensitive fingerlike toes separate inedible matter. Where many animals must swallow small prey whole, a raccoon can pick out the parts it doesn't want.

Mating Habits

Raccoons reach sexual maturity at one year, but males will probably not breed until they first establish their own territories, usually at 2 years. Mating begins in late January and

The track pattern of a raccoon running flat out over hardpack snow; note how forefeet print close together between and behind hind feet—a pattern that legendary tracker Olaus J. Murie called the "Rocking Horse."

extends through early March, peaking in February; populations in warm regions may mate in December. Males travel to females from as far away as three miles, attracted by pheromonal scents. Mating is preceded by several days of courtship, during which males den with females. Once impregnated, females reject mates and send them on their way—often to find another receptive female. Female raccoons are believed to take only one mate per breeding season.

After a gestation of 60 to 70 days, females retire to a secluded, leaf-lined den in a large hollow tree, under its roots, or sometimes in dry culverts, where mothers birth four to

Track pattern of a raccoon walking in wet sand; left to right: right front, right hind, left front, left hind, right front.

eight cubs in April or May. Cubs weigh 2 ounces at birth and are altricial—blind, deaf, and almost naked. Young open their eyes at 3 weeks and begin roving around the den. Cubs go outside the den at 2 months but never stray far from its entrance. At this stage, mothers may move cubs to an alternate den, carrying them one at a time by the nape of the neck. If a predator threatens in the open, the mother pushes her young up a tree and then follows. If cornered, females defend off-spring viciously enough to deter even desperate carnivores.

By 3 months, cubs are weaned and foraging for edible plants and small animals. The family stays together throughout the following winter but separates before the spring mating season, when the mother will probably mate again. Males leave first, seeking their own territories, followed by female siblings who will likely take mates of their own in the coming breeding season.

Behavior

Except for procreational activities, raccoons are solitary and generally nocturnal, but, where there are no humans, they may forage along shorelines in daylight. Raccoons aren't true hibernators, but extreme cold or snow may motivate them to hole up and become dormant in a warm den until the weather eases, living off a thick layer of fat and conserving energy. Denned raccoons are normally alone, but mothers and cubs from the previous spring den together, and courting pairs may stay together for a month prior to breeding.

Raccoons have well-developed tactile senses, and research suggests the sensitivity of their forepaws may be several times that of our own hands. Raccoon paws have the tactility to enable them to snatch submerged foods by feel alone. Hand-like forepaws grasp, pull, and tear with sufficient strength to pry open clams and remove the carapaces of crayfish or even of hatchling turtles.

With an ability to grasp branches, raccoons are exceptional climbers. They lack the agility to pursue prey through treetops like, for example, a pine marten can, and climb only to escape enemies or obtain fruit. Raccoons have survived falls of more than 30 feet without injury.

Procyon lotor is a born swimmer that readily takes to water to escape danger. Raccoons rarely swim without purpose, though, because their pelts lack the water-repellent oils contained in the fur of otters or beavers, and their coat becomes saturated.

Raccoon (*Procyon lotor*)

2.0"

3.0"

Note plantigrade (flat-footed) walk, typical of powerful species not designed to run fast.

The left hind (bottom) and left front tracks of a walking raccoon, probably made the day before.

Family Sciuridae

The squirrel family represents sixty-three species in North America, including marmots, chipmunks, and fox squirrels. *Sciuridae* is Latin for "shade tail," alluding to the long, bushy tail of tree squirrels, but ground squirrels, such as prairie dogs and woodchucks, have only a vestigial tail. Physical characteristics common to all species in this family include having four toes on the forefeet and five toes on the hind feet. All are plantigrade hoppers with elongated hind paws that resemble human feet. All are rodents, with chisel-shaped upper and lower incisors that are adapted to gnawing and cutting vegetation.

GRAY SQUIRREL
(*Sciurus carolinensis*)

The most common tree squirrel, with c lose cousins throughout the Americas, the gray squirrel has had no problem coexisting with humans.

The best-known tree squirrels, gray squirrels have been human food for as long as there have been people in North America. In Colonial times, it was common to refer to any long gun smaller than a .45 caliber as a squirrel gun, which infers that squirrel was probably a mainstay of our forebears. Because it is so common, the gray squirrel, also known as the eastern gray squirrel, represents tree squirrels here. The species has close cousins throughout North America, and all share similar diets and traits.

Geographic Range

Sciurus carolinensis are found throughout the eastern United States to the Mississippi River, as far south as Florida and eastern Texas, and north to the southern edge of Canada. Introduced populations also exist in Italy, Scotland, England, and Ireland, where gray squirrels have thrived to the point of becoming serious pests and threatening the survival of the indigenous red squirrel.

Habitat

Sciurus carolinensis requires a habitat with trees, so it will not be found in prairies, deserts, or places where trees don't provide forage, dens, and escape from predators. Ideal habitat includes nut trees and a variety of ground plants, with close access to water. Larger fox squirrels prefer a mixed habitat of conifers and hardwoods; smaller red squirrels are found in mostly coniferous forests.

Physical Characteristics

Mass: Gray squirrels weigh 1 to 1.5 pounds.

One of the best survivors among tree squirrels, American gray squirrels transplanted in the United Kingdom have thrived there to the point of becoming pests.

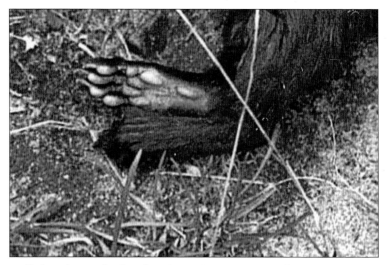

Well-clawed on each of its feet, the acrobatic gray squirrel's elongated hind feet are equipped with long, articulated toes for gripping and a knobby sole to maximize surface area and traction.

Body: Squirrels are elongated and furred, with short legs; rounded head; short, pointed muzzle; and small round ears. Body length is 16 to 20 inches. There is no difference in body size between genders (dimorphism). Differences in skull size and fur color occur between gray squirrel populations in the northern and southern parts of the species' range. North to south, skull size decreases as a regional adaptation (cline), but mandible sizes and dental arrangements remain the same. Individuals in the South tend more toward a gray coat, while populations in the North are more often black in color.

Tail: The tail is furred and more flat along its top than that of other tree squirrels. Length is 8 to 10 inches—about half the body length. The tail functions as an umbrella in rain or sun and adds insulation for sleeping in cold weather.

Tracks: There are four toes on front feet, five toes on hind. Tracks of front feet are rounded, 1 to 1.5 inches long; hind feet are elongated, 2 to 2.5 inches long. Track pattern is like a rabbit's but has much smaller hind feet prints ahead of forefeet, leaving a pattern like a pair of exclamation points (!!), typical of the hopping gait used by tree squirrels. The total length of the track pattern is 7 to 8 inches. The distance between track sets indicates gait: 10 inches for a casual hopping pace, 2 feet at an easy run, 3 feet or more when the animal is fleeing danger.

Scat: Scat consists of pellets that are dark brown to black, and 0.25 inch in diameter. Pellets may exhibit a thin "tail" of undigested plant fibers on one end, indicating fibrous browse. About a dozen pellets are found in a deposit.

Coloration: There are two color phases in *S. carolinensis*. Populations in beech forests tend to have a fur color that matches the trees' gray bark; those living among dark-trunked trees like maples and oaks are mostly black, especially in the North. Black-furred squirrels experience 18 percent less heat loss than gray-colored squirrels in temperatures below freezing, along with a 20 percent lower metabolic rate and a nonshivering (thermogenesis) capacity that's 11 percent higher than in gray individuals. Both color phases exhibit a grizzling of whitish guard hairs along the dorsal parts. Ears and underbelly are often lighter in color than the body. Although uncommon, especially in colder latitudes, albino colonies do exist in southern Illinois, New Jersey, and South Carolina. The fox squirrel is larger, with a reddish pelage; the red squirrel is much smaller, with an orangish coat and white underparts.

Sign: Sign includes beechnut husks and opened acorn, walnut, hickory, and other nuts. In autumn, nut-bearing twigs are snipped from food trees, their cut ends showing a neat, stepped bite from the squirrel's sharp upper and lower incisors. Small patches of loose soil scattered atop forest humus reveal where nuts have been buried for winter storage. In winter, hardpack snow is pocked with holes, about 6 inches in diameter, where a squirrel burrowed downward to retrieve a nut, leaving a spray of soil atop the snow.

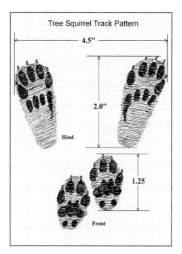

Tree squirrel track pattern as it might appear in snow (gray squirrel shown).

Vocalizations: Chirping barks come from territorial males, especially during the autumn and spring breeding seasons. Alarm calls consist of short, clucking barks that humans can imitate by sucking one cheek against their molars. The intensity of a squirrel's alarm is demonstrated by the frequency of the barks: fast chattering means immediate danger; barks become less frequent as the source alarm withdraws.

Life span: Average life span in the wild is about 12.5 years, but one captive female lived to more than 20 years.

Diet

Nuts and seeds are staples in a gray squirrel's diet, with acorns, chestnuts, and other storable nuts being favored. Tree buds are on the menu in early spring, along with stored nuts that have been frozen in the ground since the previous autumn. In summer the diet includes plants, grasses, and flowers. Pine and cedar nuts and buds are also eaten, and mushrooms are nibbled. Primarily vegetarian, gray and other tree squirrels are known to become carnivorous when plant foods become scarce. Gray squirrels gnaw on deer bones and antlers to wear down constantly growing incisors and

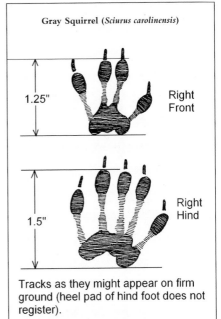

Gray Squirrel (*Sciurus carolinensis*)

1.25"   Right Front

1.5"   Right Hind

Tracks as they might appear on firm ground (heel pad of hind foot does not register).

to get the minerals they harbor. Wheat and corn are favored foods, making the squirrels a pest species in agricultural areas.

Gray (and fox) squirrels don't remember where every nut is buried, but tree squirrels possess an extraordinary sense of smell that can detect cached nuts under a foot of snow. Not all buried nuts are found, and inevitably more nuts are buried than are eaten. Unretrieved nuts take root, and squirrels help to expand their own habitats by planting trees in places where they wouldn't be otherwise.

Mating Habits

Gray squirrels mate have two mating seasons each year, in May through June, and in December through February. Males older than 11 months are drawn to preestrous females by sexual pheromones a week prior to mating and may travel as far as 0.5 miles. The testes of mating males increase in mass from their nonbreeding weight of approximately 1 gram to as much as 7 grams.

Females may breed at 6 months, especially where populations are low, but most mate at 15 months and are fertile for about 8 years. Estrus is indicated by an enlarged pink vulva that makes it easier to identify the sexes, which are nearly identical during nonbreeding months. The vulva is typically swollen for 8 hours; the vaginal cavity is closed except during estrus.

Territorial battles between mating males are common and noisy, with contenders scrapping furiously on the ground and in the trees. Where populations are high or females are scarce, males have been observed biting off the testicles of competitors. Copulation between pairs is generally over within 30 seconds, and mates then go their separate ways. Males breed with as many partners as possible, but females breed only until they become pregnant. After the female has become impregnated, a mucous plug forms within her vaginal cavity, blocking further entry by sperm and preventing further intercourse.

Gestation averages 44 days, with two to four kits born in a leaf-lined nest high up inside a hollow tree. Young are born naked (altricial) and whiskered (vibrissal,) and weigh 4 ounces each. Kits nurse constantly for the first 7 weeks, and mothers leave them only to eat, drink, and relieve themselves. During her short absences the young may fall prey to raccoons, weasels, and predatory birds that can fit through the den opening. Nursing mothers viciously defend offspring, but mothers never wander far while young are in the suckling stage and may move nursing young to a different nest if it is molested.

In cold months nests are in enclosed places, but in warm weather young may be nursed in an open nest of sticks and leaves located on a high tree limb. By 10 weeks, squirrel kits are weaned, the family separates, and mothers provide no more care. Adult size and mass are reached at 9 months.

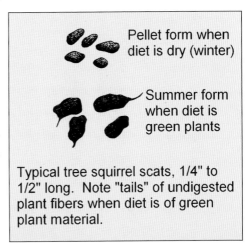

Pellet form when diet is dry (winter)

Summer form when diet is green plants

Typical tree squirrel scats, 1/4" to 1/2" long. Note "tails" of undigested plant fibers when diet is of green plant material.

Squirrel tracks atop ice that has been dusted with fresh snow show the knobby soles and claws that make tree squirrels so sure-footed in their dangerous arboreal habitat.

Behavior

With the exception of nocturnal flying squirrels, tree squirrels

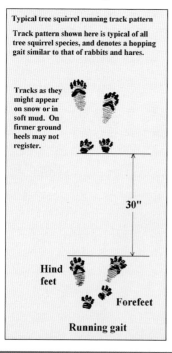

Typical tree squirrel running track pattern

Track pattern shown here is typical of all tree squirrel species, and denotes a hopping gait similar to that of rabbits and hares.

Tracks as they might appear on snow or in soft mud. On firmer ground heels may not register.

30"

Hind feet

Forefeet

Running gait

are active during daylight (diurnal), with peak activity occurring about 2 hours after sunrise and 2 hours before sunset. Hot days are spent resting in loafing platforms made from sticks and leaves and located in overhead branches. Unlike maternal nests, loafing platforms are flatter and less concave because they don't contain young that could fall out. Loafing platforms help in determining their builder's age, with those that are more haphazardly constructed usually being made by younger, less-experienced animals.

Male and female gray squirrels are identical in color and size, but an individual's activities can help to identify gender. Males are most active in autumn and spring, when food, territory, and mates make them alert for competitors and more defensive. Females tend to be more active during summer and winter, when they must work to regain energy lost while rearing a litter.

Widely differing estimates have been made of how much acreage can be required to support a healthy gray squirrel; territory size is ultimately determined by availability of resources. A single city block can be home to a half-dozen squirrels so long as sufficient food, water, and nesting sites are available, and in urban parks, where they receive regular handouts from humans, population densities may be higher. Residential areas have proved so attractive to gray squirrels that a pest-removal industry has been created in response to their invasion of attics, garages, and other places where their presence conflicts with humans. The problem is severe among transplanted populations in Great Britain, where gray squirrels are ranked second only to the Norway rat (*Rattus norvegicus*) in terms of property destruction.

Despite being pests in some areas, gray squirrels have a strong following among wildlife enthusiasts, and squirrel watching has become nearly as popular as bird watching. Gray and fox squirrels are also very popular with small-game hunters, bringing millions of dollars in revenue to state governments and the sport-hunting industry each year.

WOODCHUCK
(*Marmota monax*)

Largest of the squirrel family, the woodchuck and its close relatives, the yellow-bellied marmot, hoary marmot, and olympic marmot, are ground-dwelling burrowers that lack the bushy tail associated with tree squirrels. This species gets its common name from the Cree Indian word *woochuk*, which that tribe used to describe all marmots, but the woodchuck retained it because its burrows are most often found near forests.

Best known as the groundhog (another common name for the species) that emerges from hibernation each year on February 2 to look for its shadow, the woodchuck is the most populous marmot species in North America. Because nearly all of its habits and characteristics are shared by other marmots, the information given here is generally applicable to all species.

Geographic Range

The range of *M. monax* spreads from the Atlantic to the Pacific across North America, extending in a line to the north from New Brunswick, across the southern shore of Hudson Bay, through the Yukon Territory and into central Alaska. Southern boundaries extend from Virginia to Arkansas and northwest to British Columbia. Being burrowers, they are not found above the Arctic Circle, where permafrost prevents digging, although permafrost has been receding for more than a decade, which may in time cause woodchucks to expand their range northward.

Habitat

Like all marmots, woodchucks prefer open areas where they can bask in the sun, but they are never far from the forests that give them their common name. Burrows excavated under the roots of large trees provide protection from digging predators, such as bears and wolves, while tall trees permit a quick escape for woodchucks caught by surprise on the ground. High ground with good drainage is a necessity for woodchuck habitat, especially in northern regions that experience potential flooding from snowmelt in spring. Marmots require a source of drinking water nearby, but their excavated dens, which may extend underground as far as 25 feet and have as many as six outlets, must be in earth that remains dry year-round to a depth of at least 5 feet.

Physical Characteristics

Mass: Woodchucks weigh 4.5 to 14 pounds, with the largest individuals occurring in the North. Males are slightly larger and more muscular than females.

Body: They are chunky and stout, with short, powerful legs well adapted for digging. Body length is 16 to more than 32 inches. The skull is broad and flat on top, flanked to either side by small, roundish ears. The woodchuck's incisors continue to grow throughout its life span, and if they aren't worn down properly, the upper and lower mating pairs can grow past one another (malocclusion), where they may continue to grow until the jawbones are pierced and eating becomes impossible.

Tail: The tail is 3.5 to 9 inches long, about 25 percent of body length, and well furred but not as bushy as a tree squirrel's.

Tracks: There are four toes on the forefeet, five toes on the hind feet. The rudimentary first digit of the forepaw is covered by a flat nail; the other three digits terminate in curved claws that are useful in digging. The hind foot has five elongated and clawed digits that show clearly in most tracks. Front tracks are about 2 inches long; hind tracks are usually 2.5 inches long but can be 3 inches long or more on soft ground, where the entire heel prints. Straddle is 3.5 to 6 inches; walking stride, in which hind feet print on top of or slightly ahead of front tracks, is 3 to 4 inches. In the running stride, which may be as fast as 10 miles per hour, hind feet print ahead of forefeet, which print individually behind and between them; distance between track sets is about 14 inches.

Scat: Scat is elongated and irregular in diameter, usually tapered at one or both ends, with plant fibers in evidence. It is dark brown to black in color, lightening with age. Length is 2 to more than 4 inches.

Coloration: Woodchucks are dark brown to nearly black along the dorsal region and sides, interspersed with coarser guard hairs that are banded with alternating red and yellow, and tipped with white. Underbelly is paler; head and feet are much darker. Tail is dark and much shorter than that of tree squirrels. There is one molt, from late May to September, which begins at the tail and progresses forward. The feet are black and plantigrade. The woodchuck's long incisors are white or nearly white, lacking the dark-yellow pigmentation of other large rodents, such as porcupines or beavers.

Sign: Burrow entrances 10 to 14 inches in diameter are dug into knolls and hillsides, sometimes beneath the roots of standing trees, and occasionally into and under a hole in the trunk of a standing hollow tree. The woodchuck also possesses three nipples–anal (perineal) scent glands that secrete a musky odor, and trees, stumps, or other prominent objects around den entrances will often be marked with this scent.

Vocalizations: Woodchucks are often vocal, particularly when alarmed, which explains its nickname, "whistle-pig."

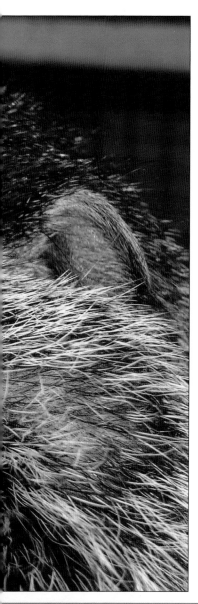

The alarm cry is a single, loud, shrill whistle, often preceded by a squirrel-like bark. The call used to attract mates, to warn intruders impinging on its territory, or from mothers calling young to the safety of the burrow is a loud whistle followed by a less-piercing call and ending with a series of softer whistles that cannot be heard except at close range. Teeth grinding, chattering, and even dog-like growls are common when woodchucks are cornered by a predator.

Life span: There is a high attrition rate for young, but woodchucks can live up to 6 years in the wild and up to 10 years in captivity.

Diet

Woodchucks are mostly herbivorous, preferring clovers, alfalfa, plantains, and grasses during the summer months but also bark and buds of wild cherry, sumac, and other shrubs in early spring, before other food plants are available. Poplar, cottonwood, and aspens are particularly important because they provide food in the form of bark, buds, and leaves throughout the woodchuck's active time of year. Woodchucks will also eat an occasional bird egg, grasshopper, snail, or tree frog, and probably the young of most small rodents, but these minor predations appear to be opportunistic in nature. Marmots aren't known to eat carrion, but they will gnaw shed antlers and bones for the nutrients they contain.

Because the woodchuck's range and habitat encompass most of the richest farming areas in North America, this species more than any other marmot has incurred the wrath of farmers. Lands cleared for planting provide good habitat, and crops like alfalfa, clover, wheat, and especially corn are relished by woodchucks, which can eat more than 1.5 pounds per animal per day, breaking down and killing plants while they feed.

In late summer, woodchucks feed more urgently. Each animal needs to gain about 25 percent of its body weight in a layer of fat that will insulate and sustain it through the winter. During this predenning period, a woodchuck becomes especially territorial and protective of its food resources. Trespassers, especially yearlings wandering in search of their own territories, will be driven off as plants become scarcer with shortening days.

Mating Habits

Breeding occurs in early spring, usually within two weeks after woodchucks emerge from hibernation, in late March or

April. Adults are normally solitary, but the territories of adult males typically overlap those of several females. This arrangement enables established males to make contact with receptive females without trespassing onto the territories of other males. When two males do compete, the battles consist of boxing matches in which both contenders stand erect on hind feet, slapping and biting one another until one withdraws.

Females are monoestrous (have only one breeding season), and accept only one mate per breeding season. Males stay in their mates' dens for about one week—the only time these normally solitary animals are social—before leaving to seek out another female. After a gestation period of approximately 32 days, females give birth to litters of one to nine naked and blind young, with five being the average litter size, in April or May. Newborns weigh about almost one ounce and measure about 4 inches long.

Females have four pairs of teats and nurse their young from a standing position, staying with them almost constantly for their first 2 weeks of life. At 3 weeks, the young begin crawling about inside the den, and at 4 weeks they open their eyes. By five weeks, the young woodchucks are fully active and begin exploring for short distances around the den entrance, scurrying back inside if the mother issues an alarm whistle.

Young woodchucks are weaned at 6 weeks but may remain with their mother until July or August, when she forces them to disperse. Yearlings must find or excavate their own burrows after leaving their mothers and will hibernate alone in their first winter. Females will probably mate on emerging from their dens the following spring, but competition may force young males to wait until the next spring, after they've established their own territories.

Behavior

Woodchucks are the most solitary marmot species, and both genders are generally hostile toward one another on meeting (agonistic). Battles are usually of short duration and relatively bloodless, but established adults do not tolerate trespassers. Reports of individuals sharing a den stem from observations made during the short mating period, when males occupy the dens of their mates or of nearly grown offspring denning with their mother.

Woodchucks are most often observed during the day, but they may become partly nocturnal if harassed by humans. The stereotypical image of this species is an animal standing erect, forelimbs held tightly to the front of its body, as it surveys the surrounding area. Standing upright is an alert posture, but woodchucks prefer to spend their time on all fours as they feed, sunbathe, and comb their fur, never far from the den entrance. If alarmed, a woodchuck retreats into its den, turning to face outward once inside. This is a defensive position from which the marmot can bite and claw with surprising ferocity. The sharp incisors of a defensive woodchuck persuade most predators to seek easier prey, but bears, badgers, and wolves can dig to the main chamber, forcing the occupant to try to escape through one of up to five escape tunnels. Woodchucks are less agile than their tree squirrel cousins but can climb trees to escape predators.

The woodchuck is a true hibernator, spending the cold winter months in a comalike slumber within a grass-lined sleeping chamber deep inside its den. The animals enter the den for the winter before the first permanent snowfall, usually in late November in the North and in December in the southern part of the species' range. Once inside and asleep, the marmot's body undergoes remarkable physiological changes: Its body temperature falls from a normal 97 degrees Fahrenheit to 40 degrees Fahrenheit, and its heart rate slows from about 100 beats per minute to just four beats per minute. It remains in this state until warming days cause it to emerge in April, although its deep slumber appears to become lighter as spring approaches. The animals do not ritually leave their dens to see if they cast a shadow on February 2, but the annual Groundhog Day festival held in Punxsutawney, Pennsylvania, creates enough commotion to awaken a hibernating woodchuck. This bit of American folklore, which coincides with Candlemas Day, is rooted in an Old World belief that sunny skies, which enabled the European badger (*Meles meles*) to see its shadow, heralded another 6 weeks of winter.

Family Erethizontidae

The family of porcupines is represented throughout the world, which demonstrates the effectiveness of their common defensive weapon (the family name comes from the Latin for "one who rises in anger"). All are slow-moving rodents that have adapted to ward off predators with the hard modified hairs interspersed in the fur on their backs and tails. These "quills" are essentially sharp needles tipped with minute barbs. Because predators have almost universally evolved to kill food animals through hard physical contact, using teeth and claws, these quills provide porcupines with a shield that can inflict serious and some-times fatal injuries to attackers. A carnivore with a mouthful of embedded quills cannot eat and does not have the means to extract them, and most such predators will suffer a serious infection.

PORCUPINE
(*Erethizon dorsatum*)

The single species of North American porcupine has been worshipped and hated by humans, protected in some states, persecuted in others. Many a hungry woodsman, including members of the Lewis and Clark Expedition, has blessed the porcupine for being the only prey he could run down and safely dispatch with a club (a hard blow across the nose usually kills it instantly).

In some places, the porcupine's value as survival food is superseded by its importance as a pest. Commercially valuable pines, particularly white pines, are favored winter foods, and porcupines frequently kill mature trees by eating the young bark from tops and saplings. Rural homeowners dislike that the porcupine's love for salt causes it to gnaw perspiration-soaked wooden tool handles and even the varnish on wooden house siding. Corn crops and orchard trees may also be damaged, but female porcupines produce only one offspring per year, keeping agricultural damage low and making populations easy to control. Evoking the most emotion are pet injuries that make even some veterinarians say they hate porcupines. In spite of prejudice toward live porcupines, Native American–made "quill boxes" crafted from bark and dyed quills fetch hundreds of dollars apiece.

Geographic Range

The common porcupine is native to boreal North America from Alaska and across Canada south of the Arctic Circle to Labrador. Its range covers the western half of the United States, southward from Montana through New Mexico, and into northern Mexico. In the eastern half of the United States, porcupines are found only in the northernmost forested regions, covering most of New England, northern Michigan, northern Wisconsin, and northeast Minnesota.

With its large, low-slung bulk, the porcupine might not appear to be much of a climber, but long claws mated to articulated fingerlike toes make it one of the best tree climbers in the animal world.

Habitat

Porcupines are found primarily in coniferous forests but may spend part of the year in deciduous woods, especially in spring, when trees are budding. Preferred habitat is mixed forest of pine, deciduous hardwoods and softwoods, and a variety of ground plants, and nearly every environment they inhabit will include tall trees and a source of freshwater nearby. There have been reports of porcupines frequenting riparian (riverfront) areas in mountainous regions and even denning in rock crevices, but they prefer woodlands that provide food, shelter, and refuge from enemies.

Physical Characteristics

Mass: Porcupines weigh 8 to 40 pounds, with the largest specimens occurring in the North.

Body: They are rodentlike, with a humped back and short legs. The dorsal region, especially the tail, is covered with coarse hairs and approximately 30,000 hollow, barbed quills that can be voluntarily detached on contact but not thrown. The longest quills occur on the rump and tail, and the shortest are on the neck; there are no quills on the underbelly. Body length is 25 to 37 inches. The head is small in proportion to the body and round, with a short muzzle, flat face, and small, round ears. Prominent yellow-orange incisors must be kept from growing past one another (malocclusion) through constant gnawing.

Tail: The tail is large, round, and clublike, with the top side heavily covered with quills. Length is 6 to 12 inches.

Tracks: There are four toes on the forefeet; five toes on the hind feet. Toes are long and articulated, each tipped with a heavy, slightly curved claw 0.5 to nearly 1 inch long. The front track is 2 to 3 inches long, including claws; the hind track is 3 to 4.5 inches long, including claws. Tracks are elongated and plantigrade (flat-footed), with distinctive pebble-textured soles. At a walk, the porcupine's usual gait, hind prints register ahead of fore prints, occasionally overlapping. In snow the porky's wide, low-slung belly often drags, leaving a trough that can obscure tracks. In sand, tracks may be brushed by the heavy tail, which typically swings back and forth, leaving striated broomlike markings.

Scat: In winter, scat consists of curved pellets with a sawdust-like texture, much like the muskrat's but not connected lengthwise. Pellets are dark brown, each about 1 inch long, and usually distinguishable by a uniquely porcupine groove running lengthwise along the inside radius. In spring, when the porcupine's diet changes to succulent green plants, pellets are often shorter, with more-squared ends, sometimes connected by grass fibers like a string of beads. Other forms seen from spring through autumn include formless blobs, with undigested plant fibers.

Coloration: Most porcupines are covered with coarse gray hairs, but some may be brown or even black. The

Revered as a survival food for humans stranded in a wilderness, the porcupine is disliked by farmers and cabin owners for its fondness of the salt found in treated wood and perspiration-soaked tool handles.

Almost beautiful to look at, the porcupine is considered a pest by timber companies because it eats the bark of young pines in the winter.

unquilled belly is lighter in color than the back and sides. Hollow quills are black tipped with white.

Sign: Most obvious are the porcupine's winter gnawing of smooth-barked pines, especially near the trees' tops, leaving irregular patches of exposed wood. In winter look for scattered twig ends lying under large pines that serve as food sources. (Red squirrels also nip off cone-bearing twigs from spruces and hemlocks.) Den openings at the base of hollow trees may have accumulations of scat pellets about their entrances. Bones and antlers are gnawed to obtain the minerals in them, leaving gouges much larger than those made by squirrels. Porcupines also gnaw processed lumber, especially wood that has been treated with varnish, which they eat for its salt content.

Vocalizations: Porcupines are usually silent, even when cornered. Most vocalizations are heard during the autumn mating season, when males may grunt, squeak, and sometimes snort while in pursuit of mates.

Life span: They live up to 8 years.

Diet

The porcupine is entirely vegetarian. In spring, before ground plants sprout, the animals climb high into poplar and aspen trees, especially, to feed on fleshy buds; buds of willow, staghorn sumac, beech, and others are also eaten. The animals prefer green plants, including grasses and sedges, plantains, beechnuts, cresses, mustard, chicory, and dandelions. As summer progresses, the diet changes to include ripening fruits, particularly apples.

When winter makes ground plants unavailable, porcupines feed on bark stripped from sumac, willows, and dogwoods, but they also climb into tall trees to reach tender bark and twig ends. White pines are a favorite, and a large tree may be occupied by a porcupine for more than a week. They also eat wood that has traces of salt, including sweat-soaked tool handles, plywood boats, decks, and wooden siding or shingles.

The right front foot of this porcupine shows the unique pebbled texture of its soles.

Legendary tracker Olaus J. Murie once described how he was forced to restrain a half-dozen porcupines that persisted in gnawing his canoe by looping cord around their necks and tying them to a tree until morning.

Mating Habits

Female porcupines may mate at 6 months of age, but competition usually prevents males from breeding until 18 months. The males' testes descend into scrotal pouches between late August and early September, and production of sperm cells (spermatogenesis) peaks during October. Mating occurs October through November, and during 60 days of breeding, males may travel several miles to pursue mates. It's during this time that normally silent porcupines are likely to be vocal, especially when several males pursue a single female into a large tree. Males are rarely violent toward one another, but arboreal pursuits can turn dangerous if a shoving and nipping match causes one of them to fall. Females are passive, attracting males with pheromonal scents but concentrating mostly on eating in preparation for pregnancy. Male courtship rituals include squeaking, grunting, a hopping dance, treeborne contests of strength, and urinating onto the female. Females are in estrus for 12 hours, so mating is urgent and brief. If a female fails to become pregnant within that period, she will come into heat again (so is polyestrous) in another 25 to 30 days.

A long-standing jocular answer to the question of just how spiny porcupines engage in sex has been "carefully," but in fact, mating occurs in the same manner as with other animals. When the female is ready, she voluntarily pulls the quills along her back downward and holds them flat against her body, then raises her tail over her back, exposing the unquilled genitalia. The male then mounts her in conventional fashion. Once she is impregnated, a mucous plug forms in the female porcupine's vaginal cavity to prevent further entry by sperm, and she loses interest in mating. Her mate, who might have come from several miles away, will set out to find another receptive female before the breeding period ends. Males take no part in the rearing of offspring.

The gestation period spans 30 weeks, which is very long for a small mammal and probably includes a period of delayed implantation. Pregnant females give birth to a single pup (twins are rare) in April or May within a den usually located inside a standing hollow tree, sometimes in a rock crevice. Young are precocial, born fully quilled and with eyes open, but quills are soft and do not harm the mother. After being exposed to open air for about one hour, the quills harden, and the youngster becomes a smaller duplicate of its mother.

In captivity, mother porcupines have suckled their young for periods spanning several months, but youngsters in the wild are able to subsist on vegetation within 2 weeks. Adolescents as young as 1 month are capable of caring for themselves, although young porcupines accompany their mothers for 5 months or more; young females may even mate with the same male as their mothers breed with. Males wander off in search of their own territories during their first summer.

Porcupine populations rise and fall in 12-year cycles; a typical cycle consists of 2 years of decline, followed by a rise over the next 10 years.

Behavior

Porcupines are normally solitary and rarely show territorial aggression. In harsh weather, several individuals may take shelter in the same hollow tree, cave, or culvert, but, when fair weather returns, they resume solitary lifestyles. Porcupines do not hibernate, but pregnant females especially seek out birthing dens. Dens are used regularly throughout the winter, and there may be several throughout a territory.

The entrance to a porcupine den is marked with scat pellets, sometimes a small mountain of them if the den has been used for several years. When the den is within a hollow standing tree, there will usually be a ledge inside, 10 feet or more above its base, where the animal sleeps. This platform is often partially or entirely constructed of scat pellets compressed by weight to a hard surface. Above this elevated platform, a small observation hole will be gnawed through the tree's shell, and trackers can often spot a porcupine peering out at them.

Porcupine scat is generally a curved pellet, about a 0.25-inch in diameter, often with a longitudinal groove along a pellet's inside radius that is seen in no other species, (Muskrats have similar scats, but no groove.) Darker scat to the left is from a small whitetail.

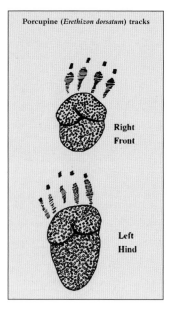

Porcupine (*Erethizon dorsatum*) tracks

Right Front

Left Hind

On hot days, porcupines escape biting flies and the heat on a thick, shaded branch high up in a tree, where they are revealed as an uncharacteristic large bump. The heavily quilled tail and rump habitually point toward the tree's trunk, the direction from which most dangers approach. This defensive position frustrates bobcats and most climbing carnivores, but the fisher can clamber past the porcupine along the underside of the branch to emerge in front of it, gaining access to the unprotected head.

Porcupines prefer to forage at night, emerging at sunset from dens and sleeping trees to forage. If a hungry or inexperienced predator threatens, the porcupine points its tail end toward the enemy, turning with the predator to keep its most potent armament positioned for a spiny slap. Given an opportunity, the porcupine will escape by climbing a tree.

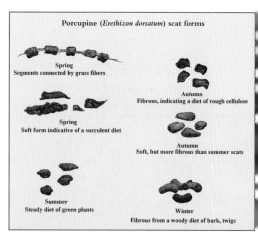

Porcupine (*Erethizon dorsatum*) scat forms

Spring
Segments connected by grass fibers

Spring
Soft form indicative of a succulent diet

Summer
Steady diet of green plants

Autumn
Fibrous, indicating a diet of rough cellulose

Autumn
Soft, but more fibrous than summer scats

Winter
Fibrous from a woody diet of bark, twigs

Family Leporidae

This is the family of rabbits and hares. Rabbits (genus *Sylvilagus*) are sometimes confused with hares (genus *Lepus*), but rabbits are generally smaller, with shorter ears and legs. The faster-running hares are more prone to open areas, while rabbits prefer brushy habitats where they can hide. Hares give birth to fully furred young in relatively open places, while rabbit newborns are born naked in a sheltering burrow or shallow hole and require a longer period of maternal care. Both are prolific breeders, with reproductive rates adapted to offset predation from numerous carnivores.

Rabbits and hares are not rodents but belong to the order Lagomorpha, a group that includes the diminutive pikas. Unlike rodents, lagomorphs have a second, smaller pair of incisor teeth directly behind the chisel-like upper incisors. This dental arrangement gives teeth a very sharp scissorlike cutting action, enabling them to chop tough cellulose into fine pieces that digest more easily. Lagomorphs are also remarkable in that males carry their scrotum ahead of the penis, instead of behind it, a characteristic otherwise seen only in marsupials.

Worldwide, there are eighty species of lagomorphs, categorized in thirteen genera, grouped into two families: Leporidae (rabbits and hares) and Ochotonidae (pikas). Native populations of lagomorphs are found on all continents except Antarctica, southern South America, and Australia. (In Australia, introduced lagomorphs have thrived to the point of becoming pests.)

SNOWSHOE HARE
(*Lepus americanus*)

Known as the varying hare because individuals in the North grow a white coat in winter, the snowshoe gets its common name from oversized hind feet that give it flotation on deep snow and mud. One of the smallest hares, the snowshoe hare is a vital food source for many carnivores, especially the lynx and bobcat.

Geographic Range

Snowshoe hares inhabit the northern United States, from New England through New York, Michigan, northern Wisconsin, northern Minnesota, and northern North Dakota. To

The snowshoe hare hasn't quite changed into its white winter coat, which has been grizzled brown all summer. (Photo coutrtesy USFWS.)

the south, their range extends only along mountain ranges that are snow covered in winter, to northern California along the Cascade Mountains, to Colorado along the Rockies, and through West Virginia and Virginia along the Allegheny and Appalachian mountain ranges. To the north, snowshoes inhabit nearly all of Canada and Alaska south of the Arctic Circle. The snowshoe hare's northern range reaches, but seldom overlaps, that of the arctic hare (*Lepus arcticus*), with a precise demarcation between the ranges of either species.

Habitat

While rabbits tend toward thickets to hide them from danger, snowshoe hares prefer more open areas where they can rely on powerful hindquarters and large feet to launch them beyond reach of predators at speeds exceeding 25 miles per hour. Secluded bogs, marshes, and swamps are preferred during daylight hours, but at night the hares venture out to feed in more open areas, such as meadows, shorelines, and roadside ditches.

Physical Characteristics

Mass: Snowshoes weigh 2 to more than 4 pounds, less than half the weight of larger hare species; it is about the same weight as an eastern cottontail rabbit, with which the snowshoe shares much of its range.

Body: The body is rabbitlike, with a humped back, long powerful hind legs, and long and wide hind feet. Body length is 15 to 21 inches. Snowshoes have a round head, blunt muzzle, and large eyes at either side of the head. Ears are 3 inches long, shorter than most other hares, to minimize heat loss. Males (bucks) are slightly smaller than females (does)—unusual among mammals but typical among leporids.

Tail: The tail is dark gray or black on top, whitish below, and 1 to 2 inches long.

Tracks: There are four toes on front and hind feet. Forefeet are comparatively round, 1.5 to 2 inches long; hind feet are very large, 3 to 4.5 inches long. In winter, tracks may be obscured by heavy fur around the pads. At a casual hop, hind feet register ahead of forefeet, leaving a track pattern that looks like paired exclamation points (!!), similar to that of a tree squirrel but several times larger. At a relaxed hop, a set of all four tracks measures 10 to 16 inches. Distance between track sets may be more than 15 feet, with longer leaps denoting a faster pace.

Scat: Scat is typical of rabbits and hares: marble- or egg-shaped pellets. Diameter is about 0.5 inch. Color is usually dark brown when fresh, becoming lighter colored and more sawdust-like with age. Scat pellets are generally found in groups of a half dozen or more. Note that rabbits and hares have a digestive process called "cecal fermentation," in which rough cellulose is eaten, pooped out in the form of green spheres, then reeaten, redigested, and finally excreted as brown, fully digested pellets. A tracker who finds green pellets can presume that their owner was frightened away.

Coloration: The snowshoe is brown in summer, becoming grizzled with age, with a darker dorsal line and longer fur than the cottontail. It has a whitish belly, brown face, black ear tips, and often a white patch on top of the head. In snow country the coat turns entirely white except for black ear tips. Snowshoes in Washington and Oregon seldom undergo this photoperiodic color change, remaining brown all year. In New York's Adirondack Mountains, there is a population that remains

This snowshoe hare demonstrates the effectiveness of its white winter coat. (Photo courtesy National Park Service.)

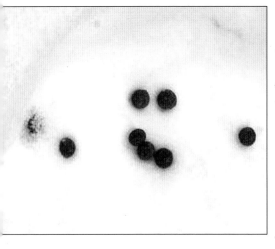

Hare and rabbit scats are generally spherical, about 0.25 inches in diameter, first excreted as green pellets (brown in winter, when diets consist of dry, woody bark and twigs), then reingested and excreted a second time as brown balls from which all nutrients have been extracted. This process is called cecal fermentation.

black (melanistic) all year. Winter molts begin in November as patchy white spots that become larger until the animal is completely white, a process that takes about 70 days. Snowshoes possess two separate sets of hair follicles—one that grows only white hairs, others growing brown and gray hairs. Color changes are regulated by daylight, not temperature, and warm winters can result in white hares that contrast starkly against snowless ground.

Sign: In winter, sign includes stripped, barkless shrubs such as sumac, dogwood, and willow. Neatly clipped grasses and stems are seen in summer. Trails are often regularly used and well packed; trails in snow may be trenches more than a foot deep, enabling hares to run fast through troughs too narrow for predators to use.

Vocalizations: Hares are normally silent. Mothers purr while nursing; newborns whimper and whine; the alarm cry is a prolonged squeal. In all cases the calls of hares are lower toned than those of a rabbit. When battling over territory, combatants growl and hiss. Thumping a hind foot repeatedly against the earth is both an alarm and a ploy to entice hidden predators into revealing themselves.

Life span: Few snowshoe hares die of old age; most become prey to a host of predators. Average life span is 4 years.

Diet

The snowshoe hare's diet is broadly varied but normally vegetarian, including grasses, vetches, asters, jewelweed, strawberry, pussytoes, dandelions, clovers, and horsetails. In winter, snowshoes forage for buds, twigs, smooth bark, and the tips of evergreen twigs. If plant foods are scarce, they have been known to raid traps baited for carnivores to get meat.

A notable trait among leporids is their need to eat the same food twice. Much of the hare's diet is tough cellulose, and because most of the hare's digestive processes are contained in the lower gut, foods must be eaten, excreted, then reeaten to extract all available nutrients. Called "cecal fermentation," this process permits the hare to quickly ingest plants where feeding may be hazardous; then the hare can retire to a safe location where the plants can be completely digested at leisure.

Although considered food by most carnivores, snowshoes are good survivors, a trait that can be seen in the lack of fat on their bodies. With a broad diet that encompasses most vegetation, as well as carrion when times get hard, the hares have little need to carry food reserves on their bodies. But they do need to maintain a lean and muscular body that can outrun fast predators, such as the coyote. Early frontiersmen for whom hares and rabbits were a winter staple often suffered from "rabbit starvation" by winter's end. Fat malnutrition occurs—as it did with the Lewis and Clark Expedition—when fat is lacking in the diet, even when plenty of other foods are available.

Mating Habits

Breeding season encompasses the summer months, beginning in March, when testicles descend, and extending through August, when testicles retract and go dormant. Males pursue females by their pheromonal scents, frequently congregating around receptive does in groups. Mating contests between males resemble boxing matches: Both contenders rise on their hind legs and bat at one another with sharp-clawed forefeet. If one is knocked onto its back, powerful hind legs kick and scratch.

Snowshoe hare
(*Lepus americanus*)

Snowshoe, or varying, hare in its all-white winter coat. Snowshoe hares in southern latitudes may remain brown all year.

Despite their apparent ferocity, these battles end quickly and are seldom injurious to either party.

Snowshoe does are polyestrous, coming into heat whenever they aren't pregnant throughout the summer months, and both genders engage in sex with any available mate (polygynandrous). This lascivious behavior ensures that these prolific breeders have a strong and varied gene pool.

Gestation takes 35 days, with litters of two to eight fully furred precocial young being birthed in a nest atop the ground, sometimes in an unoccupied burrow. Newborns are able to run within 2 hours of birth and begin feeding on vegetation within 24 hours. Mothers nurse litters for 30 days and are likely to be pregnant again before they are weaned. Does may birth as many as four litters per summer, and newborn females may mate as soon as they've been weaned. This rapid reproduction rate makes snowshoes resistant to predation from the many meat eaters that hunt it, and it's unlikely that snowshoe hares will become endangered.

Behavior

Snowshoe hares are solitary, but dense populations may force them to live together. Normally, an adult's territory may encompass up to 18 acres, but when populations peak, territories may shrink to a fraction of that size. Actual population densities may range from 1 to as many as 10,000 individuals per

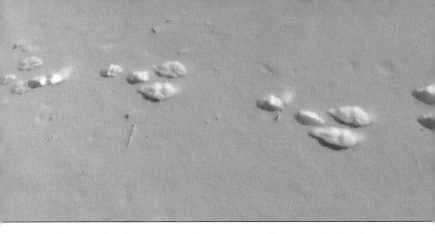

This snowshoe hare was traveling at an easy hop; note that forefeet print close together and behind more widely spaced hind feet.

square mile, with numbers typically increasing for 9 years, then drastically falling off in the 10th. Sudden population declines appear to be normal for this species and include epidemics of pneumonia, fungal infections, salmonella, and tularemia. At

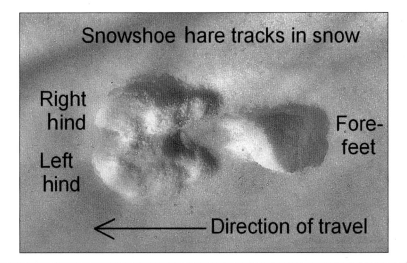

Snowshoe hare tracks in snow

Right
hind

Left
hind

Fore-
feet

← Direction of travel

the root of these plaguelike illnesses is malnutrition brought on by depletion of food resources. A secondary effect of the snowshoe's cyclic decline is a sudden decrease in populations of the lynx, which relies heavily on hares in its own diet, one year later.

The greatest fluctuations in snowshoe hare populations occur in northwestern Canada, and the least occur in Colorado's Rocky Mountains. Reasons include greater diversity among predator and prey species in warmer regions, while colder climates tend to be less varied, and relationships between hunter and hunted more critically symbiotic.

When a hare runs from danger, it zigzags through underbrush at high speed, changing direction constantly to make itself hard to follow. Hares rely on a maze of trails, each scented with frequent scat deposits, to confuse the most acute sense of smell. Snowshoes must escape quickly because they tire after a few hundred yards, while many enemies can maintain top running speed for more than a mile. When it begins to tire, a hare freezes and remains motionless, hoping to go unnoticed by its pursuer.

Hares and rabbits serve as food to many predators—like this gray wolf on Lake Superior's Isle Royale—and their prodigious reproductive rates reflect that. (Photo courtesy National Park Service.)

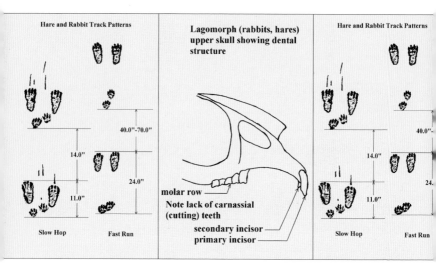

Hare and Rabbit Track Patterns

Lagomorph (rabbits, hares) upper skull showing dental structure

40.0"-70.0"

14.0"

24.0"

11.0"

molar row

Note lack of carnassial (cutting) teeth

secondary incisor

primary incisor

Slow Hop   Fast Run

Hare and Rabbit Track Patterns

40.0"-

14.0"

24.

11.0"

Slow Hop   Fast Run

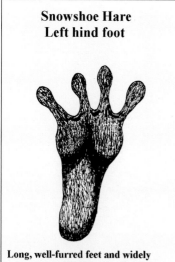

Snowshoe Hare Left hind foot

Long, well-furred feet and widely splayed toes give the snowshoe hare an unexcelled ability to run atop snow.

If open water is nearby, a hare in imminent danger will probably try to swim from a predator.

On warm summer evenings, snowshoe hares may be seen rolling about on gravel road shoulders. These dust baths loosen shedding fur and help to dislodge fleas and mites. The animals sometimes engage in this behavior in early morning, but most dust baths are taken in the evening because the majority of parasites are contracted while sleeping during the daylight hours.

EASTERN COTTONTAIL RABBIT
(*Sylvilagus floridanus*)

Able to breed continuously the year round, cottontail rabbits are a critical source of food for most American predators wherever they are found.

Immortalized by fables and songs, cottontails are the most widespread rabbit in North America. Like all rabbits, they differ from hares by having shorter, more rounded ears, a smaller body, and shorter hind legs. The cottontail is a fast short-distance sprinter that prefers to elude enemies in thick cover, rather than outrunning them across open terrain. Because it is so common, and because its traits, behavior, and diet are typical of rabbits, it has been selected to represent the genus *Sylvilagus*.

Geographic Range

Cottontails are the most widely distributed rabbits in North America. To the north, they range into southern Manitoba and Quebec. Except for Maine, they occupy all of the eastern United States from the Atlantic coast to North Dakota, south to Texas, through Mexico and into Central America and northwestern South America. To the west, cottontails inhabit the Rocky Mountains from Mexico through eastern Arizona and into Nevada.

Habitat

Supremely adaptable, the eastern cottontail is at home in any environment that provides water and cover in which to hide, including deserts, swamps, coniferous and deciduous forests, and rainforests. Currently, the eastern cottontail seems

to prefer edge environments between woods and open terrain, including meadows, orchards and farmlands, hedgerows, and clear-cut forests with young trees and brush. The eastern cottontail's range extends into that of six other rabbits and six species of hares, although, like all rabbits, it prefers less-open terrain than hares.

In winter, when green plants become unavailable, cottontails consume bark and twigs; note the neat stepped cut of this green twig, created by the scissor action of the rabbit's upper and lower incisors.

Physical Characteristics

Mass: Cottontails weigh 2 to more than 4 pounds.

Body: They have a high rounded back, ears that are 2 to 3 inches long, muscular flanks, and long hind feet. Head is rounded, with short muzzle, flat face, and large eyes at either side. Body length is 14 to 18 inches.

Tail: The tail is brown on top, fluffy and cotton-white below. Length is 1.5 to 2.5 inches.

Tracks: There are four toes on all four feet. Fore prints are round, 1 to 1.5 inches long. Hind feet are elongated, 3 to 4 inches long. Claws show in clear tracks. Toes are generally not splayed like a snowshoe hare's.

Scat: Scat consists of spherical pellets, sometimes flattened discs, usually less than 0.5 inch in diameter. Color is green to dark brown (see Diet section), becoming lighter with age. Pellets are deposited in groups of six or more.

Coloration: The brown coat is interspersed with gray and black guard hairs and is uniform over back, sides, top of tail, and head, except for a reddish patch on the nape of the neck. Ears are black tipped; the underside is buff colored. Cottontails undergo two molts

Cottontail scat is largely indiscernible from that of the snowshoe hare, except that the usually spherical pellets are slightly smaller, at just under half an inch.

Sometimes mistaken for rodents, rabbits and hares are actually lagomorphs, with a second pair of incisors located directly behind the primary incisors in the upper jaw.

per year: The spring molt occurs from mid-April to mid-July, leaving a short brown summer coat; from mid-September through October, the brown pelage is shed and replaced by a warmer grayish winter coat.

Sign: Sign includes neatly nipped-off flower and plant stems. Shrubs stripped of bark down to the cambium layer show where rabbits browsed in winter. Oblong "forms" of compressed grasses, snow, and sand show where a rabbit lay for an extended period while resting or sleeping. Disturbances on graveled road shoulders show where a rabbit took a dust bath to dislodge parasites and shed fur.

Vocalizations: A bleating distress call is intended to startle a predator into hesitating. Bucks (males) chatter and squeal loudly during and immediately after copulation. Nursing does purr while suckling young and sometimes emit a sharp alarm bark if an intruder approaches.

Life span: Cottontails live up to 5 years but usually less than 2 years because of heavy predation.

Diet

The cottontail is herbivorous, with roughly 50 percent of its summer diet consisting of grasses, and the balance is composed of a broad variety of ground plants. Its double row of upper incisors chop tough cellulose fibers into fine clippings that digest more easily. In winter the cottontail's diet turns to woody browse and bark. Deepening snows actually work for the rabbits by enabling them to reach bark and twigs that were previously inaccessible, and their gnawing makes them a pest to orchard farmers. Typical of lagomorphs, tough plant materials are digested by a process called cecal fermentation, a variation of the cud-chewing process of ruminant species. With cecal fermentation, ingested plant material is partially digested as it passes through the digestive system and is expelled from the anus as green pellets. The predigested pellets are then reeaten and pass through the digestive tract a second time, where cellulose is broken down and nutrients extracted completely. Like cud chewing, this permits rabbits to quickly eat plant foods in places that may be dangerous for them and then retire to complete the digestive process in seclusion.

Cottontails may forage at any time in places where they feel safe. In summer, they sleep away the day in cool underground burrows, sometimes in brush piles, but increased calorie needs in winter often force them to forage at all hours. In every season, activities are normally crepuscular, peaking in the first three hours after sunrise and again in the twilight hours.

Mating Habits

Serving as food for so many carnivores has given cottontails extraordinary reproductive abilities. Individuals reach sexual

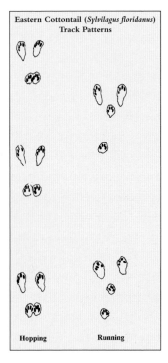

Eastern Cottontail (*Sylvilagus floridanus*) Track Patterns

Hopping

Running

Lagomorph (rabbits, hares) upper skull showing dental structure

molar row

Note lack of carnassial (cutting) teeth

secondary incisor

primary incisor

maturity by 3 months of age, and 25 percent of the rabbits born in summer will be the offspring of juveniles less than 6 months old. The start of mating season coincides with the spring molt, triggered by lengthening days (photoperiodic), warming temperatures, and the availability of green foods. Bucks, whose testicles are retracted during winter, become sexually ready in mid-February, although does don't come into estrus until mid-March.

This interval gives adult males a period in which to find prospective mates and establish a hierarchy. Both genders remain sexually active until late August or September.

Cottontail does accept numerous mates and are polyestrous, birthing as many as four litters per season. There is no bond, and mates go their separate ways after breeding; this promiscuity ensures a varied gene pool. Prior to mating, cottontails perform a courtship ritual in which the buck chases a doe until she tires and turns to face him. The pair rises on hind legs and spars briefly with the forepaws, then both drop to all fours, nose to nose, and the male jumps straight upward to a height of about 2 feet. The female replies by jumping upward, too, and both may repeat the action several times. This jumping behavior probably demonstrates the fitness of either animal to mate.

Once pregnant, does spurn further sexual advances. Gestation lasts 30 days, at the end of which expectant mothers retire to a sheltered burrow. There, in a grass-lined nest that has been insulated with fur nipped from the mother's underbelly and from around her four pairs of nipples, she births as many as eight naked and blind (altricial) young. Newborns weigh just 0.9 to 1.2 ounces but grow fast, gaining more than 0.07 ounces per day, and by 5 days they have opened their eyes.

By 2 weeks, young cottontails are fully furred and venture outside the burrow to feed on vegetation. At this point the mother is nursing them only twice a day and may already be pregnant with her next litter. Weaning occurs at twenty days, and the young rabbits, suddenly intolerant of one another, disperse.

Behavior

While not a long-distance runner, an adult cottontail can exceed 18 miles per hour through thick brush, leaping 12 feet and instantly changing direction. A flaw that human hunters exploit is that rabbits tend to run in a circle when pursued, coming back to cross their own trails and thereby confusing the noses of animal predators. Human hunters have

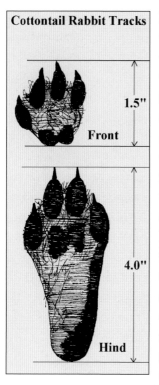

Cottontail Rabbit Tracks

1.5"

Front

4.0"

Hind

learned to take advantage of this by using dogs to chase rabbits back to where they stand. Being a sprinter with poor long-distance vision, a startled cottontail will often flee to a nearby bush and freeze. Many a cottontail has fallen to .22 rifles in this manner, because human vision is sharper than a rabbit's. Cottontails are also staples of the fur trade, although their silky pelts are made less desirable if the thin skin is torn. Uses include trimming boot tops, parka hoods, and mittens, and sometimes pelts make an entire fur coat. Rabbit fur isn't waterproof or rugged, but it is plentiful, inexpensive, and nice to touch, and a market exists for plews (prime skins).

Cottontails are not well liked by farmers, gardeners, or landscapers. Their summer feeding and reproductive capacity can mean tremendous damage to crops, while winter browsing of shrubs and fruit trees makes them pests on golf courses and in orchards. The problem is exacerbated by a human reluctance to permit the cottontail's natural predators to live near homes.

Except for brief encounters during the summer mating season, eastern cottontails are solitary and intolerant of one another. Territorial sizes are dependent on food and other resources but generally encompass between five and eight acres. Male territories tend to overlap or include the territories of local does.

Many predators consider the cottontail prey. Hawks, owls, and eagles hunt them from the air; skunks and other weasels prey on the young; bobcats pounce on them; and coyotes chase them through the underbrush. The rabbit's best defense is to sprint out of sight along a maze of trails and scents that can confuse the keenest nose. Most cottontails won't survive into their third year, but reproductive rates are high enough to ensure that this species is unlikely to be threatened by hunting or predation.

Birds

Terrestrial Birds

WILD TURKEY
(*Meleagris Gallopavo*)

When the Founding Fathers of the United States decided which bird best represented their new nation, Benjamin Franklin suggested the wild turkey. He argued that, more than any other bird, the turkey had strengthened the country by feeding American pioneers. Franklin's nomination was rejected for the more fierce image of the bald eagle, but no one disputed the turkey's importance.

The wild turkey represents a successful exercise in wildlife recovery and management. By 1920, unrestricted hunting had extirpated the birds from 18 of the 39 states they inhabited, and fewer than 100,000 still remained in the U.S. Game laws enacted after WWII helped to expand turkey populations beyond their original numbers. By 1959, populations had increased to 500,000. By 1990, wild turkey numbers exceeded 3 million, and this species now inhabits all 48 of the continental United States. Today, populations continue to grow, but the Department of the Interior's prognosis is that expansion is limited by continuing loss of habitat.

Geographic Range

Once decimated, the wild turkey now has one of the widest ranges of any game bird of North America. The species is found from the western and southern United States to the Atlantic seaboard and New England. There are six subspecies, with one additional subspecies, the Ocellated Turkey, found in Central America.

In the U.S., the most common subspecies of wild turkey are Meleagris gallopava silvestris, predominantly in the east, and Meleagris gallopava merriami, in the west. The eastern subspecies (*Meleagris gallopavo silvestris*) is distinguished by its brown-tipped tail, rump, and back feathers, whereas those feathers are tipped with tan, or sometimes almost white, on western birds.

Habitat

Wild turkey habitats are as varied as their range, and include forests, grasslands, agricultural areas, orchards, and freshwater shorelines. Overgrown brushlands where the bird's broad wingspan prohibits quick escape from danger, are usually avoided, because bobcats and coyotes find them easy prey in those places. Because the birds roost in high overhead branches through the night, suitable habitats always include tall, usually deciduous, trees with widely spaced branches.

Physical Characteristics

Mass: Wild turkey weigh 7 to 22 pounds. Weight varies considerably depending on season and food availability.

Body: The wild turkey's body is stocky. Adult males, known as toms or gobblers, have a dark, iridescent body, a reddish naked head, a wattle consisting of fleshy lobes hanging down from the chin, and a caruncle, a wartlike fleshy projection on the forehead. Thick, reddish legs have dark-colored fighting spurs projecting rearward, about halfway up. Adult males, and an occasional female, have a taillike breast tuft, or "beard," extending outward from the breast, typically growing longer as the bird ages. These beards are comprised of hairlike feathers called mesofilophumes, and are prized as trophies by sport hunters. Standing height for males averages about 48 inches.

Adult females (hens) and adolescents (jennys and jakes), are smaller and duller than adult males, lack a breast beard, have a grayish head, and the back of the neck is feathered. Standing height for adult females averages about 36 inches.

Tail: These birds have long tails, extending nearly to the ground when walking. Most distinctive is the gobbler's habit of raising his tail upright and fanning it widely during the spring mating season. Tips of the tail feathers are light brown, followed by a black band, with narrow alternating black and brown bands extending to their bases.

Tracks: Each foot has three toes, with the longer, center toe extending straight forward, flanked on either side by shorter toes that are symmetrically angled outward and forward. Claws are normally evident in tracks. Thick segments of toes are usually obvious, typically with four segments in the outer toes; five segments in the center toe. Rear toe generally prints as a round dot behind center toe, between the outer toes, but on snow or mud the entire rear toe may print. Track length is about 4 inches. Tracks are similar to those of the sandhill crane, except that the crane's digits are narrower, outside toes are asymmetrically angled, and segments are not so obvious.

Scat: In winter, when foods are drier and succulents are unavailable, scats tend to be cylindrical, unsegmented, and slightly curved, with one end rounded, the opposite flat. Dark brown, greenish, or black in color, scat is up to 3 inches long and usually less than 0.5 inch in diameter.

During the warmer months, when much of the turkey's diet consists of green plants, scats become softer and more variable in shape. Typical forms range from nearly spherical to flattened discs that are sometimes layered, similar to a cow pie, but about 1 inch in diameter.

Coloration: The wild turkey is a colorful bird, with unfeathered legs and feet that are usually pink, sometimes pink and gray. The head of the adult hen is grayish, but the head of the gobbler ranges from red to blue to nearly white, depending on the bird's hormonal status and on the season.

Flight feathers are black with brown stripes and narrower bars of white. The wattles and caruncle are pink to red, becoming more brightly colored during the mating season. The taillike breast beard, usually absent in females, is black.

Like many birds, turkeys have sharp eyesight and good color vision, and much of the communication between them is visual. The brilliant head and wattle of a dominant male in spring serves to attract females, while at the same time warning competitors that a territory has already been claimed. Fortunately, most of the turkey's most dangerous predators are color blind, while even large birds of prey, which can see colors, find the big bird too massive to be considered as prey.

Sign: Most obvious in the woods are the invariably numerous scats spattered on the forest floor under large, usually deciduous, trees. Trees that have been used as regular roosting places by several birds will have scats of varying ages beneath them, with the oldest and whitest scats being visible from a distance. Scats are usually accompanied by a scattering of feathers that fell to earth when the roosted birds preened themselves.

Scratchings and disturbances in forest humus and in grassy areas are signs of where the birds feed. Because turkeys tend to travel in flocks that may number more than a dozen birds, their foraging habits tend to leave obvious sign of their passing. Loosened soil, flattened and disturbed grasses, and displaced leaves are all signs that turkeys have been there.

Vocalizations: These vary, ranging from hollow clucking sounds to low chirping, to the distinctive gobble of mating adult males.

Life span: Wild turkeys live 5 to12 years. The mortality rate of the young can be as high as 50 percent in their first year.

Diet: Turkeys are omnivorous, eating a varied diet. They generally forage in groups, scratching the earth underfoot with their clawed toes to expose edible plants, seeds, grubs, and insects. The species also eats blueberries and other fruits in season, and may occasionally crack the husks of acorns with their strong beaks to reach the fleshy nut inside.

Wild turkeys usually forage during daylight hours, and are especially active in the early morning, after descending from their arboreal roosting places. They may also be seen feeding in open areas during the day, but are more likely to remain behind concealing cover during daylight, or in the shade of a forest on hot summer days. In the early evening, flocks will often forage in open places on the way to nightly roosting trees.

Turkeys are not migratory, but, like most animals, they change habitats out of a necessity when winter makes summer foods unavailable. Winter feeding places often include evergreen woods consisting, especially, of cedars, whose seeds make up a large portion of the species' diet during the cold months.

Mating Habits

Wild turkeys reach sexual maturity at 10 to 11 months. Females will probably mate in their second spring, but young toms may be forced by competition from larger, older males to wait until their third year. Mating takes place from February through April, sometimes extending into May in the nothernmost parts of the species' range.

Just prior to the spring mating season, the naked heads, wattles, and caruncles of mature toms take on brilliant hues of mostly red, interspersed with patches of blue, to indicate that they've reached sexual readiness. During this period, males become especially bold, frequenting open areas, from roadside meadows to hayfields, where they fan out their tails, strut, and gobble loudly enough to be heard from more than a mile distant.

The purpose of this ostentatious display is to attract females, which may come from as far as 2 miles and form harems as large as 100 individuals, although most mating flocks number about 20. Dominant gobblers will gather and hold as many hens as competition from other males will allow, herding them from behind, often with tail fanned, wings held slightly away from the body, and with a strutting walk intended to make the gobbler look as large as possible. Harems may include adolescents, and even young males are tolerated so long as they don't try to usurp the dominant tom's authority. Only a single male will mate within each flock, however, and that alpha male will at least attempt to breed with every receptive hen in his harem.

If a dominant male is challenged, the toms square off with fanned tails and outspread wings, and stalk around one another in a display of body language. If neither contender is discouraged, the contest becomes more physical, with both toms flying at one another, feet extended and spurs raking. The spurs, which are similar to those seen on domestic roosters, are the toms' main weapons, and may reach lengths of more than 1 inch. Spurs are primarily stabbing instruments, used for jabbing with a downward motion when their owners fly upward and descend on top of an opponent. As natural weapons go, they aren't very effective, and probably most of a gobbler's real power lies in the bludgeoning force of its powerful wings. As with most wild species, mating battles are seldom more than mildly injurious to either party.

After copulation, hens gestate for roughly 18 days before leaving the flock to lay an average of eight eggs (clutches as high as fifteen eggs have been reported) in a leafy depression on the ground, usually under a concealing shrub, low evergreen bough, or within the thicket of branches formed by wind-felled trees. Wild turkey eggs are about 50 percent larger than chicken eggs, with most measuring more than 3 inches long, and have shells that are beige in color.

Despite being on the ground and seemingly vulnerable, few large predators can reach most turkey nests, and smaller egg-eaters, like raccoons, skunks, and ermine, are unwilling to risk the wrath of a protective mother hen, so predation on eggs is minimal. Nesting hens leave their clutches periodically to feed during the warmth of the day, but never for long periods. After an incubation period of about 28 days, the eggs hatch. Hatchlings are precocious, and within days are able to follow their mothers, who rejoin the flock., where the entire family enjoys the protection of a group.

Behavior

Turkeys are active only during daylight hours, roosting at night in tall trees. The turkey is a wary bird with keen eyesight and good hearing, able to detect most predators at a distance in their open feeding areas. Adults can run in excess of 10 miles per hour, and, when pressed, can fly at remarkable speeds, up to 55 miles per hour, for several hundred yards or until reaching the safety of tall trees.

In autumn, usually September or October, turkeys gather in wintering flocks of several males and sometimes more than twenty females. There appears to be no animosity between adult males at this time, with none of the strutting displays seen during the spring mating period, and members are generally silent unless the flock gets separated. The goal at this time is to feed and put on fat reserves against the coming winter, and the turkeys concentrate on eating to the exclusion of all else.

Since their comeback, turkeys have become perhaps the most popular game bird in the United States, bringing in revenue that numbers in the millions of dollars each year to states that allow them to be hunted. Turkey hunting actually helps conservation efforts by prompting governmental and sporting organizations to preserve or create habitat where turkeys and numerous other species can thrive. Although hunting seasons are strictly regulated, *M. gallopavo* is not endangered, and thanks to good conservation efforts, it can today be found in habitats where it historically didn't exist.

RUFFED GROUSE
(*Bonasa umbellus*)

Ruffed grouse, sometimes incorrectly referred to as "partridge," are the most widespread of the grouse family, which includes sage hens, prairie chickens, and spruce grouse. All of the grouse prefer a four-season environment, where winters include snow, and none are migratory. The scientific name *Bonasa* means "like a bison," which probably alludes to this bird's stout physique, and the manelike collar of feathers that both genders can voluntarily "ruff" outward to make themselves look larger to an adversary.

Geographic Range

Ruffed Grouse are a northern species, found from Newfoundland on the Atlantic seaboard, across Canada on the southern shores of Hudson Bay, and extending northward into central Alaska. To the south, their range covers New York to Michigan, Wisconsin, and northeastern Minnesota, with populations extending southward through the Allegheny and Appalachian Mountains into Tennessee, Virginia, and northern Georgia. Their range also includes the Rocky Mountains south into northeastern Nevada, and the Cascade Mountains down to northern California. All of the places where ruffed grouse are found will be places where winters are snow covered but south of the Arctic Circle.

Habitat

Ruffed Grouse prefer mostly coniferous forests in the rugged north woods, especially thick swamplands of red and white cedars, which provide most of its winter foods. These birds are rarely seen in deciduous forests, and then only when passing through to a coniferous woods.

They also avoid fields and other open areas, unlike their cousins, the prairie chickens. The ideal ruffed grouse habitat is overgrown, sheltered from wind, and canopied enough to be shaded at all times of day. The species generally avoids human habitation.

Physical Characteristics

Mass: Ruffed grouse weigh 2 to 3 pounds.

Body: The ruffed grouse is a stoutly built bird that stands approximately 18 inches tall. The lowest segment of the leg (tarsus) is partially feathered on both legs. A ruff of feathers around the neck, larger on males, can be erected when the bird is excited or agitated to make it appear to be larger than it is. A white stripe extends from the base of the beak, around the eyes, to the rear of the head. The top of the head is partially crested, with about three short, upright feathers that angle backward.

Tail: In the resting positon, the tail is wedge shaped wider at the end and tapering inward toward the body; consists of roughly twenty wide feathers that have wide black bands at their outer ends and are tipped with gray. Males fan their tails widely, much like a tom turkey, to help attract females during the mating season.

Tracks: Tracks of grouse usually show three toes, with the longest toe, center one, extending straight forward, flanked on either side by shorter toes extending forward and outward at symmetrical angles. On softer soils and in snow, the rear, grasping, toe will print lightly and partially behind the three forward toes; on firmer soil the rearmost toe might not print. Forward toes exhibit three obvious segments per toe. Tracks are about 2 inches long (discounting rear toe), similar to but much shorter than those of a wild turkey. Aside from the usually obvious size difference, there's little danger of confusing tracks from a large grouse with those of a small turkey, because turkeys tend to travel in flocks and prefer open areas, while ruffed grouse are solitary and keep to canopied woods.

Scat: Winter scats are usually brownish and elongated, of even diameter throughout their lengths, and crescent shaped. One end will normally be flat, the opposite end rounded. Like its tracks, ruffed grouse scat is very similar to that of a wild turkey, but usually less than half the size at about 1 inch long, and nearly always found in deep woods that turkeys tend to avoid.

Summer scats tend to be softer, less pelletlike, revealing a more succulent diet of greens and insects. Color is generally black or dark brown, usually with a chalky white (calcareous) substance at one end, sometimes throughout. In any season, scats become lighter and more crumbled with age, deteriorating more quickly than the scats of mammals.

Coloration: Although considered to be the same species, ruffed grouse exhibit two distinctive regional color phases (morph): A red morph occurs in the Appalachian range and in the Pacific northwest, while the gray morph is predominant in the northern range east of the Pacific. Both color phases wear the same black collar (ruff), with a wide black band at the end of the tail, a light colored breast speckled with darker horizontal crescent shapes, and an almost scaled appearance on wings and back.

Sign: Scats beneath cedar, hemlock, and spruce trees. Collections of scats of varying ages on a large downed observation log. Green pine needles, pieces of poplar buds or catkins, cedar nut husks on the ground beneath trees a partridge has fed from.

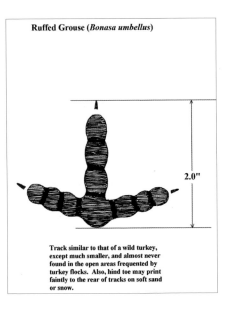

Ruffed Grouse (*Bonasa umbellus*)

2.0"

Track similar to that of a wild turkey, except much smaller, and almost never found in the open areas frequented by turkey flocks. Also, hind toe may print faintly to the rear of tracks on soft sand or snow.

Vocalizations: Clucks and chirps, difficult to distinguish from the sounds made by other birds. Most distinctive is the trademark drumming sound made by territorial males during the spring mating season. This drumming sound is made by beating the wings rapidly against the breast while standing atop a wide downed log. The sound has been likened to that of a two-stroke engine that sputters but refuses to start, and many have mistaken it as the noise made by a poorly tuned chainsaw.

Life span: Ruffed grouse live 3 years in the wild.

Diet

More than a quarter of the adult ruffed grouse's diet is made up of seasonal fruits, including strawberries, serviceberries, blueberries, and wild cherries. Prior to fruiting, the sugar-rich blossoms of these shrubs and trees are also eaten, as are grass sprouts.

Insects are also eaten opportunistically, from moths that cling to tree trunks during the daylight hours to grasshoppers, crickets, grubs, and ants found in the forests where ruffed grouse forage. Young chicks too small to fly and forage in the trees make insects most of their diets, using these protein-rich foods to grow quickly.

When winter snows make most food plants and fruits unavailable, grouse continue to feed on withered berries so long as they're available but also find good sustenance in the winter buds. Many shrubs and trees produce preleaf sprouts by mid-winter, leaving the grouse with a normally plentiful diet of tender buds from river willow, cedar, beech, and other shrubs or trees.

Mating Habits

Ruffed grouse breed throughout April and May, although a warm spring might cause males to advertise for mates as early as mid-March, and chicks born the previous spring may take part in their first mating season, at about 10 months of age. The mating season appears to be initiated mostly by a photoperiodic response to lengthening days, although warming weather undoubtedly plays a part as well.

Male ruffed grouse play the most active part in mating, advertising their availability by standing atop an elevated position, usually a downed log or large stump, and "drumming," beating their wings rapidly against the breast to produce a sound similar to that of a small piston engine. Drumming posts are above ground to make the sound audible from more than a mile distant, as well as to permit males a good view of the surrounding terrain, but are rarely higher than 4 feet above ground. Receptive females respond to the sound and come to where the male has stationed itself. Copulation normally takes place on the ground within a few yards of the male's drumming post.

Adult male ruffed grouse (roosters) frequently compete for prime drumming stations, particularly in areas where there are numerous females. Battles between them consist mainly of shoving matches in which contenders fly at one another atop the drumming site, attempting to push one another off. A few dislodged feathers mark the ground where these contests took place, but battles are usually bloodless, and the weaker male withdraws to find another drumming spot.

After mating, male and female ruffed grouse separate, the male to find another mate, if one is available. The eggs grow quickly inside the female, and, after a gestation period of 1 to 2 weeks, she begins laying them, one per day, in a bowl-shaped ground nest constructed of grasses, twigs, and pine needles. Clutches average about eleven eggs, and, when all have been laid, the female sits on them almost constantly until they hatch, about 24 days later.

Not all eggs hatch. Cold spring weather, especially combined with rain or late snows, can kill embryos within the eggs, and also new, unfeathered hatchlings. Many small predators prey on both eggs and hatchlings, even though mothers attempt to locate their nests in places that are inaccessible to raccoons and larger egg-eaters. Smaller predators, such as ermine and mink, will dine on eggs if the opportunity arises but prefer to avoid the flailing wings of a protective mother grouse if more easily obtainable foods are available.

Chicks are fed a diet of mostly insects by their mothers for the first month, after which they begin foraging near the nest site on their own, but always under their mother's watchful eye. A high-protein diet of bugs causes the young birds to grow quickly, and by 10 weeks all surviving chicks can forage on their own, and fly away from danger. At this point the family separates, and no more maternal care is given.

Behavior

The most memorable, and probably the first, encounter a typical hiker has with ruffed grouse is a startled reaction to the birds' explosive and noisy eruption from cover. Grouse have an instinctive tendency to sit tight until a potential enemy has approached to within just a few feet, then burst into flight with a sudden loud flapping of wings. This defense uses the bird's very good camouflage to conceal it from sharp-eyed predators, then, if a predator approaches too closely, the grouse's almost violent blast from cover nearly always guarantees a short head start while the enemy recoils involuntarily.

Except for the spring mating season, ruffed grouse are solitary birds. Males especially seem to claim terrritories, but there are almost no disputes beyond mating season, and territorial boundaries are respected. Drumming from territorial males helps to reinforce the peace, and may continue well past the mating season, through the month of June.

Despite its popularity as a game bird, the ruffed grouse is not endangered, although populations in some areas dipped noticeably in the late 1990s. More dangerous to ruffed grouse populations than hunting is deforestation of the species' natural habitat. Cutting timber from large tracts of forest insures that grouse will neither mate or live mate there.

AMERICAN WOODCOCK
(Scolopax minor)

This member of the sandpiper family (Scolopacidae) is perhaps best known as a migratory game bird to sport hunters. Often confused with the common snipe, which which it shares most of its range, the American woodcock is a shorebird that actually prefers wet, overgrown woodlands and mostly-dry swamps, while true snipes tend toward shorelines.

Geographic Range

The American woodcock is native only to North America, where its range covers all of the eastern states to a rough line extending from Minnesota south to eastern Texas. To the north, woodcocks are found in southeast Manitoba, eastward along the southern borders of Ontario and Quebec. A few individuals are reported to winter on islands in the Caribbean Ocean.

Habitat

Woodcock habitat is primarily in damp, mostly deciduous woods and overgrown thickets, where moist soil with moderate to low acidity provides an abundance of earthworms. Small meadows and glades surrounded by forest are its preferred mating grounds in spring, while the leaf-covered floors of deciduous forests are best for foraging. Nesting areas include coniferous and mixed forests that provide good cover, as well as older clearcuts. Despite being classed as a sandpiper, this shorebird always tends toward woodlands, although never more than a mile from a source of open water.

Physical Characteristics

Mass: Woodcocks weigh 4 to 10 ounces; adult females about 10 percent larger than males.

Body: The American woodcock is short and stout compared with the closely related snipes, with a thick body, comparatively large, rounded head, and very short neck. Also distinguished from other sandpipers by three large blackish bands that run across the top of the head, instead of the lengthwise stripes found on snipes. Large brown eyes are set far back on the skull to provide good rearward vision. The slender, sharply pointed bill is specialized for probing into soil, and measures 2 to 3 inches long. Body length is 10 to 12 inches from tip of beak to end of tail. The wings are broad and rounded, spanning 17 to 19 inches when spread.

Tail: Very short and wedge shaped, the tail is 2 to 2.5 inches long, and composed of twelve narrow feathers that taper to rounded ends.

Tracks: American woodcocks have three forward-pointing toes and one rearward-pointing grasping toe that angles to the inside, enabling the bird to grasp small branches when perched. The rear toe prints lightly in soft soil, sometimes not at all. Track length is 1.5 inches, discounting the rear toe.

Scat: Seldom seen, scat is most likely to be found on the ground beneath low shrubs. The typical form is cylindrical, rounded at one end, slightly crescent shaped. Dark brown to nearly black in color, scat is about 0.125-inch long and up to 1 inch in diameter. Scats usually lack seeds and vegetable matter.

Coloration: Plumage is patterned with brown, buff, and black, which camouflages the bird extremely well in its woodland habitat. Wing feathers give the appearance of black scales when folded against the sides. A narrow dark band extends from the front of the eyes forward to the base of the beak. Legs are tan to gray. Both sexes are monomorphic, exhibiting the same patterns and colors.

Sign: Woodcocks leave little sign of their presence. Most often found, especially during the summer molt, are feathers that have been discarded under low-lying shrubs and bushes. Leaf litter below these bushes will often show evidence of having been disturbed when the bird probed for earthworms, but this sign is easily missed and difficult to discern from sign left by other small local animals.

Vocalizations: The most commonly heard vocalization, especially in spring and early summer, is a nasal beeping sound that has been described as an unmelodious "peent" that lasts for about 1 second. This call is usually heard from males that are attempting to attract females during the spring mating season but apparently serves as a territorial claim in summer as well.

Also commonly heard is the tremolo whistling of the woodcock's wings in flight. With each downbeat of the wings, the flight feathers make a high pitched whistle that is especially apparent to hikers who approach a quietly sitting bird closely enough to cause it to burst into flight. A variation of this sound is heard from adults during the spring mating season, when males fly upward 200 to 300 feet, their wings issuing a rapidly repeated "woo-woo-woo" sound, then fall earthward a 100 feet or so, and repeat the process.

Life span: American woodcocks live 3 to 4 years, on average.

Diet

An estimated 50 percent to 90 percent of the woodcock's daily diet consists of earthworms, but numerous other insects are eaten as well, including beetles, moths, flies, centipedes, and the larvae of most insects. Because the woodcock is a ground forager, nearly all of the insects it eats are on the ground or under leafy humus; it doesn't pursue flying insects or snap them out of the air the way flycatchers and some other birds are adept at doing.

Woodcocks are extraordinary earthworm hunters, able to sense minute movements under the ground. Most sensitive is the long beak, which is kept in contact with the earth almost constantly. An earthworm moving within several inches of the woodcock creates minute vibrations that are detected through the bird's beak, and the woodcock makes an unerring stab beneath the forest duff to grasp the worm before it can escape underground. If no movement is detected, a woodcock may stamp the ground with one foot to incite lethargic worms into motion, all the while keeping the tip of its sensitive beak in contact with the earth. And although there's no data to confirm this, it seems apparent that woodcocks also possess an acute sense of smell and are able to narrow their searches for worms through odors.

Woodcocks also eat some vegetation, particularly seeds, grass sprouts, and buds in early spring, when they migrate northward. Earthworms and insects are preferred in any season, but if spring weather arrives late in the woodcock's summer habitat, causing these small animals to remain dormant for an extended period, vegetation is made to suffice until temperatures rise.

Mating Habits

Both genders of woodcock reach sexual maturity at 10 to 12 months. Courtship and nesting span the warm weather months, from spring to early fall, beginning as early as late February in southern latitudes, as late as May in the northermost regions. Mating is preceded by a northerly migration of sometimes large flocks of these normally solitary birds.

Males may begin courting during that migratory flight, but breeding takes place only after the birds have reached the forests in which they were born.

Woodcocks are territorial, with males and females staking out territories in their winter and summer ranges that they'll continue to use throughout their lifespans. The species is also among the most nonviolent of animals, and there's no record of either sex battling over territory. Females seem content to nest within as little as 50 yards of one another, and can sometimes be seen foraging for worms in such close proximity that it makes them appear friendly to one another. Males who find themselves in competition for the same territory resolve their disagreements with puffed-up displays and excited chirps, but never fight.

Male woodcocks assume the most active role in mating, and their advertisement for mates is one of the most obvious in the bird world, even though most courting is done during the hours of darkness. On reaching their summer range, males find a clearing, sometimes referred to as a "singing site," where they can fly upward and descend freely, with no interference from an overhead canopy. There, the male begins displaying by flying 200 to 300 feet upward on wings that make a high-pitched twittering sound when flapped rapidly against the air. On reaching the apex of its flight, the woodcock falls or glides earthward to a height of about 100 feet, then rises again on twittering wings. Between aerial displays, males rest on the ground and utter their distinctive "peent" cries.

Receptive females are drawn to the male's courting display from a mile or more distant, initially by the distinctive whistling of its wings, then, as the female draws closer, by its silhouette against the sky. On meeting, the pair engage in a brief courtship in which the male again plays the most active role, peenting and occasionally flying upward for several yards on twittering wings. Copulation generally occurs within an hour, then the female leaves, and the male returns to advertising for mates. There is no lasting bond between mates, and both will likely breed with several partners over the course of the summer.

Impregnated female woodcocks withdraw to their own, usually heavily wooded, territories almost immediately after mating. Those not fertilized by their previous matings will probably respond to the calls of another male and mate again, but those whose eggs have begun to develop will seek out a suitable nesting site.

Like turkeys and grouse, female woodcocks are ground layers, making rough nests of available leaves and debris directly atop the forest floor, always behind or under covering foliage, and usually in a place that's difficult for most predators to access. A few, usually inexperienced, mothers may lay their eggs directly on the forest floor if the weather is warm.

Eggs are laid within a week or so of mating, and the usual clutch size is four eggs that are gray-orange and measure about 1.5 inches long. Incubation lasts about 21 days. Newborn woodcocks are precocious, walking around the nest within hours after hatching, but they cannot feed themselves for the first 3 to 4 days, and must be fed earthworms by the mother. By 4 days, the hatchlings will have begun feeding themselves with small insects and plant sprouts, and will begin probing for earthworms with their long beaks. By 30 days the young are nearly fully grown and disperse to find their own territories.

Behavior

The American woodcock is a normally solitary bird that avoids bright daylight. Most active at dusk and dawn (crepuscular), woodcocks spend the sunlight hours sleeping in shaded undergrowth, usually on the ground, where their mottled camouflage makes them virtually invisible. When darkness falls, the birds leave their seclusion to probe the forest floor for earthworms and nightcrawlers, which are also most active at night.

The woodcock's large eyeballs give it exceptional night vision, while their placement near the rear of the head provide a field of view that permits the woodcock to see movement from behind, a valuable ability for birds that spend much of their time facing downward. Being primarily nocturnal, the woodcock's greatest danger comes from above, usually in the form of hunting owls. Terrestrial predators, especially foxes and bobcats, also prey on woodcocks, but it appears that relatively few birds are taken by these carnivores.

Like ruffed grouse, most of a woodcock's defense against predators lies in the mottled camouflage pattern of its feathers and an instinctive reluctance to reveal itself. When approached by a potentially dangerous animal (including a human) the bird remain almost stubbornly motionless under shading foliage, virtually invisible to even the sharpest eye, until the predator is mere feet from its hiding spot. Then, the woodcock bursts from cover in a flurry of twittering wings that startles the enemy into hesitating for the brief second the woodcock needs to become airborne.

Escape flights seldom cover more than 100 yards before the woodcock again settles into an obscure hiding place, a habit also seen in ruffed grouse. This method of escape is effective against animal predators, but human researchers and sport hunters can exploit it by noting in which direction a woodcock flew, then very slowly following, knowing that the bird has gone to ground again within a few dozen yards.

Woodcocks have been referred to as "timberdoodles" by hunting-magazine writers, but this monicker rightfully belongs to the closely related common snipe (*Gallinago gallinago*), whose marshland habitat frequently overlaps that of the true woodcock. The name alludes to the corkscrewing flight pattern used by flushed snipes, whose spiraling escape over relatively open marshes is designed to make them a difficult target for hawks that are adept at plucking prey birds out of the air. The woodcock's forested habitat doesn't require such evasive maneuvering, and in fact often prohibits such aerobatics. A woodcock often flutters while flying away from an enemy, but isn't known to employ the corkscrew flight used by snipes.

COMMON RAVEN
(*Corvus corax*)

Largest of the family Corvidae, which also includes crows, magpies, and jays, the raven may be the smartest bird species in the world, arguably second to the smaller American crow (*Corvus brachyrhynchos*) in terms of social structure and a rudimentary language. This innate intelligence has made both crows and ravens popular in zoos and as pets, where some individuals have even been trained to speak simple words, like "hello." Some cultures have revered these birds enough to incorporate them into their heritage—raven with wings spread was once the icon painted on the sails of ships belonging to the Scottish clan MacDougall.

The raven's historical range was once broader than it is today, but for centuries the big, bold birds were easy targets for farmers who blamed them for crop damage, and for varmint hunters who eradicated them for sport. Today ravens enjoy legal protection in many states, and the species appears to be rebounding.

Geographic Range

Ravens are common throughout most of the world, and especially in the northern hemisphere, where they range well above the Arctic Circle. Outside the United States, ravens are native to northwest Europe, Great Britain, the shorelines of Greenland, Iceland, northern Scandanavia, central Asia and the Himalayas, northwest India, Iran, northwest Africa, the Canary Islands, and Central America South to Nicaragua.

In North America, the species is found throughout Canada and Alaska, throughout the western states and southward into Mexico. It is absent throughout all but the northernmost eastern states, except along the Appalachian Mountains, where it extends southward to Georgia.

Habitat

Ravens are adaptable to almost any environment, but are partial to cooler climes where winters include at least some snowfall. These birds are capable of withstanding extreme cold, and it might not be coincidental that the rugged, cold habitats that ravens seem to prefer are places that are sparsely populated by humans.

All suitable raven habitats include elevated places where females can nest well above ground, out of reach of most predators. In mountainous terrain, rocky crags and cliff faces are used for nesting, but it appears that ravens most prefer to nest in the tops of standing trees, particularly conifers.

Physical Characteristics

Mass: The common raven weighs 1.5 to 3.5 pounds, with the heavier individuals occurring in the north.

Body: The raven is the largest of all-black birds, standing 24 inches or more, or roughly 50 percent larger than the closely related common crow. Wingspan is about 46 inches. The all-black bill is comparatively larger than the crow's, with the upper side covered with short, black nasal feathers about halfway out from the head. Neck, and especially the throat, is more thickly feathered than the crow's. The genders are nearly identical, except that females tend to be roughly 10 percent smaller than males.

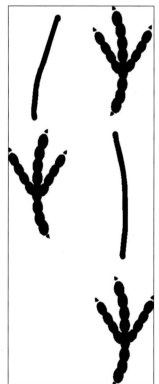

Tail: The common raven's tail is wedge shaped and much longer than that of the crow, extending nearly to the ground and sometimes dragging when the bird is walking.

Tracks: Three thick, segmented toes face forward, with the center toe longer than outer toes; one toe, facing rearward, is used for grasping. The forward-facing toes are less splayed than in some species (such as the turkey), with less of an angle between the outer toes and the center toe. The rear toe is usually in line with the center toe, not offset as in crows and many other species. The claws are exceptionally long compared with most nonpredatory species, measuring up to 0.5-inch, and normally showing in tracks. Track length (excluding claws), is about 3.5 inches from the tip of the rearward toe to the tip of the center forward toe.

Although very strong fliers, ravens tend to walk from one place to another with a strutting gait that might be described as almost cocky in nature. The typical pattern is a staggered line of left and right tracks, evenly spaced, and all pointing forward—as opposed to the pigeon-toed (inward-pointing) or duck-footed (outward-pointing) tracks of many other species. The distance between left and right tracks averages about 6 inches, with a narrow straddle of about 2 inches between the left center toe and the right center toe. Note that the rear toes tend to drag as the bird steps forward, leaving scrape marks behind them and revealing its habit of angling the forward toes upward as it walks.

When taking flight, ravens, like most birds, prefer to get a running start that consists of a series of hops in which paired left and right tracks print closely together but with 2 to 3 feet of space between pairs. Tracks tend to point forward, not angled, and rear toes seldom leave scrape marks.

Scat: Scat is varied—sometimes solid, but most often watery and formless. Solid scats are typically dark, brown or blackish, unsegmented, evenly cylindrical in shape, and curved. The diameter less than 0.5-inch, and length ranges from less than 1 inch to more than 2 inches. Solid scats are often indicative of a poor diet that lacks good nutrition and moisture. Scats turn white as they become drier with age.

A more succulent diet of fresh carrion and other animal flesh results in a semiliquid scat form that's most often found beneath trees and other elevated perches. These splattered scats may be up to 2 inches across, and usually have a mucous-like consistency, with traces of yellow or white. Occasionally there will be more solid segments included, as well as insect legs and carapaces in summer.

Coloration: The common raven's feathers and bill are black. Legs and feet unfeathered and black. Feathers have an iridescent quality because of oils, making the bird shiny in sunlight, and causing it to have a purplish cast under bright conditions.

Sign: Scat accumulates under roosting trees, and is especially obvious atop snow. Discarded, all-black feathers are usually under roosting trees, especially in summer. In winter, the bird's wingtips often brush against snow when it is taking flight, leaving imprints of flight feathers, as well as a good indication of wingspan; the same phenomenon may be seen on dusty roads and sandy shorelines.

Vocalizations: Classified as a songbird by ornithologists, ravens are among the loudest and most vocal of birds, making them easy subjects for study. Less easy is deciphering the precise meaning of the species' numerous calls, which range from the familiar croaks and caws to short whistles and clucks. It's commonly accepted among ornithologists that both ravens and crows have a rudimentary language, but the process of defining vocalizations is a work in progress.

The call heard most often is a croaking "awwk" that keeps members in touch with others of the same flock. A call used to alert others to the presence of food is a higher-pitched and less hoarse "ock."

A less commonly heard raven voice consists of a repeated clucking sound that has sometimes been mistaken for the mating call of a male grouse. This sound, which humans can imitate by placing the flat of the tongue against their upper palates, then sucking it abruptly downward, is a hollow cluck, almost a popping noise. The call is usually in two stages, a lower-toned cluck followed by a slightly higher-pitched one, but different combinations are sometimes used. The call is apparently a communication, but is often issued from lone ravens perched on a low branch, and its exact meaning has yet to be determined.

Another raven call that often goes unidentified or mis-identified is a hollow whistle that sounds much like the noise humans make by blowing across the mouth of a glass sodapop bottle. The exact meaning of this call has yet to be deter-mined, but it seems to be uttered mostly in the early morning, and from lone individuals perched overhead.

Life span: Ravens live about 6 years in the wild.

Diet

Ravens, like the related crows, jays, and magpies, are best known as scavengers of carcasses, but the species' diet is actu-ally broadly omnivorous. Carrion, especially the carcasses of larger animals such as deer, represent a large, easily obtained source of food, but ravens, like most of the birds in their taxonomic family, are versatile feeders that can subsist on nearly any digestible organic material.

Being scavengers that rely on vision, ravens possess extraordinary eyesight and good color discrimination, which enables them to see dead or dying animals from great distances. A very long beak filled with olfactory receptors gives the birds an ability to detect the spoor of blood from several miles distant; among birds, only the turkey vulture (*Cathartes aura*) has a more acute sense of smell.

Much of the reason ravens are known primarily as carrion eaters has to do with the birds' habit of frequenting roadways, where large numbers of animals are killed by motorists. Smaller road kills, like squirrels, are simply carried off in the birds' talons to be eaten in a less hazardous location. Deer and other animals too large for transport draw sometimes large congregations of ravens and crows, although rarely both at the same time, because ravens are loathe to share a bounty with their smaller cousins.

Ravens do share large carcasses with coyotes and wolves, and in fact intentionally advertise the presence of large dead animals to these more powerful carnivores by giving a raucous display in which a flock of them, sometimes 10 or more, circle above the carcass with a cacophony of croaking calls. Before the larger carrion eaters respond, attendant ravens busy themselves eating a carcass's soft parts—eyeballs, nose pad, and around the anal cavity—but the birds lack the strength necessary to tear through tough hide to reach fleshier, more preferred portions. Coyotes and wolves have learned to recognize the ravens' display as a sign of easily obtained food. After the larger carnivores have eaten their fill, the ravens descend to peck the remaining flesh from nooks and crannies.

Large dead animals that are in places too open to attract carnivores may remain inaccessible to ravens, although they have learned that carcasses at the roadside are often split open from impact, but the birds also frequent carcasses after they've begun to decay. Rotted flesh isn't generally eaten, but fly and insect larvae, beetles, and other invertebrates that feed on decayed organic matter can make up a large portion of the diet of ravens that feed along roadways.

Although not known for their hunting prowess, ravens also have a predatory side. Raids on the eggs and newborns of smaller nesting birds, especially those that nest on the ground, are fairly common, and ravens frequently make meals of hatchling turtles in early summer, as well as snakes, frogs, mice and voles. The birds can often be seen foraging in meadows for grasshoppers and mice, and in freshly plowed fields for earthworms. Few small animals are excluded from the diet of this opportunistic hunter. In some areas, predation of ravens on the young of endangered species, such as desert tortoises and least terns, has caused ravens to be considered pests.

Ravens are also fond of fruits and seeds. Raspberries, blueberries, and most other berries are eaten in season, but the birds dislike having their vision hampered by the dense foliage of a berry thicket, and often will fly up into nearby trees to survey the surrounding area for danger. More favored are fruiting trees, such as crabapple, serviceberry, and wild cherry, which enable ravens to have an unrestricted view while they feed. Cornfields are sometimes plundered, and cobs carried off in the birds' feet to a safer, more open feeding spot. Ravens and crows also incur the wrath of farmers by eating seeds from freshly planted fields.

Like most species in the Corvidae family, ravens are known to carry off and store foods in elevated larders that range from cracks in cliff faces to holes in standing trees, and even church belltowers. It doesn't appear that foods are cached for long-term storage but rather to provide a safe place for them to be retrieved and eaten within a few days.

The tendency to cache items also extends to nonfood objects. Ravens and, to a lesser extent, crows, are known for stealing small shiny objects, like watches, marbles, and even coins, then flying off with them clutched in their feet to stash the objects in an elevated cache, which might also be used for storing food. The purpose behind this behavior isn't known, but the thievery of ravens has been well documented.

Mating Habits

Ravens reach sexual maturity at 11 to 12 months. Mating takes place from late February through early March, later in the north than in the south. It appears that the breeding season is initiated by several factors, including lengthening days, warming temperatures, and probably pheromone scents emitted by receptive females.

Both males and females become territorial at the start of the breeding season, driving off other ravens of the same gender and becoming generally intolerant of all larger birds within their claimed domains. Males tend to pursue females, and their territories are generally sited to overlap those of several females, even though both sexes are typically monogamous, accepting only one mate per breeding season.

Courtship between prospective mates is a ritualized affair of elaborate displays and dances. The female indicates her readiness to breed to an attendant male by crouching low to the ground and extending her wings, their tips drooping to the ground, in a posture of submission. The male struts around her, breast and neck feathers ruffled to make itself look as large as possible. If the male is an acceptable mate, the crouched female raises her tail, exposing her genitalia, and shakes it rapidly. The male then mounts her from behind in typical bird fashion, pressing her to the ground and holding her in a submissive position be covering her outspread wings with his own. Copulation lasts less than a minute and may be repeated several times before the pair fly off together.

Mated pairs are highly territorial, remaining together and defending their nesting area from intruders throughout the summer, and often longer. Both mates participate in building a broad, dish-shaped nest, about 3 feet in diameter, of large sticks encasing a more densely intertwined wall of smaller sticks, and lined with feathers, fur, grass, and other soft materials. The raven's larcenous nature and innate intelligence sometimes result in nests that are lined with socks and small articles of clothing stolen from clotheslines, while the nest walls may include wire, plastic drinking straws, string, or other suitable manmade objects.

The raven's best-known nesting places are rocky ledges on high cliff faces, out of the wind, but other equally elevated and sheltered locations are also used. Nesting ravens have been sighted atop power poles, farm silos, microwave towers, and once even on the roof of an abandoned car. In forested country, the birds often nest at the tops of tall pines, especially those standing in open marshes.

Pregnant females begin laying their eggs almost immediately after their nests are completed, within about 10 days of mating. Clutch sizes average four to five blue-green, brown-spotted eggs, each about 3 inches long. Eggs are incubated by the female, although some reports claim that males may sit on the eggs for short periods while their mates leave to drink and feed. Males also bring their nesting mates food.

Raven eggs hatch after an incubation period of about 18 days, in late March to early April. Similar in size to chicks of the domestic chicken, hatchlings are born naked in the south, and covered with a fine fuzz in the north. Both parents care for the young, bringing them insects and scraps of meat.

Young ravens learn to fly at about 8 weeks, and leave the nest with their parents. Adolescents can be differentiated from their parents by being slightly smaller, and by their lack of the blue-black iridescence of an adult, especially around the head and shoulders.Parents and young remain loosely together throughout the summer and following winter, with the family growing progressively less cohesive as the young ravens approach maturity. Yearling ravens leave their parents to establish their own territories and to find their own mates in the following spring.

Behavior

Ravens are complex birds, which historically led to some disagreement about their habits and behaviors among ornithologists and laymen alike. Adult birds are indeed solitary, but only until they find mates. Mated pairs probably remain together for life, yet widowed mates will rarely remain alone past the next spring mating season, and widowed parents of immature, nest-bound young will probably find a new mate to help raise the offspring soon after losing the parental mate.

Although described by some authorities as being solitary in nature, ravens are most often seen in flocks that can number 15 birds or more. The explanation behind this seeming contradiction is that only unmated adults in search of their own territories are solitary. Mated adults tend to remain together throughout the year, probably until one of them dies, and the bond between parents, offspring, and siblings seems to diminish very little as the birds age.

The primary reason that related ravens flock around a carcass is to create an intimidating show of force to discourage other ravens, and even eagles, from attempting to appropriate a good source of food. Bald eagles and other large raptors have little to fear from individual ravens, and in fact consider them prey, but a half-dozen or more ravens gathered at a deer carcass is more trouble than even a pair of eagles can contend with. Too intelligent to engage a larger, better-armed eagle in individual combat, the ravens persist in harassing the raptor by jumping from all sides to peck at it. Unable to enjoy its spoils, the eagle eventually abandons the carcass to find a less annoying meal elsewhere. That same tactic works against smaller carnivores, such as foxes and opossums, but not coyotes or wolves, which ravens rely on to tear through tough hide that their own beaks can't penetrate.

Historically, ravens have been persecuted by humans for superstitious reasons, which in turn spawned erroneous, but persistent, beliefs that ravens were somehow bad birds. Edgar Allen Poe's immortal poem, "The Raven," refers to the bird as a "devil" and "demon," and even the legendary John James Audobon incorrectly accused the raven of preying on lambs. Prompted by these and other myths, and perhaps intimidated by the raven's bold curiosity and obvious intelligence, farmers in the New World made a point of shooting the birds on sight for centuries. By the first quarter of the 20th century, this once-common species had all but disappeared from much of its historical range in the eastern United States. Today raven numbers are rebounding, especially in the western states, but many eastern states still classify them as endangered or threatened.

BLACK-CAPPED CHICKADEE
(*Poecile atricapillus*)

This tiny but endearing bird has long been a favorite among birdwatchers. Chickadees have been described as the toughest birds in the forest, because when eagles, hawks, and other species known for their fierceness have fled south to warmer climes, the little chickadee remains, energetic and seemingly cheerful in the coldest, most hostile weather.

Geographic Range

Black-capped chickadees are native only to North America, where they range from central and western Alaska, and throughout Canada. In the West, the species ranges south to northern California and Nevada, and through the Rocky Mountains as far south as New Mexico. In the eastern and central United States chickadees are found as far south as Indiana and New Jersey.

Habitat

Black-capped chickadees prefer open deciduous woodlands, but are not uncommon in mixed or mostly coniferous forests, cedar swamps, or among willow and dogwood thickets along river and lakeshores. Many sources list them as being most common at the edges of forest and field, but this may be due more to the number of observers in those places than to the actual number of chickadees living there.

Physical Characteristics

Mass: This chickadee weighs about 3 ounces.

Body: This species is easily recognized by its short, plump body, solid black cap and bib, and white cheeks. Its standing height is 5 to 6 inches; wing span is 6 to 8 inches. The bill is proportionally short, about 0.25-inch long. The sexes are alike in color and size. This chickadee is difficult to differentiate

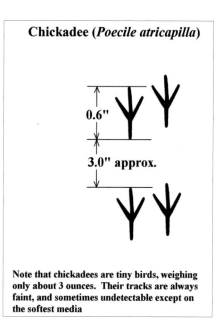

Chickadee (*Poecile atricapilla*)

0.6"

3.0" approx.

Note that chickadees are tiny birds, weighing only about 3 ounces. Their tracks are always faint, and sometimes undetectable except on the softest media

from the Carolina chickadee, whose range slightly overlaps that of the black-capped in the southeastern edge of the latter's range, except that the true black-capped chickadee's breast bib is more irregular along its lower edge.

Tail: Proportionally long, dark gray.

Tracks: Small and very faint, even on snow or mud. 3 toes pointing forward, center toe slightly longer than outer toes; outer toes arrayed at outward-pointing angles to either side. Rear toe typically points straight backward, used for grasping. Track length about 0.5-inch, discounting rear toe. Black-capped Chickadees hop rather than walk, leaving paired side-by-side tracks with 3 to 4 inches between pairs.

Scat: Difficult to find, but usually on the ground below branches where the birds perch. Solid form is cylindrical and blackish when fresh, rapidly becoming white as it ages; length about 0.125-inch, diameter about equivalent to a Number 2 pencil lead.

Coloration: The black-capped chickadee has a black skull cap, black bib, white cheeks, and a greenish-gray back, with streaks of white and black. Wings and tail are dark gray, flanks buffy. The upper wing feathers have white edging.

Sign: Signs include seed husks, and sometimes discarded feathers on the ground below perches. Chickadees leave little evidence of having been in a place, but their energetic activities and vocal nature usually make their presence obvious.

Vocalizations: Black-capped chickadees have a range of vocalizations that this species uses to communicate not only among themselves, but apparently with grosbeaks and other small bird species commonly seen feeding with chickadees. The simple-sounding calls have been found to be surprisingly complex and language-like, encoded with information on identity and recognition of other birds, and including predator alarms and gathering calls. The call for which chickadees are best known suggests their common name: "dee-dee-dee-dee." The black-capped chickadee's song consists of two or three whistled notes, the first higher in pitch, described as "fee-bee-ee."

Life span: Chickadees live an average of 2.5 years in the wild, although birds up to 5 years old aren't uncommon. The oldest wild black-capped chickadee on record lived 12 years and 5 months.

Diet

Black-capped chickadees are omnivorous, feeding on most forest-dwelling insects, and their larvae, and spiders, many of which are snapped up as the birds hop about on the trunks of rough-barked trees, such as oak, ash, and white pine. Fat-rich grubs and caterpillars are especially preferred during the birds' mating season. Chickadees are an important species in terms of mosquito control, with insects making up roughly 70 percent of their diets during the summer months. Because chickadee communities tend to be large in the habitats where they live, this species' impact on the numbers of parasitic and agricultural insect pests can be significant.

During the growing season, flowers, fruits, and seeds make up the other 30 percent of a chickadee's diet. Summer plant foods include nectar-rich flowers, numerous seeds, and many types of berries, including serviceberry, blackberry, goldthread, rosehips, and blueberry. Chickadees have also been observed eating waxy berries, such as soapberry and the autumn fruits of poison ivy. It's believed that chickadees play an important role in dispersing undigested, scat-borne seeds throughout their habitats, thereby helping many plants to propagate.

In winter, chickadees eat seeds of cattails, cedars, and dogwoods, as well as the tender bud ends of river willow, pines, and most other trees, sometimes hanging upside down from twigs as they feed. Hibernating spiders and insects are plucked from recesses in the bark of trees, where they've taken refuge until spring.

Chickadees also eat carrion when they can get it, especially in winter. Many hunters have noted that their skinned and hanging deer are a major attraction for chickadees, which focus most of their attention on fats, rather than meat. They also help to clean the bones of larger prey animals brought down by carnivores.

Mating Habits

Black-capped chickadees generally reach sexual maturity at about 12 months, although it appears that some females born in early spring may mate later in the same breeding season in which they were hatched. Mating extends from April to early July, earlier in the south than in the north, and adults mate only once each year. Chickadees probably do not possess a keen sense of smell, so mating is most likely triggered by warming and lengthening days, less by pheromone scents.

Male and female chickadees are typically already paired from the previous autumn. Unpaired males and females are drawn to one another through vocalizations, which studies suggest are complex enough to be considered a form of rudimentary language. Courtship appears to have no ritual but consists of much flitting around one another. Mating competitions between breeding males is usually brief and limited to shoving matches in which contenders vie for possession of a perch. Breeding season is the only period of the year in which these social birds exhibit territorial behavior.

Once paired, mates retire from the rest of the flock to find a nesting site, usually inside a standing hollow tree or a knothole in a large dead branch. Females do all of the nest building, while their mates bring them gifts of food. Nests are constructed of grasses, animal fur and feathers, and pine needles.

Fertilized females begin laying as soon as the nest is completed, with clutch sizes ranging from 5 to 10 roundish marble-size eggs with white shells and red-brown spots, especially around their larger ends. Both mates watch over the nest, but only the female sits on the eggs, leaving for brief periods that seldom exceed 5 minutes to drink and relieve herself. After a short incubation of about 12 days, the eggs hatch.

Chickadees are born blind and naked (altricial), but they grow quickly on a diet of mostly insects that are brought to them by both parents. By 9 days the chicks will have grown feathers, and by 16 days they'll have learned to fly. Both parents continue to feed them a high-protein diet of insects until the young are 3 to 4 weeks old, at which time they'll have matured sufficiently to fend for themselves.

Behavior

The black-capped chickadee is a social bird, except during the spring-summer mating season, when pairs withdraw from their flocks to incubate and rear young, rejoining the flock between May and August, typically later in the north than in the south.

Before and after their mating season, black-capped chickadees exhibit some of the most social behavior in the animal world, gathering together in flocks that may number in the dozens. Further adding to the size of a chickadee flock are numerous similar-size but unrelated bird species that fly, feed, and often roost—but are not known to interbreed—with the chickadees. These friends of the chickadee include grosbeaks, nuthatches, warblers, vireos, and small woodpeckers. Aside from an occasional squabble at birdfeeders, there seems to be no animosity between the different species, and it's thought that this communal behavior, like schooling fish, provides safety from predators by making it difficult to isolate a single individual from the confusion of a large flock.

Probably in large part because of its social flocking behavior, the chickadee suffers relatively few losses from predation. Bird predators include small forest-dwelling owls and hawks, red squirrels and arboreal snakes that prey on eggs and hatchlings, and occasionally a pine marten or fisher that catches a chickadee roosting in the darkness of night. Being active by day, chickadees have relatively poor night vision, but their habit of sleeping on small-diameter end twigs, where vibrations from an approaching arboreal predator can be felt, ensure that the tiny birds aren't easy prey at any time of day.

Black-capped chickadees are not migratory, and, although they possess the ability to fly from an unsuitable environment to another, better habitat, the species prefers to remain within as small an area as possible, sometimes living their entire lives within just a few acres. This quality has helped to endear them to bird lovers, because chickadees remain in the same territory throughout the coldest winters and are regular visitors to bird feeders.

To help them resist cold, chickadees' metabolisms slow while sleeping in cold weather, and their body temperatures drop slightly, much the same as a hibernating mammal. This phenomenon doesn't appear to have an effect on the birds' ability to react to danger, but it does serve to conserve energy in very cold weather. Despite this ability, subzero weather is said to be the greatest killer of chickadees, which frequently die of hypothermia while roosting.

Chickadees are not threatened, and their numbers are at healthy levels throughout the species' range. Continued logging of forested habitat, with subsequent loss of nesting sites, is the biggest threat to populations of black-capped chicka-dees. A positive note is that chickadees have shown themselves willing to use manmade nesting boxes in lieu of natural sites.

Shore and Water Birds

This section deals with bird species whose lives are spent mostly or entirely around water. These include geese, swans, and ducks, herons, cranes, and bitterns, and many species of hawks and eagles. The water birds selected for coverage here represent only a small number of the species that fall into this category, but they are some of the most important, from an ecological standpoint, and many of the characterics of each are applicable to other members of the same family.

GREAT BLUE HERON
(*Ardea herodias*)

One of our most magnificent shorebirds, the great blue heron is an icon of marshalnds throughout North and Central America. The great blue heron is a seasonally migratory species, wintering and breeding during the summer months in northerly climes, then migrating to warmer regions with their young before snowfall. A less migratory, all-white subspecies, the great white heron, is found almost exclusively in shallow shoreline habitats around the Florida Keys. In places where both white and blue heron populations meet, another intermediate subspecies, the Wurdemann's heron, can also be found.

Geographic Range

The great blue heron breeds throughout North America, Central America, the Caribbean, and the Galapogos Islands. A migratory species that avoids snow, the great blue heron moves northward in spring to mate and live in more northerly climes that range from the Pacific coast of southern Alaska to throughout the southern half of Canada, across all of the lower forty-eight states, and south through most of Mexico and into Central America.

In late autumn, usually November and December in the northernmost parts of its range, blue herons and their now-grown young fly southward to winter in warmer regions that extend from Canada's coast up to Nova Scotia, through the southern half of the states, Mexico, and into South America. In winter, the more northern populations are concentrated around the Pacific and Atlantic coastlines, where temperatures are kept warmer by latent heat from the oceans.

Habitat

The great blue heron's habitat will always be at the edge of a body of water, including rivers, lakes, beaver ponds, marshes, and saltwater and Great Lakes shorelines. Smaller streams are sometimes frequented, but these will nearly always be tributaries of a larger body of water nearby.

Herons, like most large stilt-legged shorebirds, take flight more slowly than smaller birds, and they prefer a running start of several steps. They tend to avoid overgrown shorelines where willows, dogwoods, and other tall shrubs inhibit the bird's freely spreading its wings to a span that can exceed 6.5 feet. For these reasons, most herons can be found in relatively open shallows, where cattails and reeds provide cover, and most of the heron's favorite prey animals can be found.

The habitat of the great blue heron can usually be relied on to reward field researchers and naturalists with a diversity of other stilt-legged shoreline species, such as bitterns, egrets, and cranes. The same habitat nearly always yields an abundance of other species that have a part in the aquatic food chain, from ducks and geese to mink and otters, to fish and frogs.

Physical Characteristics

Mass: Great blue herons weigh 4.5 to more than 5.5 pounds.

Body: The great blue heron is the largest heron in North America, standing 38 to 54 inches from its large feet and long, comparatively spindly, legs to the top of its black-crested head. The skull crest consists of two blackish stripes that extend from the eyes at either side of the head, back to the nape of the neck, and terminate in black, upward-curling plume feathers. Wings span 66 to 79 inches. The long daggerlike bill, is about 8 inches long. The long, slender neck is carried in an "S" shape, even when in flight. A line of almost shaggy-looking plume feathers extends along the spine from neck to tail. Genders are identical, except males are likely to be slightly larger than females.

Juveniles resemble adults, but lack the crest, and instead have a dark-gray to black cap extending from the nape across the top of the head, around the yellow eyes, and to the top of the characteristically rapier-like bill. Juveniles also have a dark upper bill, rust-colored edging on the back and wing feathers, and lack the mane of long plume feathers that encircle the adults' lower necks.

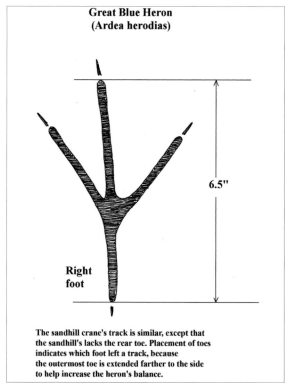

**Great Blue Heron
(Ardea herodias)**

6.5"

**Right
foot**

The sandhill crane's track is similar, except that
the sandhill's lacks the rear toe. Placement of toes
indicates which foot left a track, because
the outermost toe is extended farther to the side
to help increase the heron's balance.

Tail: The great blue heron's tail is comparatively short, squared at the end, with a blackish tip.

Tracks: Each foot has four toes, with three toes pointing forward, and one gripping toe pointed rearward. The total length, from tip of rear toe to tip of center front toe, is about 6.5 inches. Note that the outermost front toes of either foot are widely splayed from the inner two toes, which are themselves held nearly parallel to one another. A track with a splayed outer toe that points left was made by the left foot, and vice versa.

Scat: Scat is sometimes cylindrical, dark brown when fresh, 0.5-inch in diameter, and about 1 inch long. More often, scats are semiliquid, mucous-like spatters among shoreline grasses, sometimes with evidence of fish scales, but often indistinguishable from those of other large shorebirds.

Coloration: A white stripe extends across the crown from the front to back of the skull, bordered at either side by a black plume extending from behind the eye to off the back of the neck. Back, wings, and breast are bluish gray, often appearing all gray from a distance. The bird has a brownish patch is under the leading edge of both wings and black patch at the elbow wing joint. Flight feathers are black-tipped, contrasting with the wing centers, and with a spinal tuft of gray-blue plume feathers when the wings are folded. The neck is long and gray, and is sometimes marked with rusty brown, especially in younger birds. The breast is streaked with white, black, and red-brown, and the bill yellowish. The legs are brown, sometimes dyed green from wading through algae, and the thighs may be marked with brown. The eyes yellow, round, and obvious.

Sign: Signs include cattail and other reeds that are pushed aside, leaving a trail of foliage displaced by the bird's large body. These trails are often marked by blue-gray feathers pulled free as the heron pushed through foliage.

Vocalizations: The great blue heron is less vocal that most members of its family, usually going about its business in silence. The most common call between mates is a hoarse, low-toned, and relatively quiet croak, not greatly different than that of a raven. A guttural "rawk" sound is made when the bird is distraught, and sometimes while it's in flight. When disturbed near its nesting site, a parent of either sex may utter a nasal "rawnk" that sounds similar to the call of a Canada goose.

Life span: Great blue herons live about 7 years.

Diet

Although generally thought of as a daylight operator, blue herons also frequent shorelines at night, especially warm, moonlit nights, when many of the birds' prey remain active through the night and lunar glow makes hunting by night easier. A typical heron spends about 90 percent of its day hunting for food in the shallows.

The great blue heron's hunting technique is effective and relatively simple. Able to wade shallows more than a foot deep without getting its feathers wet, the heron spends most of its waking hours standing motionless inside the concealment of a reed marsh. If no prey wanders within the bird's reach, it may move to a new location with slow, stealthy steps, placing each foot softly to avoid disturbing food animals and fine silt that can swirl up in clouds and obscure the bottom. Perhaps because of their shapes, neither movement of the heron's legs or the silhouette of its body against the sky seem to disturb smaller animals that make up most of this species' diet.

Edible animals in the great blue heron's diet include small fish of about 4 ounces, crayfish, snails, small clams, frogs, snakes, and small rodents. Because most of these creatures are crepuscular in their habits, herons and other shoreline birds tend to be most active in the twilight hours of predawn and dusk.

Larger prey is captured by the heron's long, sharply pointed bill, which shoots forward, propelled by unwinding the spring-like "S" shape of its neck, and impaling the target with sometimes unerring accuracy. The prey, which is now actually holding the heron's bill from opening, is then thrown straight upward into the air with a toss of the bird's head, where it slides free of the tapered bill and is caught in the heron's wide open mouth on the way down. Maybe most impressive is that prey animals tossed into the air are caught by their heads nearly every time, which generally disposes of their biting ends first, and orients small fish so that their spiny fins will lie back and down as they slide into the bird's gullet. In a few rare, and usually well-heralded, instances, herons have choked to death when fish became lodged in their throats, but the vast majority of great blue herons become superbly skilled at skewering and flipping prey into their own mouths.

Smaller prey, like snails and small clams, are held down with one of the heron's large, strong feet, and pecked or pried at with its bill until the the shell's occupant has been consumed. Besides being an effective stabbing weapon and a good prybar, the heron's long, pointed bill can serve as needlenose pliers, reaching through chinks in natural armor—including the carapaces of turtles small enough to be gripped and held by one foot. Crayfish are sometimes pecked apart to get at the meat beneath their carapaces; other times, especially when their shells are softest, which is right after molting, they're simply swallowed whole. Snakes are pecked on and around the head until they die, then swallowed whole like a string if spaghetti.

While few small animals are beyond a great blue heron's dietary bounds, the birds also eat seeds and tender sprouts found around their shoreline habitats. Like most meat eaters, herons appear to require at least some of the nutrients and vitamins that can be obtained only by eating plants.

Blue herons and their cousins are often blamed whenever a favorite fishing hole becomes depleted of game fish. In reality, overfishing by sport anglers and death from parasites or disease are the most common reasons for diminished fish populations. As in every predator-prey elationship, fish taken by herons are almost exclusively small, weak, and slow, often sickly, individuals that are, by nature's standards, genetically deficient.

Mating Habits

Solitary by nature, blue herons gather to breed at different times, depending on the latitude in which they live. Some adults, including chicks born the previous spring, may remain in southern latitudes year-round, and these populations begin mating early, from November through April. In the northern parts of the species' range, where herons and other shore birds don't live during the winter months, breeding is delayed until after the birds arrive at their summer habitats, with most mating occurring from March through May in the coldest climes. The instinct appears to be triggered mostly by warming, lengthening days in the north, but the heron's long bill probably endows it with an acute sense of smell that permits locating responsive mates by pheromonal scents, too.

Blue heron mating territories vary in size with the environment—wooded lakes, for example, have smaller areas of open shoreline—but a strong male heron tries to claim as much open space as it can hold from competitors, including claim to females whose own territories overlap those boundaries. Even so, claimed territories seldom exceed more than 3 or 4 acres.

Disputes between breeding males are resolved by a display of stalking one another, stiff-legged and with feathers fluffed outward to make themselves appear larger. If one of the contenders doesn't concede to being overmatched, the two may fly at one another, feet extended for clawing, and sometimes stabbing with their beaks. Territorial battles are seldom more than mildly injurious to either party, and less-able males move on to find territory that is not so well defended.

Females are often regaled with dances that consist of a male leaping straight upward to a height of 3 or 4 feet, wings outspread, then fluttering back to earth. These mating displays aren't as ritualized as those of the whooping crane, but they're no less spectacular to watch.

Mated pairs of herons often stay together throughout the breeding months, but more polygamous behavior may be seen in areas where there are fewer males than females. Males aren't remarkably paternal, but they do sometimes sit on the eggs while their mates take a break, and they defend nesting sites from small predators.

Great blue heron nests are large, dish-shaped platforms of intertwined reeds, lined with softer pine needles, cattail fluff, grasses, and feathers. The overall diameter may exceed 6 feet. Nesting places are often difficult to find, as nests are often constructed atop dry grass hummocks above standing water, and concealed by a forest of bulrushes and cattails.

Great blue herons have also been observed nesting within the branches of standing trees near water. These nests are bowl-shaped, with a rough outer wall of sticks, and cushioned on the inside with an insulating layer of softer materials. Some tree nests may be constructed atop existing raven or other large nests, but the prevalence of tree nesting is probably limited by the presence of raptors, like ospreys and bald eagles.

As the size of the great blue heron's nest indicates, this bird's eggs are roughly 50 percent larger than a chicken egg. Females begin laying eggs in batches every 2 to 3 days until reaching an average clutch size of three to seven pale-blue eggs, with the larger clutch sizes occurring more frequently in the north—a natural adaptation to counter increased mortality from predation and cold. Both parents, but especially the mother, incubate the eggs and defend the nest site.

After an average incubation of 28 days, the eggs hatch. Heron chicks are semialtricial, born with eyes open and covered with pale-gray down, but are easy prey for their first 7 weeks, when they learn to take refuge by hopping into overhead branches. By 9 weeks, the chicks will usually have gained sufficient strength and feathers to fly short distances.

Both parents provide meals for their chicks, with voles and mice making up most of the hatchlings' diet in many cases, followed by fish, insects, and snakes. Parents also provide aggressive protection against predators until the young reach 10 weeks of age and about 2 feet of height, when the rapidly growing herons can fly and feed themselves. By summer's end, the young will have mostly or entirely dispersed to seek out their own territories.

Behavior

While great blue herons are solitary by nature and generally tolerant of each other, during the breeding months, except in the breeding months. In habitats where food and other resources are abundant, adult males may forage the same shoreline with a few yards between them. In some especially good habitats, heron populations can increase to a point where some biologists consider them colonies.

Places where great blue herons can make a nuisance of themselves include fish hatcheries and rearing ponds, where fry and small, tank-raised fish are easy prey. Commercial and governmental fish hatcheries generally defeat the birds by covering their stock tanks with a roof to lessen the amount of sunlight striking the water in them, or by adding a roof of light fencing. Pond owners have had good luck with discouraging herons by placing heron decoys, flags, and other scarecrows around their shorelines.

Unlike most large herons and cranes, the great blue heron was saved from plume hunters who once harvested large numbers of long fluffy feathers to adorn hats and clothing worn by refined society. Its drab feathers didn't hold the appeal of the brightly colored plumes taken from flamingos and great white egrets, which kept the blue heron from being subjected to the overhunting that endangered those and other prettier species. Today, great blue herons in the United States are protected under the Migratory Bird Treaty Act.

Great blue herons are the most widespread and commonly seen large shorebirds in North America, and they have never been endangered. Despite that, the species faces danger from loss of marshland habitat, which is even today being filled and developed. A number are also killed by collisions with power lines during migratory flights, prompting some communities to install orange, basketball-size spheres over the wires at intervals to make them more apparent to flying birds.

SANDHILL CRANE
(*Grus canadensis*)

Sandhill cranes are the second-best-known of North America's large shorebirds. Standing as large or larger (depending on subspecies) than the great blue heron, sandhills are also migratory, flying hundreds of miles north each spring to summer breeding grounds, then flying with their grown young south to warmer regions before winter snows set in. Adults wear a distinctive cap of short reddish feathers that make them unlikely to be confused with any other species.

Sandhills are closely related to the whooping crane (*Grus americana*), which has long been an endangered species. Both birds wear a red skullcap, but the adult whooping crane is marked by a black trangular stripe extending rearward from its eyes, and by all-white plumage.

Geographic Range

During the summer months, sandhill cranes range as far north as Alaska's northern coastline, throughout the northern half of Canada, and into Michigan, Wisconsin, and northeastern Minnesota. To the west, their range extends southward along the Rocky Mountains, and west to Oregon. Perhaps notably, the Pacific coast is devoid of sandhill cranes to a distance of at least 100 miles inland.

In winter, sandhills and their grown young return to their winter habitats along the southern border of the United States, from Florida to California and southward into western Mexico. Populations have been reported as far south as Cuba, and as far north as Russian Siberia. In spring, before the full heat of summer sets into their southern wintering grounds, the cranes fly hundreds of miles north to mate, incubate, and rear the next generation in a cooler climate.

Habitat

Sandhill cranes are always within walking distance of a freshwater shoreline. Active by day, they're most often seen frequenting fields and meadows in search of insects and rodents. By night, the cranes retire to a nearby shoreline, often the same marsh where they nest, to sleep and keep eggs or young warm through the chill of darkness. Sandhill cranes tend to avoid dense forests, where trees and vegetation inhibit spreading their wings, and prefer to live well away from human habitation.

Physical Characteristics

Mass: Sandhill cranes weigh 8 to 9 pounds, with larger individuals occurring in the south.

Body: These cranes are heavy bodied, with long necks and legs, and a long rapierlike bill typical of herons and cranes. Body length from the tip of bill to claws averages between 4 and 5 feet. Wings are about 22 inches long; total wingspan is 5.5 to more than 6 feet. Males and females are indistinguishable, except that males are normally slightly larger.

Tail: The crane's tail, sometimes referred to as a "bustle" because of its shape, consists of feathers are about 1 foot long and drooping, downward with an almost ragged appearance when the bird is standing erect.

Tracks: Tracks show three forward-pointing toes, each tipped with a claw that is about 0.5-inch long. Middle toe is longest, 2.5 to 3 inches, and points straight forward. Outer flanking toes point forward at outward angles from the center toe. The single rearward-pointing toe, about 1 inch long, is located higher up on the ankle and doesn't print in tracks; this short toe also prevents sandhills from roosting in trees like blue herons. Tracks may be mistaken for those of a wild turkey in meadows where both species forage, except that wild turkey tracks tend to be slightly longer and more robust, with obvious segmentation, whereas the crane's toes are more slender and lack obvious segments.

Scat: The sandhill's scat can easily be mistaken for that of other large birds with similar diets, especially great blue herons, except that sandhills tend to forage in dry meadows and fields, while most shorebirds remain near water. In solid form, scats are cylindrical, dark brown when fresh, roughly 0.5-inch in diameter, about 1 inch long. Scats are often semiliquid spatters among meadow grasses where the cranes hunt, and sometimes include insect parts, but are often indistinguishable from those of other large shorebirds.

Coloration: Sandhill cranes are easily identifiable by their bright-red skullcaps, which cover the tops of their heads from the base of the long bill, around the eyes, and halfway to the rear of the skull. Directly below the red cap are near-white cheek patches of near-white that contrast with the gray feathers covering the rest of the body. Wing and tail feathers are edged with darker gray to nearly black. Older adults also tend to become stained with a brown color on their wings and back, the result of algae and minerals in shoreline waters where they nest and sleep.

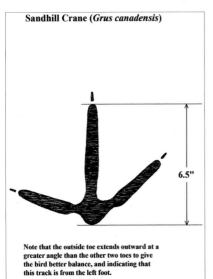

Sandhill Crane (*Grus canadensis*)

6.5"

Note that the outside toe extends outward at a greater angle than the other two toes to give the bird better balance, and indicating that this track is from the left foot.

Juvenile sandhills have wing feathers tipped with brown, and all-brown head and neck, but lack the red skullcap of the adults. By their second year, most juveniles will have grown their full adult plumage. Sandhill cranes in juvenile plumage are virtually indistinguishable from juvenile whooping cranes.

Sign: Depressions, football-size or larger, are left in

tall grasses where the cranes have sat down. Discarded large grayish feathers in grassy areas are a reliable indication of sandhill cranes.

Vocalizations: Most identifiable is a high-pitched, staccato cooing sound, heard most often from marshy shorelines, and especially in early spring, when groups of migrating birds are establishing territories and advertising for mates. Other voices in the same timbre include a short "awwk" that serves as an alarm, and a more prolonged version that indicates greater fear or agitation.

Life span: Sandhill cranes live 20 years or more in the wild.

Diet

Like other herons and cranes, sandhill cranes eat an omnivorous diet that consists of mostly animal matter, but also includes seeds and young vegetation. Like the much smaller woodcock, sandhills use their long bills as probes to unearth and find worms and insects, but also as a spear for impaling small rodents, snakes, and frogs. The sandhill is a capable fisher, but prefers to spend its daylight foraging hours in open fields, rather than along shorelines, where it might need to compete with great blue herons.

In northern latitudes, especially, sandhill cranes make vegetation and berries a large part of their diets. Their long bills are used to winnow seeds, to nip off young grass and other shoots, and to pluck sugar-rich berries. During the spring migration, when flocks of cranes travel northward to summer mating grounds, their arrival often coincides with the spring planting season, and many farmers complain that sandhills eat the seeds from their freshly planted fields.

Mating Habits

Sandhill cranes are sexually mature in their second year, but some individuals, especially males, may be forced by competition to wait longer before breeding. The most active breeding ages span between 2 and 7 years of age.

Most sandhill cranes are migratory, leaving wintering grounds in warmer latitudes in spring, before the heat of summer, and flying several hundred to more than 1,000 miles to reach the northerly latitudes where they were born. The mating season begins immediately after the birds arrive in their summer habitat, preceded by a brief period in which males, in particular, engage in relatively nonviolent territorial battles that consist primarily of flying at one another with flailing wings and outstretched feet. Although cranes spend most of their active days on dry land, preferred nesting territories are always at the edges of or near marshy shorelines.

After territories have been established, usually between mid-March and early June, depending on the latitude, the rituals of mating begin. Most spectacular of these rituals are the mating dances that are performed to some degree by all large cranes and herons. Much like the whooping crane, which it closely resembles, the sandhill male woos a prospective mate by jumping high into the air, wings outstretched to make its size appear more impressive, and fluttering to the earth. These leaps are accompanied by the birds' staccato cooing, and dances may continue for an hour or more, until the female becomes enamoured enough to accept the male, or leaves to find a more suitable mate. Frequently the female will dance, too, but most displaying is done by the male.

After mating, crane pairs set to work constructing a nest. A few incidents of sandhills nesting on dry land have been reported, but nearly all nesting sites are along remote shorelines with standing water and emergent (surface-growing) vegetation that includes bulrushes, cattails, and hummocks of rough grasses. Large grass hummocks, or "deadheads," that stand well above water are favored nesting spots not only for cranes, but for most waterfowl. Nests are constructed from sticks, reeds, and grasses taken from the surrounding area and consist of a walled platform, up to 6 feet across, in the center of which is a smaller egg cup that has been lined with softer grasses, cattail fluff, and down feathers. Time from start to completion of the nest is about 7 days. It should be noted that sandhills sleep in nests at all times of year, but those used by males or used outside of the brooding period are flat, with only a residual egg depression in their centers.

Expectant female cranes begin laying a clutch of one to three eggs, usually one per day, as soon as the nest is completed. Eggs are oval and about 4 inches long, with dull brown shells that are irregularly spotted with rust-colored markings. Incubation begins as soon as the first egg is laid, and both parents assume responsibility for sitting on them, and for defending the nest against raccoons and other egg-eating predators. Note, however, that males sit on the nests only during daylight; from dusk to dawn, all incubation is done only by the female.

After an incubation of about 30 days, the young hatch, one every 2 or 3 days. Chicks begin wandering from the nest as young as 6 hours after hatching, sometimes swimming for short distances, but never far from the watchful eyes of at least one parent. The first hatchling is dominant and frequently bullying of its younger siblings, so parents use their own bodies to keep chicks from fighting. Chicks are fed a diet of mostly insects for their first 30 days, after which the mother feeds them bits of their own broken eggshells, probably for the nutrients they contain. At this point the parents begin leading their offspring away from the nesting site to teach them the hunting skills they'll need in coming years. The family returns to the nesting site each evening, often calling loudly to one another as they settle in to sleep in relative safety among the marshes. By their 5th week, chicks will have become strong fliers, but both parents continue to look after their brood for about 9 months, separating just prior to the migratory flight south.

Although sandhill cranes are perenially monogomous, it appears likely that established pairs may reunite each breeding season for several consecutive years. The strong family bond shown during the summer months dissipates once the birds have migrated to their southerly wintering grounds. Yearling chicks may remain with their mothers for a month or more, but will normally have become independent before the spring flight north.

Behavior

While sandhill cranes are essentially solitary, adults 2 years and older spend three-quarters of each year with mates and offspring, separating only for the roughly 3-month period spent in their winter habitats. Although sandhills are considered a migratory species, the distances they travel between warm wintering grounds and cooler summer habitats may vary considerably; some cranes might fly many hundreds of miles, while other populations merely migrate from lowlands to mountaintop lakes. Most individuals tend to return to the places where they were hatched.

During annual migrations, sandhills flock together in survival groups, relying on numbers to discourage predators that might prey on the young, especially. These groups are not cohesive, and there's little social stability among their members. On reaching the places where they'll spend the summer or winter seasons, the birds break away from their flocks to establish individual territories.

Like most heron and crane species, sandhills are diurnal by nature, sleeping through the night on large, dry nests concealed within marshes. The birds are most active during the twilight hours of dusk and dawn (crepuscular), when small rodents are traveling to or from foraging places, and when most cold-blooded reptiles, amphibians, and insects are sluggish. On hot summer days, the birds may retreat from the open places where they hunt to the cooler breezes of their nesting marshes, standing silently for hours, often on one leg in typical crane fashion, and feeding on an occasional frog or snake.

Unlike the related whooping crane, sandhill cranes aren't considered to be threatened, and are in fact considered pests by farmers who complain that flocks of migrating birds can pick clean newly seeded crops. Because of real or supposed damage to crops, and despite the species' diet of insects and rodents that are harmful to agriculture, sandhill cranes are legally hunted in Texas, Kansas, and seven other states along the birds' migratory flyway. At the time of this writing, Wisconsin authorities are debating whether to open a hunting season for sandhill cranes.

Hunting sandhill and other cranes isn't a recent development; by the beginning of the 20th century, private and commercial hunters who killed the birds for the roughly 3 pounds of rich, red meat contained in their breasts had reduced sandhill populations to the point of causing concern. In 1918 the practice was banned under federal law, but continued lobbying from the agricultural community caused those protections to be relaxed. In the early 1960s crane hunting was again made legal in New Mexico when that state staged a "depredation hunt," and a precedent was set for the states that followed. Today, hunting sandhill cranes is becoming increasingly popular among sport hunters, even spawning a market for crane calls, crane decoys, and guided crane hunts.

CANADA GOOSE
(*Branta canadensis*)

The Canada goose is one of the most easily recognized birds on the North American continent. There are four recognized subspecies, *B. canadensis occidentalis, B. candensis hutchensii, B. canadensis minima, and B. canadensis leucopareia,* all of which are smaller than the true Canada goose but share its distinctive markings. In general, individuals are larger in southern populations, and breasts are darker in western populations.

Geographic Range

Canada geese are found throughout their native North America, with specific subspecies being more regional. The larger, pale-breasted *B. canadensis canadensis* is found mostly along the eastern portions of North America, while the equally large, brown-breasted *B. canadensis occidentalis* inhabits the west. The smaller, pale-breasted *B. canadensis hutchensii* is found in central and western Canada. *B. canadensis minima,* as its name implies, is the smallest of Canada geese, and is found in western Alaska. *B. canadensis leucopareia,* of the Aleutian Islands, is threatened, and is distinguished from *B. canadensis minima* by its larger size, paler breast, and, often, a wider white neck ring. All subspecies tend to winter in the southern parts of North America, then fly north in spring to mate and raise the next generation. This migratory habit has been artificially changed in many locales by humans who feed waterfowl throughout the winter months, making it unnecessary for flocks to travel south in search of food.

Habitat

Every goose habitat (as well as those of their duck cousins) will include a relatively large body of open freshwater—usually a lake or pond, but sometimes large, slow-moving rivers—where the birds can escape or avoid terrestrial predators by swimming into deep water. In midsummer and in their southerly wintering grounds, Canada geese are often seen swimming along the shorelines of larger bodies of water, including the Great Lakes, but nesting areas will always be along marshy shorelines of, usually, smaller lakes and beaver ponds, where cattails and reeds provide cover, grassy hummocks provide dry nesting sites, and calm shallows hold an abundance of edible aquatic vegetation.

Like most large birds, including herons and turkeys, the terrestrial portion a Canada goose's habitat will always be in open places, where spreading its large wings won't be inhibited by trees or undergrowth. Grassy, open meadows along shorelines are especially preferred.

Physical Characteristics

Mass: Weight of Canada geese ranges from slightly more than 2 pounds for *B. canadensis minima*, the smallest of the subspecies, to more than 19 pounds for *B. canadensis canadensis*.

Body: The Canada goose has a large, heavy body with massive breast muscles, and a neck that is long and comparatively thin. Females tend to be slightly smaller than males, although both genders share the same colors and patterns. Short, stout legs positioned close together under the bird's body cause it to waddle as it walks. The feet are large and webbed. The flat bill is lined around its outer edges with teethlike projections, called lamellae, that are used for cutting grass and other stems that serve as food. The wings are long and very strong, spanning 50 to more than 65 inches when spread.

Tail: The tail is short, black-tipped, and ends in a blunt point. Seen from above while the bird is in flight, the tail exhibits a white semicircle just forward of its black tip.

Tracks: Canada geese have three toes, with thick webbing extending from the tip of one toe in a semicircle to the tip of the next. The webbing normally shows in tracks, with the heaviest impressions being made by the center toe, which is longest and points straight forward, and the outer flanking toes, which also point forward, but at outward angles from the center toe. Track length is about 4 inches; width from the end of the outermost toe to the tip of the innermost toe, about 4 inches. The walking track pattern exhibits an extreme toe-in (duck-footed) stride in which all toes point inward. Stride length from one track to that made by the opposite foot is about 6 inches.

Note that Canada goose tracks are very similar to those of the smaller ducks and the larger swans, with the only obvious difference being one of size and stride length. A typical large (for example, mallard) duck leaves a track roughly 3 inches long, with a stride of about 4 inches. A mute or trumpeter swan has a very large track that can exceed 6 inches, with a much longer stride of 9 inches or more.

Scat: Scat is cylindrical, with a consistent diameter from one squared (flat) end to the other, occasionally with a larger, bulbous form at the end that was excreted first. The diameter is about 0.5-inch; length is up to 3 inches, but often shorter. The color is typically

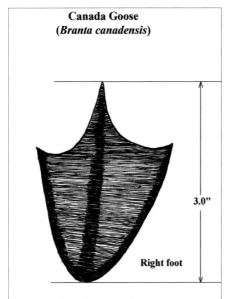

Canada Goose
(*Branta canadensis*)

3.0"

Right foot

3 forward-pointing toes print most heavily on soft ground, but webbing between them will print more faintly, often not at all.

olive-brown when fresh, becoming darker with age. Grass and other plant fibers, clipped short by the goose's toothed bill, are usually obvious in fresh deposits. Dimensions given are for *B.c. canadensis,* the largest of the Canada geese, and vary downward in size for the smaller subspecies.

Coloration: The neck, bill, head, legs, and feet of *Branta canadensis* are black. A white patch, sometimes called a chin-strap, extends from behind the eye, under the chin just rearward of the bill, to the rear of the opposite eye. The upper body and back are brownish gray, with whitish breast and under-belly (breast is brown in the western subspecies *B. canadensis occidentalis*). The smaller subspecies *B. canadensis leucopareia* and *B. canadensis hutchensii* have a distinctive white ring around the base of the neck, just above the breast. Wings are brown, with darker tips. These color patterns are unique to the Canada goose and its subspecies, making it unlikely to be confused with any other bird.

Sign: Flocks of geese often gather in open, grassy areas, especially during migratory flights, and the grasses in these places can be clipped nearly to ground level when large numbers of birds feed on them. Such places may exhibit a trampled look from the flattening effect of having been walked over by many flat, heavy feet and are usually well marked with scats.

Vocalizations: The call of the Canada goose histori-cally is described as a honk, but only the high-pitched call of migrating Canada geese in flight accurately matches that definition. When this species is nesting, the call between mates might be described as a high-pitched "rrrawwnk." The call of an agitated or threatened goose is a rapidly repeated

"awnk–awnk–awnk," which becomes quieter as the source of agitation withdraws. Like swans and ducks, geese can also make a loud hissing sound, heard especially when the birds are attempting to drive off intruders during the mating and nesting seasons.

Calls of the Canada goose (also ducks) are normally heard only during daylight hours. An exception occurs during the spring hatching season, when the nested birds, eggs, and hatchlings are preyed on at night by bobcats, coyotes, and an occasional large otter.

Life span: The reported maximum lifespan in captivity is 28 years, although the typical lifespan in the wild is about 8 years.

Diet

Canada geese are believed to be entirely herbivorous, although there have been accounts of the birds eating grasshoppers and other small insects. On land, the birds eat a variety of plants, including most grasses, plantains, dandelion shoots and flowers, and wild strawberry plants and fruits. Most types of nontoxic berries are eaten when in season and when in proximity to the birds' feeding areas—they will never venture into woods or brushy places where opening their wings in escape might be impeded.

Despite having no true teeth, Canada geese are able to snip off small, more easily digestible sections from rough grasses and other stems using the serrated, teeth-like lamellae that border the outer edges of their bills. By pinching leaves and stems in their bills, then pulling with a quick jerk of the head, geese are able to cut free small mulch-like snips of rough vegetation, which digest more easily than would longer blades of grass or stems.

Aquatic plants also make up a large part of the Canada goose diet, especially during the nesting season, when parents prefer to remain close to their eggs. Pondweeds, and pond-lilly and waterlily leaves, are eaten, along with tender cattail sprouts, wapato, and feshwater seaweeds. As the summer progresses and plants begin to mature, most types of seeds are eaten, including wild rice and grass seeds of all types.

A notable characteristic displayed by geese and ducks while feeding on aquatic vegetation is the tail-up posture assumed by them while plucking food plants from the bottom of shoreline shallows. By tipping their bodies 90 degrees, with tails pointing skyward and heads underwater, the birds are able to extend their long necks to reach food plants growing in the muddy bottom. Sometimes this feeding method will be observed with lone geese or ducks, but most often there will be a pair or more, which take turns foraging underwater while companions remain upright to watch for potential danger.

Mating Habits

Canada geese, like ducks, swans, and other migratory waterfowl, breed in the spring, returning to the same waterways where they were born. Mating begins as early as March in southern latitudes, but as late as June in the northernmost parts of the species' range. Individuals born the previous spring are sexually mature but may not mate until 2 years old if competition is strong. Fortunately for the geese, there exists an almost even ratio between geese (females) and ganders (males), and adults of either sex take only one mate per season, so breeding rivalries are less common than with some waterfowl species.

Canada goose mating rituals are unremarkable compared with those of many other waterfowl species. When two males do compete for a female, the contest consists mostly of hissing and flying at one another with outspread wings that are used as bludgeons. Battles are short, and neither contender is likely to be injured. When the vanquished suitor withdraws, the winning male approaches the female with head down, and neck outstretched and undulating from side to side.

Most older geese will arrive at their breeding habitats already paired with a mate. Sometimes the pairs will have joined during the flight north, but the majority of adults will be with the same mate they had the year before, and perhaps for several years prior to that. Some biologists believe that Canada geese mate for life, but an adult whose mate is killed by hunters or predation will find another mate prior to or during the following breeding season.

Copulation between Canada geese is unusual in that it takes place on the water, and the female may be partially or wholly submerged during the act, held underwater by weight of the male when he mounts her from the rear and covers her body with his own. However, coitus is quick, lasting only a few seconds, so there is no danger of the female being drowned during mating.

Choice of a nesting site is at the female's discretion; her mate simply follows where she leads. Likewise, the male takes little part in actually building the nest, and his role is generally limited to offering bits of reeds and grasses to his mate. Preferred nesting sites are on a raised point surrounded by water, especially grassy hummocks, snags of wind-felled trees, and occasionally atop a muskrat house. Nests tend to be quickly made, simple affairs, usually little more than a rounded depression in the grass, formed by the female's large feet and heavy body. (In one unusual instance, a particularly inexperienced goose tried nesting atop a raised platform that had been constructed for ospreys, 15 feet above the surface of a beaver pond; none of her eggs escaped predation from the ospreys).

Females begin laying eggs within a day or so of mating, laying one egg about every 36 hours until a clutch of two to as many as nine eggs have been deposited in the nest's center. Eggs are slightly larger than a large chicken egg, almost 4 inches long, and are cream colored. Mothers partially cover their clutches with an insulating layer of down feathers plucked from their own breasts, which help to keep the ova from becoming too cool or too warm, and the ova are turned regularly to ensure even exposure all around.

Ganders remain close by during the nesting period but don't take part in incubating the eggs. When the sitting goose leaves to feed or relieve herself, the gander's job is to guard the nest against predators. Smaller egg-eaters, such as foxes, skunks, and crows, are chased, away by loud honking and the male's bludgeoning wings. Larger carnivores such as coyotes, are led away on a "wild goose chase" when the gander pretends to be injured, enticing predators to follow by flopping pathetically and giving the impression of being easy prey.

After an incubation period of 25 to 28 days, the eggs begin hatching. Despite having been laid as many as 3 days apart, all eggs begin hatching within 24 hours. Hatchlings break free of the shell using their single egg tooth, and by the end of 48 hours, all goslings will have freed themselves. Hatchlings are born covered with downy, yellow coats that are marked with patches of greenish gray atop the back and neck. Their legs, feet, and bills are blueish gray, but grow darker as the birds mature.

Goslings are able to swim within hours after hatching and leave the nest with their parents immediately, usually on the same day they were hatched. The young are imprinted on their mother, and follow her wherever she leads, while the father generally follows behind. The goslings grow quickly, and by summer's end have become slightly smaller replicas of their parents. In autumn, the entire family joins with other groups of migrating geese to form the sometimes large flocks that we see flying southward each year. When the flocks return to their northern summering grounds the following spring, goslings will have reached full adulthood and seek out their own mates.

Behavior

The best-known characteristic of the Canada goose is the distinctive V-shaped formation of a migrating flock. These flocks, which may number more than 30 birds, are made up mostly of families that have been joining the same flock to make annual migratory flights to the same places for many generations. By flying together in large groups over long distances that may span more than 1,000 miles, the geese find safety in numbers when they land in a strange place to spend the night each evening.

A benefit of flying in the trademark V formation is that it creates a slipstream behind each bird, beginning with the foremost—and generally the strongest—gander, which leads the flock. This arrangement permits every bird following the leader to "draft" behind the goose immediately in front of itself, much the same as race-car drivers employ the vacuum generated by the vehicle in front of them to lessen the amount of fuel their own cars expend while maintaining an equal speed. Drafting behind one another permits adolescents and other less-strong geese to keep pace with the most powerful individuals, while at the same time ensuring that the long flight is much less taxing to flock members than it would be if the big birds were making the same trek alone.

Although Canada geese flock only during annual migratory flights, individuals are seldom seen alone. The birds aren't social in the same way that turkeys tend to live their lives as members of large groups, but mated pairs typically remain together throughout each year until one of them dies, and parents look after their broods throughout most of the youngsters' first year of life.

Canada geese, particularly those of the smaller subspecies, are frequently preyed on by carnivorous mammals, large raptors, and an occasional alligator in their southern winter habitats. Large fish of the pike family have been observed eating goslings, as will most types of hawks and owls. Raccoons, skunks, opossums, and ravens are known for preying on unhatched eggs—but always with respect for the bludgeoning power of an irate parent's wings—while bobcats, especially, make a habit of patrolling spring nesting grounds at night, when the geese are effectively blind.

Nested geese are seldom preyed on during the day, when their keen hearing, and eyesight, and the panoramic field of vision provided by placement of eyeballs at either side of the head, permit them to see approaching danger from the air or ground. In most nesting habitats, Canada geese are too large and strong to be considered prey by daytime predators, and the birds' aggressive defense of nests and hatchlings is sufficient to discourage carnivores even as large as a coyote. An interesting behavior exhibited by nesting mothers is their tendency to lie flat, neck outstretched atop their eggs, when they spy an approaching enemy, thus lowering their conspicuous head and neck below the predator's line of sight while their mates lead it away on the proverbial wild goose chase.

Another threat to nesting populations of Canada geese comes from swans, particularly the much larger and notoriously aggressive Asian mute swan (*Cygnus olor*). Introduced to the United States as a replacement for dwindling populations of native trumpeter swans (*Cygnus buccinator*) the mute swan's powerful physique places it beyond the abilities of most wild predators, enabling it to become firmly established around the Great Lakes region and along the northern Atlantic seaboard. An unforeseen result of this aggressively territorial species' success has been the displacement of native ducks and geese from their historical nesting areas. The presence of mute swans also inhibits the return of native swans, which has caused wildlife authorities to consider eradicating them from the Great Lakes region.

Although protected from spring hunting under the 1918 Migratory Bird Act Treaty, and again by the imposition of autumn bag limits in 1960, the Canada goose in general has never been threatened. The smaller Aleutian subspecies was once listed as endangered by the U.S. Fish and Wildlife Service after populations were reduced to just 800 birds by the introduction of a nonnative fox in 1967, but good recovery efforts and steadily increasing numbers caused them to be downlisted to "threatened" in 1990, and the danger appears to have passed. In 1999, populations of the Aleutian Canada goose were estimated at 15,000 individuals nesting on eight islands.

In fact, Canada geese populations in general have increased to the point of making them a serious pest along many urban and suburban waterways. In some places, flocks that can number in the hundreds leave large volumes of scats sufficient to create bacterial infestation of land and water, including the fungal infection known as "swimmer's itch." Adding to the problem are goose populations that have become year-round residents in areas where they should migrate. In both these instances the troubles are caused, or at least exacerbated, by human populations, because Canada geese inhabiting remote northern waterways do not overpopulate, nor do they remain through the winter. Canada geese, like deer, squirrels, and numerous other species, have learned to occupy territories close to human habitation because those places are shunned by wild predators, and many well-meaning people contribute to these problems by feeding wild species.

Predatory Birds

While most species of birds can be considered predatory, some are exclusively so. Eagles, ospreys, hawks, and owls make up this large group of hunting birds whose diets consist almost entirely of the flesh of other animals. All are strong, fast fliers with very keen eyesight, powerful feet with sharp talons evolved for gripping prey, and hooked beaks designed to tear flesh from bone. Most are active during daylight, but the owls are possessed of extremely good night vision that enables them to be uncannily accurate night hunters. Some, like the bald eagle and the osprey, are famed for their ability to snatch fish from water, while others are skilled at catching other birds in flight. All prey on rodents and, depending on their own size, rabbits, and all have an indispensible role in controlling populations of prolific animals that would otherwise multiply beyond the capacity of their environment.

BALD EAGLE
(*Haliaeetus leucocephalus*)

Best known of the predatory birds, the bald eagle has become a symbol of fierce independence and strength, and has been the national bird of the United States since 1872. Benjamin Franklin had argued that the national bird should be the uniquely American wild turkey, stating that the bald eagle was a bird of poor moral character because of its habit of stealing food from other predatory birds. Certainly Franklin was right in his assertion that the turkey had played a much more important role in the forging of a new nation by feeding early pioneers, but the poor homely turkey just didn't evoke the same image of strength and pride as the eagle.

Despite being the emblem of the United States, the bald eagle was nearly extirpated by the widespread use of the insecticide DDT (dichlorodiphenyltrichlorethane) in the mid–20th century. DDT spread through the food chain to bald eagles and other accipiters, where it caused females to lay eggs that had weak shells, or sometimes no shells at all, cutting reproduction to almost zero. By the time the U.S. banned DDT in 1972, the bald eagle's numbers had fallen from an estimated 50,000 individuals to about 800 breeding pairs in the lower 48 states. Enactment of the Endangered Species Act of 1973 prompted a concerted, and ultimately successful, recovery effort.

By 1995, bald eagle numbers had risen to about 3,000 breeding pairs, hatchling rates were up, and the species was downlisted from "endangered" to "threatened." By the beginning of the new millenium, some biologists were suggesting that it was safe to remove bald eagles from the endangered species list altogether.

Geographic Range

The bald eagle is native to North America and was once common from central Alaska, throughout Canada and the United States, and southward to the Mexican border and the Gulf of Mexico. Today bald eagles may still be found over much of that original range, but there are fewer of them, especially in the southern U.S., than there once were.

Habitat

Bald eagles are able to live anywhere on the North American continent where there are adequate nest trees, roosts and feeding grounds. Suitable habitats include temperate forest, rainforest, prairies, desert, and mountains. Being especially capable fishers, open water is a necessity in every bald eagle habitat, and this may include large rivers, lakes, or oceans.

Physical Characteristics

Mass: Bald eagles weigh 6.5 to 14 pounds; females are typically larger than males.

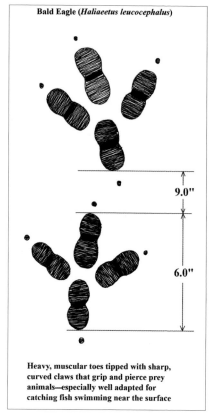

Bald Eagle (*Haliaeetus leucocephalus*)

9.0"

6.0"

Heavy, muscular toes tipped with sharp, curved claws that grip and pierce prey animals—especially well adapted for catching fish swimming near the surface

Body: Males are 30 to 35 inches long, females 34 to 43 inches long. Legs are feathered halfway down the tarsus. Wing span may exceed 7.5 feet. Sexes are identical in plumage.

Tail: Moderately long, the tail is 6 to 8 inches, and slightly wedge-shaped.

Tracks: Bald eagles have massive feet, short and powerful grasping toes, and long talons. The talon of the hind toe is used to pierce vital areas while the prey is held immobile by the front toes, and is powerful and highly developed in all eagle species.

Scat: Typically the scat is birdlike, but larger than that of most birds. The solid form is irregularly cylindrical, dark brown in color, usually white at one end, sometimes bulbous at one end, about 3 inches long, and less than 0.5-inch in diameter. Alternately, scat form may be massed, sometimes nearly liquid. Look for undigested fish scales, fur, or feathers.

Coloration: Bald eagles aren't truly bald; the term is an abbreviation of the word "piebald," which describes a spotted or patchy color pattern, especially in black and white. The adult bald eagle's dark-brown body—which can look black against the sky—stands in stark contrast to the white feathers of its head, neck, and tail. The long, hooked bill is and the cere (the fleshy swelling at the base of the upper beak) are yellow, as are the eyes and feet; the legs are yellow and unfeathered.

Immature eagles are irregularly mottled with brown and white until 4 or 5 years of age, but, like adults, their feet, and legs are bright yellow. The eyes of immature eagles are darker yellow or brown, the bill and cere, dark gray.

Sign: Large, brushy nests at the tops of usually dead standing trees. The ground around these nesting trees is typically scattered with a variety of feathers, fish fins and scales, and small bones and fur.

Vocalizations: The call is probably best described as a screeching whistle that's often heard while the bird is in flight. Eagles can also croak or squawk much like a crow.

Lifespan: Bald eagles live approximately 15 years in the wild, up to 50 years in captivity.

Diet

Bald eagles are strict carnivores. Best known as fishers, eagles swoop down onto the waters of a lake or large river to snatch shallow-swimming fish in their powerful, hooked talons, then fly off with the prize to feed at leisure on some lofty perch. Although not so skilled at catching fish as its slightly smaller cousin, the osprey (*Pandion haliaetus*), the eagle is larger and stronger, able to carry away fish and other prey weighing in excess of 8 pounds.

In fact, the eagle's large size can work against it while fishing. Ospreys and smaller hawks that share the waterways found in every bald eagle habitat are better suited to catching bluegills, perch, and young bass, which aren't easy targets for an eagle's large feet. This has led to the larcenous behaviors that Benjamin Franklin found so objectionable, in which an eagle waits for its smaller, more nimble cousin to capture a fish, then steals that fish for itself—or, as the Odawa Indians say, "The osprey catches the fish, then an eagle eats."

Despite being most commonly known as a fisher, the bald eagle is an efficient hunter of other prey as well. With the "eye of an eagle," this raptor can spot a foraging rabbit from more than a mile distant, then swoop down onto the unsuspecting prey at a diving speed of nearly 200 miles per hour—or about the same speed as a WWII fighter plane. When just a few yards above the target, the eagle applies brakes by spreading its wings wide to catch air like a parachute, and, with a bit of luck, lands directly atop its next meal with sharp-clawed talons that pierce its prey's body with a viselike grip.

In fact, not every strike results in a kill, but with the power to take hares, muskrats, young beavers, and most other small animals, the eagle usually finds sufficient opportunity to keep itself and its young well fed.

Other birds also serve as eagle prey. Smaller species, like bluejays and redwinged blackbirds, are too undersized and quick, but ducks, immature geese, swan cygnets, and an occasional young heron or crane are taken if an opportunity presents itself. Often these prey birds are taken with the swooping attack while on the water or ground, but bald eagles are agile enough on the wing to take most shore and water birds out of the air, too. Crows and ravens are also preyed on, and these birds will often alert a tracker to the presence of hunting eagles by gathering in a tree whose branches prevent the wide-winged raptor from diving, then cawing loudly.

Other eagle prey includes large snakes, especially water-snakes and cottonmouths, small alligators, and large bullfrogs. Carrion is sometimes eaten, especially in winter, and eagles are occasionally seen feeding on roadkilled deer, but the birds generally prefer to hunt or steal fresh meat.

Mating Habits

Bald eagles become sexually mature at 4 years, but may not mate until age 5. In the northern part of the species' range, mating takes place between mid-February and mid-March, but in the South eagles may mate until August. Mating appears to be initiated by the female, who typically approaches a suitable male with ducking gestures of her head. Both eagles then take to the air, flying up to an altitude of several hundred feet, usually over water, then turning toward one another and locking their talons together. With feet locked in this manner, both birds freefall nearly to earth before relinquishing their grip and flying upward again to repeat this behavior. The precise reason behind this activity is unknown, but it appears to be a test of strength and agility to determine if a male is physically strong enough to be a candidate for mating. The male must be able to keep up with the female as she flies upward, and his eligibility to mate—as well as his personal safety—demands that he have strength enough to recover from the freefall.

If a male is deemed acceptable, the receptive female repeats the head-down gesture, raising her tail and presenting her cloaca (genital cavity) to the male. The male then mounts her from behind with his talons instinctively closed into fists to protect her from being harmed by his claws. The male maintains his position atop her by pressing his closed fists firmly against her sides, gripping her body tightly between his feet during copulation. As with most bird species, intercourse is completed within a few seconds.

Historically, bald eagles have been thought to mate for life, although it appears that may not be true in all cases. What is certain is that mated pairs will remain together for at least as long as it takes to rear the next generation. Immediately after mating, the pair seeks out a suitable nesting site high in a large tree (usually a conifer), or sometimes on a cliff ledge, and always near open water.

Nests consist of a rough outer shell of interwoven sticks, with a softer interior lining of grasses, moss, fur, and feathers.

Newly constructed nests measure about 6 feet in diameter by about 1 foot deep.

Pairs that have mated in previous years will probably use the same nest for many years, building onto it with each passing year, so the size of a nest is indicative of the number of generations that have been reared there. Some very old nests have reached huge dimensions, measuring more than 20 feet across, 10 feet deep, and weighing in excess of 1 ton. Providing a nest isn't toppled by wind, or doesn't crush the tree onto which it's built, it will continue to be used year after year, sometimes by succeeding generations who were themselves hatched there.

Impregnated females occupy the nest as soon as it's finished, laying their first creamy-white, 5-inch-long egg within about 3 days, usually in late March or early April. They will lay another every 1 to 3 days thereafter until a clutch of usually two, but sometimes three, eggs have been deposited.

Incubation of the eggs is performed mostly by the female, and exclusively by her at night, while her mate sleeps in a nearby tree. After an incubation period of 35 to 42 days, the eggs begin to hatch, with the oldest hatching first, and its siblings hatching every 2 or 3 days thereafter in the same order in which they were laid. By mid- to late June, all eggs will have hatched.

Sibling rivalry is fierce, and sometimes violent, between eagle chicks. The eldest hatchling is typically the largest, and will try to steal food from its younger and smaller nestmates. Parents will not intervene, leaving the younger chick to fend for itself in a real example of survival of the fittest. In a clutch of two, both eagle chicks will probably survive to the fledgling stage, but a third chick's odds of survival are greatly decreased.

Feeding duties are performed by both parents, and one will always be nearby when the other is away hunting. Hawks, and especially ravens, that might prey on the chicks are driven off vigorously, and predation on eaglets is virtually nil. By 60 days of age, the chicks will have grown to become fledglings and will fly short distances with their parents. Parents will continue to hunt for and feed their brood for an additional 30 days, when the eaglets will have become educated and strong enough to fend for themselves. The family remains together until autumn, when the offspring strike out to establish their own territories.

Behavior

Native only to N. America, the bald eagle is as big or slightly smaller than the golden eagle (*Aquila chrysaetos*) of Eurasia, North Africa, and North America, but it is no less a predator. Stories of eagles carrying off small children and lambs are groundless, but the big raptors have often incurred the wrath of farmers—and a few pet owners—by occasionally snatching up small dogs, cats, chickens, and rabbits.

Bald eagles are migratory only by necessity; if they possess access to open water, they will remain near their summer nesting sites the year around. Those in the north that don't have access to open water in winter fly to southern latitudes, or to coastlines where waters remain unfrozen enough to permit fishing. In northern latitudes where small mammals and other prey remain plentiful, adults have been known to remain all winter, even though lakes and rivers are frozen.

Unlike adults, juveniles that have been emancipated from their parents and are in search of their own territories have been known to migrate more than 1,000 miles in search of mates or habitat. These youngsters may remain nomadic for as long as 5 years, or until they find a mate and settle down to raise their own offspring.

Eagles rarely fly at night, but the reason has less to do with lack of night vision than with air currents. Like vultures and other long-winged raptors, bald eagles prefer to glide rather than fly because gliding requires less expenditure of energy. Thermal updrafts, which these birds rely on to hold them aloft for hours at a time, are normally present only during the daylight hours, when a warming sun causes heated air to rise.

An unusual behavior among eagle mates is their occasional tendency to copulate outside of the mating season. Except for humans, sexual intercourse for the pleasure of it is virtually unheard of in the animal kingdom, and some biologists believe that this behavior might be related to the strong bond that exists between eagle mates.

Today, the bald eagle remains a symbol of strength and courage. It's the main icon of the Presidential Seal of the United States, and, among most Indian tribes, it's the messenger that carries prayers to the Creator. So strong is the image of power conveyed by this most striking of raptors that many states have found it necessary to protect the species by making it illegal to possess their feathers.

Reptiles and Amphibians

Snakes

Probably the most widely feared animals in the world, snakes are among the most important animals in nature. Often cast in a negative, even demonic, role in stories throughout history, every species plays a keystone role in its native environment, although a few invaders, like the anaconda in the southeastern United States, have assumed destructive-pest status.

All snakes are carnivorous; many are constrictors that asphyxiate prey by grasping it headfirst in their jaws, then coiling around the victim, squeezing it to death.

Some snake species are venomous, equipped with teeth or hollow fangs that inject poison. Most are nonvenomous, but many possess teeth that can inflict wounds.

All snakes are hairless, cold-blooded, and limbless, accomplishing locomotion through muscles in scaled (armored against injury) undersides that push in succession against the earth, propelling their bodies in a slithering motion. None can crawl backward, but long, flexible spines enable them to change direction, even doubling back on themselves, instantly.

Some snakes literally hang out above ground in the branches of trees, safe from enemies, but most can be found warming themselves in open places under a morning or afternoon sun.

No snake harbors animosity toward humans, and the most venomous will withdraw from conflict if allowed to do so. Small humans are rarely prey for the largest snakes, and most are too small to eat animals larger than a rat. Snakes seldom eat, and can subsist on one meal for weeks, even months.

COMMON GARTER SNAKE
(*Thamnophis sirtalis*)

Beautiful and harmless to humans, the garter snake is an important predator of rodents.

There are thirteen species of garter and ribbon snakes in North America, including: *Thamnophis sirtalis parietalis* (Red-sided Garter Snake), *thamnophis sirtalis similes* (blue–stripe garter snake), *thamnophis sirtalis pallidulus* (maritime garter snake), *thamnophis sirtalis semifasciatus* (Chicago garter snake), *thamnophis sirtalis dorsalis* (New Mexico *garter snake)*, *thamnophis sirtalis annectens* (Texas garter snake), *thamnophis sirtalis fitchi* (valley garter snake),

thamnophis sirtalis infernalis (California red–sided garter snake), *and*
thamnophis sirtalis tetrataenia (San Francisco garter snake).

Geographic Range

The common garter snake (*Thamnophis sirtalis*) is the most common of the garter snakes that live in North America, and it's the only snake native to Alaska, ranging farther north than any other reptile. Absent only from the desert southwest, this snake is native from Texas and Florida to Canada.

Habitat

The common garter snake can survive cold better than any species in the world. Always near water, it occupies a variety of habitats, including forests, marshes, and suburbia. Its importance in controlling fast-reproducing populations of

rodents and large insects is demonstrated by a ban on killing snakes on military bases.

Physical Characteristics

Mass: The common garter snake usually weighs usually less than 1 pound, but very old individuals may reach more than 3 pounds.

Body: The body is usually less than 1 foot, but may exceed 3 feet.

Tail: Tapered, the common garter snake's tail is unadorned by rattles or by markings dissimilar to those on the body.

Tracks: As with most snakes, tracks are undulating grooves.

Scat: Scat is seldom seen, but watery, with black, white, and brown. Often excretes feces when threatened to make itself less attractive as food.

Coloration: Lateral stripes—white, yellow, green, blue, orange, or red—against a darker background of black, dark green, or brown. Common garter snakes can be distinguished from other *Thamnophis* species by location of the lateral stripe, which is always limited to the second and third rows of scales forward of the ventral scales, with a double row of black spots between the lateral stripes. Identifying subspecies of *Thamnophis* requires a detailed field guide.

Sign: Garter snakes shed their skins during summer months.

Vocalization: Garter snakes are usually silent, but may emit a low hissing sound when threatened.

Life span: Little data exists for establishing a mean lifespan, but several contradictory studies conclude that an average lifespan is about two years. Lifespan in captivity has reached 14 years.

Diet

Diet of a common garter snake varies with habitat. They subsist on earthworms and grasshoppers, frogs, toads, birds, rodents, and an occasional fish or tadpole. Having no meaningful teeth or venom, *Thamnophis sirtalis* ambushes prey, snatching it by the head with a fast strike. With its head engulfed, and held in place by small, serrated teeth while being constricted, prey struggles little as it is slowly swallowed whole. Digestion may take several days.

Mating Habits

common garter snakes are ovoviviparous, bearing live young incubated from fertilized eggs carried in the mother's lower abdomen. Sexual maturity is 1.5 years for males, 2 years for females. Mating occurs just after snakes emerge from winter dens in April or May. Males emerge first, and immediately congregate around den entrances of females, where they emit sexual pheromone scents.

Male snakes are polygynandrous (promiscuous), seeking a new mate as soon as they've finished breeding. Females are able to store a partner's sperm, ejecting it if a more suitable mate comes along.

After mating, females retire to birthing dens, continuing to hunt and feed over a gestation period of 2 or 3 months (depending on cold) before bearing a clutch of about fifteen to fifty young, depending on a mother's size and health. Baby garter snakes are immediately abandoned.

Behavior

Garter snakes are most active during the day, and on especially warm nights. With evening's chill, they crawl under logs, debris, even in garages, to await the warmth of morning. In the morning, they move to open places, including roads, railroad grades, and hiking trails, where the sun enables them to regain a normal body temperature of about 30 degrees Centigrade. In the middle of the day, if the sun makes these basking places too hot, the snakes seek shaded spots, taking refuge in the same enclosed places where they sleep.

Common garter snakes are sociable, though they spend much time alone during summer. When two snakes meet, they communicate through a system of chemical scents, composed of lipids (fatty acids), exuded through their skins. These scents are used to advertise sexual availability and gender, although a number of male snakes are endowed with female lipids that cause other males to court them. Lipid-borne pheromones help garter snakes to meet when they gather for denning in the fall.

At the onset of winter, garter snakes congregate in a single large burrow below the frost line, where the heat generated by constantly writhing bodies helps to keep them from freezing until spring. Trails used by garter snakes are well established and permanent around mating and denning places, and are followed by newborns when they leave the den.

Garters are both predator and prey; newborns may be eaten by frogs, toads, turtles, and even some insects, larger snakes by hawks, foxes, raccoons, opossums, and other snakes.

With a flight speed of 3 miles per hour, garter snakes are easily caught. When cornered, they coil like a viper, and may hiss. When handled, they often bite, harmlessly, to frighten off captors. Perhaps most effective is the habit of exuding foul-smelling chemicals through its skin.

Garter snakes are popular pets, and biologists warn that overcollection for that reason has already caused a decline of this environmentally important species. That problem is especially serious in the north, where denning snakes gather in large numbers and are therefore more easily collected. One subspecies, the San Francisco garter snake (*Thamnophis sirtalis tetrataenia*), was placed on the endangered species list in 1967.

CORN SNAKE
(*Elaphe guttata*)

Variegated body markings make corn snakes popular as pets.

This member of the rat snake genus (*Elaphe*) is also known as the red rat snake. Often mistaken for vipers because of blotched markings on their backs, they are nonvenomous, but larger individuals may inflict a painful bite when handled. The orange-colored eastern race is sometimes mistaken for a copperhead (*Agkistrodon contortrix*). The darker brown-on-gray western, or Great Plains, race resembles a rattlesnake (*Crotalus*), except that it has no rattles. True rat snakes (*Elaphe obsoleta*) exhibit considerable color variation, or race, within the same species, being black, yellow, gray.

Geographic Range

Eastern corn snakes are found from southern New Jersey south through Florida, and west into Louisiana and parts of Kentucky. The species is most abundant in Florida and the southeastern U.S.

Habitat

Corn snakes inhabit woodlands, rocky sunlit hillsides, and meadows. They also occupy crawlspaces under barns and outbuildings. Preferred habitats include a stream or pond, but they are frequently found far from water.

Physical Characteristics

Mass: Corn snakes usually weigh usually less than a pound, occasionally in excess of 4 pounds.

Body: Typically slender, the body is 2 to 6 feet long.

Tail: The tail is slender, without rattles.

Tracks: Corn snakes leave undulating grooves in loose sand on dirt roads and trails.

Scat: Seldom seen, scat consists of small, elongated blobs that are black and white with varying shades of brown or gray, depending on the snake's diet.

Coloration: Nonvenomous, corn snakes mimic venomous species, such as the copperhead, ranging in color from orange to brownish yellow, with large black-edged red blotches down the middle of the back. Alternating rows of black and white marks on the belly resemble an ear of Indian corn, and are believed to be the origin of the common name. Considerable variation occurs in the coloration and patterns of individuals, depending on age and region. Hatchlings are more subdued, lacking the brighter color and contrast of adults.

Sign: Corn snakes shed skins during summer months. Skins retain markings, but without coloration.

Vocalizations: Normally silent, corn snakes may hiss when threatened. They are also among several species that vibrate their tails against foliage to make a sound that mimics rattlesnake rattles.

Life span: Corn snakes live up to 23 years in captivity, generally much less in the wild.

A female corn snake with a clutch of eggs.

Diet

Corn snakes don't feed every day because their digestive systems work slowly. Hatchlings feed on small lizards and tree frogs; adults feed on mice, nesting birds, and roosting bats. This snake's small, inward-pointing teeth cannot kill prey, so this species constricts its prey, using their coils to suffocate animals before swallowing them whole, usually head first.

Mating Habits

Corn snakes breed from March to May, earlier in southern climes. Impregnated females deposit a clutch of about twenty eggs from late May to July in rotting stumps, decaying vegetation, and other moist locations that will remain at about 80 degrees Fahrenheit until they hatch, in about 60 days. Eggs are abandoned soon after they're laid, and hatch from July through September, earliest in the north. Hatchlings are about 3 inches long at birth and mature at about 2 years. Little real data has been established about the reproductive behaviors of corn snakes.

Behavior

Corn snakes are active day and night so long as temperatures remain near 70 degrees, and are more nocturnal than many North American species. Good climbers, they ascend trees to capture birds, stealing eggs that are small enough to swallow. Although secretive and seldom seen, they enter barns and outbuildings in search of rodents, slithering through burrows to find litters of newborn mice and voles.

When it's too hot or cold, or if the snake has a full belly, it conceals itself under fallen trees, under farm outbuildings, or in rock cracks until it must hunt or mate. Corn snakes are not endangered, but they are listed by the state of Florida as a species of special concern because they face habitat loss in the lower Florida Keys.

EASTERN HOGNOSE SNAKE
(*Heterodon platirhinos*)

Often mistaken for a venomous species, the big eastern hognose snake is harmless to humans, and extremely beneficial for rodent control.

The family of hognose snakes, so called because of their distinctive upturned snouts, is composed of twenty species that inhabit both North and South America, with at least one species being present from southern Canada to Patagonia. Only the eastern hognose is showcased here, but all members share the moniker "puff adder," an allusion to their ability to rise up, spread their necks like a cobra, and hiss loudly in a display of ferocity. Despite their apparent aggressiveness, hognose snakes are harmless to humans, and the eastern hognose especially is known for playing dead when confronted with danger.

Geographic Range

The genus *Heterodon* is endemic to North America and includes the eastern hognose snake and five other species. The range of the eastern hognose includes most of the eastern portion of the U.S., from southern New Hampshire south to Florida, and then extends west to Texas and up to southeastern South Dakota and Minnesota.

Habitat

All species of hognose snake prefers woodland environments, although the eastern hognose is sometimes found in brush-lands and overgrown clearcuts. All habitats include forest debris under which the snakes can root with their upturned noses in search of prey. A temperate species, *H. platyrhinos* can tolerate four-season environments down to winter temperatures below 20 degrees Fahrenheit.

Physical Characteristics

Mass: The eastern hognose is stout, sometimes weighing in excess of 4 pounds.

Body: This snake's body is up to 3 feet long, occasionally longer. It is a short, thickly built snake with a pointed, upturned snout and wide neck. The anal scale plate is divided into halves. Although considered nonvenomous to humans, the hognose possesses a pair of enlarged teeth at the rear of the upper jaw that inject venom into prey as it's swallowed. These teeth puncture and deflate toads that swell with air as protection against being swallowed; they give the genus its name, *Heterodon*, which translates to "different tooth." Humans would need to insert part of their anatomy into the back of the snake's mouth to receive a venomous bite.

Tail: The tail is blunt, with no rattles.

Tracks: Hognose snakes leave serpentine grooves in dry sand, unusually wide compared with snakes of similar length.

Scat: Seldom seen, the scat is mucous-like, elongated blobs of black, white, and varying shades of gray and brown.

Coloration: The eastern hognose is yellow to light brown or grayish, and often tinted with rust-red. The species exhibits considerable variation in color and markings; some herpetologists believe this is because it is a relatively new member of the hognose genus, and hasn't yet evolved a permanent camouflage color scheme.

Sign: Eastern hognoses shed skins with keeled (ridged) scales in rows of twenty-five scales per row.

Vocalizations: Generally silent, the eastern hognose will hiss loudly when cornered and is more vocal than most snakes. The snake also vibrates its tail against ground debris to imitate a rattlesnake.

Life span: This species can live 10 to 15 years, but most do not survive their first year.

Diet

The forest-dwelling hognose snake's diet reflects its habitat. senses of smell and heat detection can locate prey hiding beneath leaf litter, which it unearths by rooting with its namesake hog nose.

The hognose's diet consists of toads, frogs, mice, salamanders, and small lizards. Hognoses are especially immune to toxins excreted from a toad's parotid glands and are among few species that eat toads predominantly. After unearthing toads from their daytime burrows with its snout, the hognose swallows them, usually, head first. The toad inflates its body by gulping in air to prevent itself from being swallowed, but a pair of venom-producing teeth located at the rear of the snake's upper jaw are adapted to defeat that defense by puncturing the toad's skin, deflating it. Deflated and paralyzed by venom, the toad becomes easy to ingest. Enlarged adrenaline glands enable the snake to resist the bufotoxins secreted from parotid glands.

Mating Habits

Little data has been established about the hognose snake's mating habits, making it an ideal candidate for field research.

What is known is that eastern hognose snakes generally mate between May and June, depending on temperature and latitude, but in southern regions, where temperatures remain warm year round, they mate a second time in August or September. There is no bond between mates, and they separate after breeding. Females seek out depressions or abandoned dens in soft soil in late June or July, depositing a clutch of whitish, ovoid, thin-shelled eggs that are about 1.25 inches long. Clutch sizes appear to reflect the mother's size and state of health, varying widely in number from four to sixty eggs. Eggs are abandoned after being laid.

Sun-warmed earth causes the eggs to hatch after 50 to 65 days, usually in August or September. Incubating eggs actually grow during the gestation period, resulting in large hatchlings that may be from 6 to 10 inches long. Generally lighter colored than adults, hatchlings are otherwise duplicates of their parents.

Young snakes spend their time in hiding, feeding on small insects, and grow quickly their first year. Other snakes prey on hatchlings, as do opossums, skunks, ravens, and birds. Toads that are eaten by adult hognose snakes will also prey on

The eastern hognose is a big, aggressive-acting snake, but it's actually harmless to humans. (Photo by Jeff LeClere.)

hatchlings. If a hatchling survives until it reaches adulthood at 3 years, it fears only large predators.

Behavior

Hognose snakes are best known for the way they react when threatened. The hognose first tries to withdraw, but, if cornered, it coils its body like a rattlesnake, raises its head, and spreads its neck like a cobra. The image is enhanced by loud hissing as the snake undulates, waving its head back and forth as it writhes. These behaviorisms have earned it monikers like "puff adder," "blowsnake," and "American cobra."

If an enemy persists, the snake secretes mal-odorous lipids from glands in its skin and defecates, smearing unpleasant odors over its body. The snake may strike at an enemy, but this is a bluff; its nose might butt the assailant, but its mouth remains closed.

If an attacker isn't discouraged by these feints, the snake falls onto its back, with tongue lolling out, and plays dead.

Rarely seen with its mouth open, this hognose displays the two venomous fangs at the back of its throat, designed to puncture inflated toads.

If the snake is rolled onto its belly, it immediately turns over onto its back again. The belly-up position is thought to keep the snake's most distasteful side presented to an enemy. When an enemy has withdrawn, the snake rights itself and moves off.

The scenario just described, though typical, isn't absolute; large, old snakes that are accustomed to being near the top of the food chain may refuse to play dead, while younger, less confident hognoses may feign death at the sight of a human.

Like garter snakes, the eastern hognose is active in temperatures cold enough to send most serpents into a den. Resistance to cold makes it one of the first snakes out of hibernation in spring, and one of the last to den in autumn, which gives the hognose a survival advantage over other snakes.

Eastern hognose populations are stable throughout their range, but there is concern about the southern hognose (*Heterodon simus*), which is thought to have become extinct in some habitats. Development of woodlands on which the snake depends is blamed, but also a factor is the spread of fire ants, an aggressive predator of hognose hatchlings. At the time of this writing, there are fewer than 10,000 *Heterodon simus* snakes, and the species is considered threatened.

EASTERN DIAMONDBACK RATTLESNAKE
(*Crotalus adamanteus*)

Like all rattlesnakes, the eastern diamondback possesses tail rattles to warn off threats, but the rattling often goes unnoticed in wind-rustled underbrush. (Photo by Barbara Magnusson and Larrry Kimball.)

Considered by many to be the most dangerous snake in North America, the eastern diamondback has earned that reputation by proving fatal to 40 percent of people who are bitten. Its close cousin, the western diamondback (*Crotalus atrox*), inhabits open areas in the desert southwest, but this

rattlesnake occupies more junglelike terrain, where surprise encounters with humans are more likely.

Slightly larger than its western cousin, the eastern diamondback is disproportionately more dangerous because its venom contains both a tissue-dissolving hemotoxin common to all rattlesnakes, but also a fast acting neurotoxin, like that a cobra. Together, these poisons ensure that prey is overcome swiftly, before escaping into dense foliage.

Because human encounters are likely to be at close range, hikers should exercise extreme caution where this species lives. The snake will normally advertise itself by buzzing rattles on its tail, but, like the deadly fer-de-lance (*Bothrops atrox*) snake of SothAmerica, eastern diamondbacks are known to remain quiet under foliage in hope that an enemy will pass. With either species, hikers are well served by carrying a long walking stick with which to poke inside shadowed places, thereby forcing hiding snakes to reveal themselves, or to retreat.

Geographic Range

Eastern diamondbacks inhabit coastal lowlands, from southeast North Carolina down through Florida and its keys, and westward to eastern Louisiana. (Western diamondbacks are found from central Texas through southern New Mexico, Arizona, and California, extending southward into central Mexico.)

Habitat

Eastern diamondbacks prefer foliated environments, including dry swamps, palmetto groves, and pine forests. They're seldom found in wet swamps or marshes, but may inhabit dry shorelines. Despite an apparent aversion to water, they have been seen swimming in shallow waters of the Atlantic as they migrate between islands off the Florida coast.

Physical Characteristics

Mass: Eastern diamondbacks usually weigh about 6 pounds, but may exceed 14 pounds.

Body: Although they can grow up to 8 feet long, they are usually about 4 feet. long. It has a broad, triangular head with large sensory pits located below and between eyes and nostrils. Long, tubular fangs are normally folded backward to lie flat against the upper palate.

Tail: The tail is white with black peripheral rings and tipped with segmented rattles stacked atop one another in a cone shape. Each rattle is a remnant of the last scale, left when the snake molted. End rattles may be broken on older individuals.

Tracks: The diamondback's tracks are serpentine undulations.

Scat: Typically snakelike, this snake's scat is an elongated mass of white, black, and brown.

Coloration: A row of large dark diamonds with brown centers and cream borders run down the the length of the back. The background color of the body ranges from olive to brown, to almost black. The tail is usually a different shade, brownish or gray, and banded with dark rings. The head has a light-bordered dark stripe running diagonally through the eye. The young are similar to the adults in color pattern.

Sign: Signs include shed skins and discarded broken rattles.

Vocalizations: The diamondback is generally silent, but its tail vibrates with a buzzing rattle when agitated.

Life span: This species lives up to 20 years.

Diet

Carnivorous. and primarily nocturnal, *Crotalus adamanteus* and its western cousin prey on small mammals, birds, reptiles, amphibians, large insects, and sometimes fish. Larger snakes may prey on rabbits or muskrats.

Specialized to prey on small, warm-blooded animals, eastern diamondbacks and other pit vipers use thermal sensory pits to detect animals from minute differences in temperature. Prey is also detected by scent through the snake's forked tongue, which flicks outward constantly when the snake hunting.

Prey is stalked quietly by slithering in close, then swiftly lunging forward with mouth open and fangs poised to strike. Striking distance is up to 75 percent of the snake's body length, meaning that an 8-foot rattler may strike a victim from as far as 6 feet. Fangs are driven into the prey's body, and a dose of venom is injected. Venom flow is metered by voluntary muscles, permitting the snake to regulate dosage to match prey size, but there appears to be no preference about where a bite is administered. Fangs are sometimes broken off to remain in the victim, but rattlesnakes can replace lost teeth up to four times per year from reserve teeth carried in the upper jaw.

Once bitten, prey animals are typically released, and fangs return to their resting position against the upper jaw. This helps to ensure that a snake isn't injured by holding a victim that may bite or scratch. Released prey attempts to escape, but is quickly overcome by venom. The neurotoxic component immediately paralyzes heart and respiratory systems, while hemotoxins degrade blood vessels, causing internal hemorrhaging. The hemotoxin literally softens a prey's tissues, making it easier to swallow and digest.

After ingesting prey head-first in typical snake fashion, the now lumpy, sluggish snake retires to a secluded hollow to digest its meal. Digestive processes are very slow but efficient, assimilating bone, hair, and other body parts that would pass intact through the intestines of most predators. Presuming a prey animal as large as the diamondback could swallow, 2 weeks may pass before it needs to eat again, and during that interval the rattler will remain sedentary unless disturbed.

Habitats of the eastern diamondback provide access to water not available to desert-dwelling cousins, but either species can survive a year on an amount of water equivalent to its own body weight. More water is required during seasonal molts, when skin is shed to accommodate body growth, and new skin loses moisture through desiccation as it toughens. As with the western diamondback, much of the water needed to survive is absorbed from the bodies of prey.

Mating Habits

Eastern diamondbacks of either gender attain sexual maturity at 3 years. Mating occurs in spring soon after adults emerge from hibernation. Ritualized territorial fights are common among males, but the combatants rarely bite one another. Instead, they wrestle, entwining one another in a contest of strength. When it becomes obvious that one is the stronger, the weaker diamondback retreats to seek another prospective mate.

Females are passive during courtship, remaining inactive while the male slithers in jerky movements atop her body, flicking his tongue continuously. Copulation occurs when the male forces his tail beneath the female's tail, and she accepts by raising her tail to allow insertion of his forked hemipenis. Intercourse typically lasts several hours, with numerous resting periods.

Gestation is a comparatively long 167 days. Being ovoviviparous, young are hatched from eggs carried within the mother's womb. The ten to twenty young break free of the thin membranes encasing them in a process that may last up to 5 hours. Newborns are fanged and venomous, and remain with the mother for no more than a day. Mothers provide no care or protection.

Born at the onset of autumn, young snakes must immediately learn to hunt and find suitable shelter (an existing rodent burrow) in which to spend the coming winter. Probably most will become prey to birds, lizards, toads, and other snakes. Young grow fast, at roughly 1 foot per year until reaching puberty.

Behavior

Like western diamondbacks, eastern diamondbacks are quick to adopt a defensive posture, but often prefer to lie motionless, hoping that an enemy will pass without notice. This passive reaction actually increases the danger they pose to humans, who might inadvertently walk close enough to panic a hidden rattler.

Diamondbacks are often touted as causing more fatalities than any venomous snake in North America, but casualties are infrequent enough to be nearly insignificant, and nearly all bites are caused by victims. No snake considers humans as prey, and none is eager to risk certain death in a conflict with a foe twenty times its own size. The best way to avoid a coiled rattlesnake is to take one step backward—sound advice for dealing with any species of venomous snake.

The rattles that give diamondbacks and other rattlesnakes their names are actually the terminal scales of a snake's tail, left behind each time a growing snake sheds its skin. Rattles were once thought to be a means of communication, but we now know that snakes are deaf, able only to detect vibrations through the ground. Instead, it appears that rattles were evolved for communicating with larger animals, as a means to avoid being stepped on.

The frequency at which rattles are shaken indicate their owner's level of fear: a slow shaking like that of a maraca (a rattle used in music) is used to alert intruders to the snake's presence; rattling increases in frequency as the snake's level of agitation increases, until the sound becomes a buzz at about 50 cycles per second. This sound, which has been described as the sound of sizzling of bacon, is accompanied by a coiled body that presents an enemy with a smaller target, and a tongue that flicks rapidly to gather as much scent information as possible from the surrounding air.

A successful predator in its own right, the eastern diamondback also serves as prey to a number of carnivores. Larger individuals are preyed on by hawks, owls, and eagles, and at least some coyotes have a limited immunity to venom. Perhaps most dangerous to snakes of any species are pigs, both wild and domestic; swine are especially resistant to snake venoms, and any serpent unlucky enough to attract the attention of a pig is almost certain to be killed and eaten.

While neither eastern or western diamondbacks frequent regions that receive snow in winter, they tend to gather in communal dens, called hibernacula, during the coldest months, and may be found at elevations as high as 2,400 feet. Suitable hibernacula include caves and rock cracks, hollow logs, and animal burrows. The snakes don't actually hibernate but rather gather in a lethargic mass that uses little energy, while keeping all members warm enough to survive until spring.

Demonized by Old World immigrants, the eastern diamondback and its cousins were revered by most tribes of American Indians. Rattles were used as religious and ceremonial icons, and some tribes practiced rituals in which a vision-seeker would be purposely bitten, in the belief that venom-induced illness would carry him to the spirit world. While few accidental snakebites prove to be fatal, allowing oneself to be bitten numerous times is very dangerous, and some of those who traveled to the spirit world remained there.

While not victimized by the carnival-like "roundups" that have driven western diamondbacks to the brink of extinction in places, eastern diamondbacks also face danger at the hands of humans. Continuing destruction of their habitat from housing and other development is forcing the reptiles to occupy increasingly smaller areas, while widespread fear of snakes evokes an unwarranted kill-on-sight response from people who find a snake near their homes. Eastern diamondback populations also face danger from commercial snake hunters who gather them (under permit in Florida and North Carolina) for sale as pets.

Turtles

All turtles and tortises belong to the order Testudines, which includes all reptiles that have a hard, plated carapace over a bony shell on their backs, and a hard, plated underbelly, called a plastron.

Tortises spend their lives on land, have vegetarian diets, and are equipped with flat feet that are adapted to walking and digging. Turtles spend their lives in or near water, have webbed feet evolved for swimming, and eat a more carnivorous diet.

Turtles are considered to be cold blooded, but at least one, the blandings turtle (*Emydoidea blandingi*) has been observed swimming under ice on frozen ponds. All turtles and tortoises

are hatched from eggs that have been buried in soft soil, then abandoned, by their mothers.

Families that comprise the order of turtles include Carettochelyidae (pignose turtles), Chelidae (Austro-American side-necked turtles), Cheloniidae (sea turtles), Chelydridae (snapping turtles), Dermatemydidae (Mesoamerican river turtle), Dermochelyidae (leatherback turtle), Emydidae (pond turtles and box turtles), Kinosternidae (mud turtles and musk turtles), Pelomedusidae (Afro-American side-necked turtles), Testudinidae (tortoises), and Trionychidae (softshell turtles).

COMMON SNAPPING TURTLE
(*Chelydra serpentina*)

Second only to the painted turtle *(Chrysemys picta)* as the most widespread turtle in North America, the northern snapper is the dominant aquatic carnivore in most habitats where it lives. This species is second in size only to the alligator snapping turtle *(Macroclemys temminckii)* of the southeastern U.S.

Snapping turtles, and the northern snapper especially, also differ from most turtles and tortoises by having a carapace and plastron that are too small for the animal to retreat into completely.

Whether a too-small shell is the cause of this species' legendary ferocity when cornered on land is left to conjecture, but an adult northern snapper has little need to fear any animal except humans.

Geographic Range

Chelydra serpentina's northern range extends from southern Alberta, Canada, eastward to Nova Scotia. To the south, the species' range covers all the United States from the Rocky Mountains eastward to the Atlantic coast, and along the Gulf of Mexico into central Texas.

Habitat

Because they spend their lives in water, northern snapping turtles require a body of freshwater in their habitats. The species is not found in saltwater, nor does it inhabit swift-running streams or rivers. Most preferred are backwaters and beaver ponds, where muddy bottoms and an abundance of aquatic vegetation provide good places to hide, forage, and hibernate.

Physical Characteristics

Mass: This snapping turtle can weigh up to 70 pounds, but typically is 35 to 40 pounds at maturity.

Body: The snapper has a comparatively large head that cannot be withdrawn under the carapace, as with most turtles and tortoises. Carapace length is up to 19 inches. The snapper has powerful jaws, hooked beak, and a long neck that is normally retracted. The skin on its upper surface is covered with bumpy projections (tubercules). Legs are thickly built and powerful, covered with scaly skin and tubercles, and terminating in large, webbed feet. The plastron is small, covering only the vital organs in the belly, leaving extremeties exposed.

Tail: The snapper's tail is nearly as long as its carapace, thickly muscled, and topped with sawtoothed keels, reminiscent of an alligator's tail.

Tracks: Five toes are on the forefeet, four on the hind feet; each toe is tipped with a thick, sharply pointed claw. The snapper's tracks are generally not perfect but show scrape marks where the foot slipped as the turtle's heavy body was pushed forward, usually with claw marks evident. Tracks print individually, without overlap, in pairs, with the hind print behind front print, because the stride is short, reflecting short legs. In soft mud or sand, the carapace drags intermittently, leaving a shallow trough. The tail also drags, leaving a serpentine channel between tracks. The straddle is variable, depending on a snapper size, but always comparatively wide because of the snapper's plastron. Stride is also variable, depending on size, but equates to roughly one-half of the carapace length.

Scat: The scat is misshapen but generally cylindrical. Color varies with diet but is usually dark brown or black. Adult scats are generally 1 to 1.5 inches long. Scats are usually deposited in water, but are sometimes found along shorelines and on partially submerged logs where the turtle basked and marked territory.

Coloration: Carapace color varies from dark brown to tan, and may even be black. Snapping turtle necks, legs, and tails are olive or yellowish, with heads being a darker shade. The plastron is white or yellow, darkest in older individuals.

Sign: In spring, usually May or June, look for narrow excavated holes, or large disturbances in sandy soil, where egg-laying females buried a nest, usually near water. Flattened trails in grasses indicate a snapper's passing. Clouds of silt under stream banks indicate a snapping turtle burying itself in mud.

Vocalizations: Silent unless cornered on land, a threatened turtle may hiss and snap its jaws.

Life span: The exact lifespan of this species is unknown, but it lives at least 40 years. In many cases, turtles have outlived their owners.

Diet

Like all turtles (and unlike tortoises), snapping turtles are omnivorous and will eat nearly anything organic, especially meat. Diets are dictated by available foods, but northern snappers consume aquatic and shoreline vegetation, carrion, and nearly any small animal that comes within reach of their powerful jaws. Being able to subsist on a broad variety of foods increases the species' chances of survival under changing environmental conditions.

Northern snapping turtles are efficient hunters. Favored hunting spots include undercut banks and beneath sunken logs, because these places offer concealment for the turtle, and are preferred hiding places for small fish and crayfish that serve as food.

Unlike its larger cousin, the alligator snapping turtle, which lies in wait with mouth open wide and its pink, wormlike tongue waving as bait, the northern snapper relies on stealth and camouflage. When a fish swims within range, the northern snapper's powerful jaws shoot out, propelled by its muscular, extendable neck, and its beak snaps shut on the prey's body. The prey is gripped tightly by the jaws, while strong, sharp clawed forefeet shred its body into pieces small enough to swallow. The snapping behavior appears to be instinctive, because captive turtles raised from hatchlings lunge at even inanimate foods.

The size of a snapping turtle's prey changes as it grows: hatchlings subsist on insects, fish, and crustaceans, but large turtles have been witnessed snapping ducklings and goslings from the surface of shallow waters, along with snakes, frogs, and an occasional young muskrat.

Although air breathers with lungs, snapping turtles, like frogs, can absorb the oxygen they require through their skin while under water. They will raise their snouts slightly above water to breathe air from time to time, but can remain submerged for hours at a time.

Snapping turtles grow continuously throughout their lives, with some old individuals reaching a carapace length of 2 feet or more. Their feeding habits are more voracious than most other reptile species, and snappers are nearly always hungry.

Mating Habits

Male northern snapping turtles become sexually mature at 5 years, females not until 7 years. Mating occurs in April or May among northern populations, but may occur as late as November in the southernmost part of the species' range. Sexual maturity seems dictated more by size than age. Malnourished individuals may take longer to reach puberty, whereas those that are especially well fed may breed earlier.

Similarly the mating season depends more on warming temperatures than dates. A cold spring will delay procreational activities. Because snapping turtle eggs are incubated in an underground nest, the earth must maintain a constant temperature between 60 and 70 degrees Farenheit.

How male and female snapping turtles attract one another is under study, but urine-based pheromones probably play a large part. Females may not mate every year, carrying live sperm from a previous mating within their reproductive organs for several years before laying eggs. This process, called delayed implantation, is seen in numerous species, and helps to ensure that females are physically strong enough to withstand the demands of gestation and birth without draining their own reserves.

Copulation between snappers generally occurs at or near the eater's edge. Mating is conventional, with males mounting receptive females from behind. If a female accepts the male's advances, she pushes her long tail to one side and allows him to climb onto her carapace, where he uses strong, clawed forefeet to firmly grasp the edges of her shell. He then curls his own tail downward until their genitalia meet, and deposits his sperm within her cloaca (roughly, a female turtle's vagina).

No lasting bond exists between snapping turtle mates, and when a female becomes impregnated, she abandons the male. Precisely how long is required for a clutch to develop within the female is dictated by her state of health, but 3 to 4 weeks is average, and egg laying always coincides with warm weather.

When she's ready to lay eggs, typically in late May or early June, a female leaves the water to find a nesting place on dry, digable ground well above the water table. Preferred nesting sites are in sandy soil along shorelines, but females have been observed laying eggs a half mile from open water, sometimes crossing paved roads. Loose soil is necessary, because nests are excavated to a depth of roughly 8 inches with the hind feet, but cinder-filled railroad grades are among favored nesting places.

An egg-heavy female snapping turtle looking for soft sand, near water in which to dig a nest to deposit her clutch.

Nests begin as a broad, shallow hole wide enough to accommodate the female's rear, then taper to a narrow, downward-sloping tunnel about 2 inches in diameter. At the bottom of this tunnel is an enlarged chamber that receives the eggs.

When her nest is ready, a female settles her rear over the hole and lays her clutch of round eggs, each about the size of a ping-pong ball. Clutch sizes depend on the size and health of the female; average is 40, but a clutch of more than 100 eggs was recorded from an exceptionally large turtle in Nebraska.

Eggs are creamy white, with a flexible shell, like a ping-pong ball, but softer. A flexible shell permits the eggs to roll down the tunnel-like nest opening and land atop one another without sustaining damage. After depositing her eggs in a process that may take several hours, the female refills the nest with loose soil and leaves. Elapsed time from start to

completion may take 4 hours. She may return to the same nesting site in subsequent years to lay a new clutch.

Hundreds of eggs may be laid within a single square mile, but few will hatch. With a taste and texture very much like a small chicken egg, snapping turtle eggs are a favorite food for every carnivore capable of excavating them. Skunks, raccoons, badgers, and bears take a heavy toll by eating whole clutches, and I've personally been guilty of eating a dozen fried snapping turtle eggs for breakfast while backpacking. Despite heavy predation, snapping turtle populations remain healthy.

Most snapping turtle eggs hatch after about 9 weeks, usually in late July or August, but cool weather can delay hatching as much as two months. Hatchlings, about 1 inch in diameter, tear free of their eggs using a typically reptilian "egg tooth" (also seen in snakes, lizards, and birds) that later falls out, and dig upward to the surface. For their first 2 weeks, newborns carry a fat-rich yolk sac under their plastrons as they learn to forage for plants and insects.

Like hatchlings of every turtle species, young snappers face a host of predators that range from muskrats and snakes to raccoons and most birds. Instinct compels the little turtles to immediately head for water, where they'll find sanctuary from most terrestrial predators. But even in the relative safety of a pond, hatchlings must hide from large fish, watersnakes, herons, otters, and larger turtles for their first 3 years of life. Presuming an abundant supply of food is available, a good rule of thumb for growth is about 1 inch of length per year for the first 5 years. At 5 years of age, few predators pose a danger to the snapper's powerful beak and strong armor.

Behavior

Turtles aren't especially gregarious, but northern snapping turtles are the least social of any. Excepting brief sexual encounters, neither juveniles nor adults of either gender are tolerant of one another. Obedient to the natural law that prohibits willingly killing one's own kind, territorial battles are seldom more than slightly injurious to either party. Lacerations from claws, and bites to the tail or hind legs of a retreating opponent, are most common, but combatants rarely injure one another.

Snapping turtles don't give the same consideration to other species. Large, usually female, painted turtles, especially, are frequently found decapitated along shorelines during mating and egg-laying seasons. Such beheadings result from lopsided territorial battles in which painted turtles face off against much stronger snapping turtles over territorial or nesting rights. Painted turtle heads are never found with the body, and are apparently eaten by the snapping turtles who bite them off. The fact that decapitated turtles are typically found with their meaty legs and tails intact indicates that this behavior is territorial.

Snapping turtles on land can be very aggressive, and will bite hard given an opportunity. In the water, snapping turtles are docile, and swimmers need not fear them. But a snapper cornered on land may stand its ground, even attack. With a running speed of about 1 mile per hour, there's not much danger of being run down by a charging turtle, and most such attacks are attempts to escape, or to frighten a foe into withdrawing.

Snapping turtles are a known vector for salmonella bacteria. If a snapper must be handled, wear leather gloves, and grasp it firmly at either side of the carapace, keeping hands and forearms away from its sharp claws, and especially away from its long, extendable neck. Turtle hunters who take snappers as meat (turtle soup is a delicacy) recommend carrying the animal by its tail, but researchers consider this method inhumane and injurious to a turtle's spine. However a turtle is handled, always wash your hands thoroughly afterward, and especially before eating.

About the Author

Len McDougall is a professional outdoorsman with four decades of sometimes hard experience in the north woods. Len is an internationally recognized survival instructor/tracker, and author of the books *The Encyclopedia of Tracks & Scats, The Log Cabin: An Adventure, Practical Outdoor Survival, Practical Outdoor Projects, The Complete Tracker, The Outdoors Almanac, The Snowshoe Handbook, The Field & Stream Wilderness Survival Handbook* and *Made for the Outdoors*. He teaches survival, snowshoeing, kayaking, dogsledding, and tracking classes, and works as a wilderness guide.

Len's interest in all things natural began early. Having grown up with youngsters of the Odawa and Ojibwa tribes in Northern Michigan, the elders considered him more Nish-na-bee (Indian) than Chee-mook-a-mon (white), and accepted the Scots-Irish kid as one of their own. With that status, he received the teachings of the grandfathers, who are obligated by culture to pass what they know to the next generation. With no written language, the tribes had already lost much, but what remained was enough to strike young Len's heart with a passion that would subsequently consume his life.

At twelve Len was backpacking solo for a week at a time in summer. At thirteen he was running a trapline to provide his family with meat and with money from the sale of pelts. At sixteen, he nearly died of hypothermia during his first solo winter camping trip when an unpredicted blizzard buried his camp. The following summer he was bitten by a Massasauga rattlesnake and survived three days alone in the woods before finding his way back home ("Snakebitten!," *Michigan Out-of-Doors*, October 1985; *Woods-N-Water News*, July 2004). At twenty-three, he was given up for dead by local authorities while backpacking in -35 degree windchills. At twenty-seven, he was again given up for dead under similar conditions. At thirty-eight, he was stranded for three days alone in a blizzard with windchills below -65 degrees, but no one considered him to be in danger. At age forty-five, he built a log cabin homestead, with hand-dug well, using only hand tools, "just to see what the old-timers went through" (*The Log Cabin: An Adventure*, Globe Pequot Press, June 2003).

In March 1997, Len discovered the first pair of mating timber wolves to migrate south to Michigan's Lower Peninsula in 100 years. For the next five years, he guided biologists from the Natural Resources Commission of the Little Traverse Bay Band of Odawa Indians into local wolf habitats to gather data on what has now become a thriving population. Len also served as Team Tracker for the Northern Michigan Wolf Detection and Habitat Survey Team.

Having forged a career in Manufacturing Quality Control for ten years prior to becoming a writer, Len has found a niche in evaluating and writing about outdoor products. He has evaluated products for more than 150 manufacturers, including Coleman, Vasque, Winchester, Current Designs, Pelican International, Atlas Snowshoes, La Crosse, Kelty, MSR, Jansport, Kodak, Pentax, Nikon, Slumberjack, Tasco, Timex, Simmons, Buck Knives, Brunton, and Remington. His real-life, long-term field tests find flaws that were not apparent in less rigorous trials, and his findings have been used numerous times to improve existing products. He has been called on to evaluate conceptual designs and prototypes before they reach the marketplace, and Consumers Digest has hired him to award its coveted Best Buy rating to more than twenty outdoor products.

Born in 1956, Len says he's had more financially lucrative jobs than working in and writing about the great out-of-doors, but none have been more fulfilling. He likes to think that what he writes is a contribution to the well-being of fellow outdoorsman, and he openly admits to being an idealistic fool who's out to change the world into a better, nicer place for tomorrow's generations.

A grandfather himself, Len has assumed the obligation to pass along what he learned from his Indian mentors. He smiles without humor at the recent trend toward being "green." "I've always known that if Hollywood said it was cool to be an environmentalist, everyone would be one." Although considered a loner by the people who know him, Len prides himself on lending a helping hand to those in need. In his own words, "There are only two rules to a good life: Always do the right thing, and always be the Good Guy. Everything else will follow."

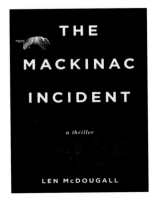

The Mackinac Incident

A Thriller

by Len McDougall

Fifteen miles off the coast of New Brunswick, Canada, a Soviet-era diesel submarine off-loads four men before being intercepted by a US Navy vessel patrolling the area. The men make up a team of Al Qaeda–trained specialists skilled in the black arts of terrorist warfare and are headed by a man who has billions of dollars in oil money with which to indulge his murderous fantasies. What they do next will determine the fates of thousands of Americans.

Rod Eliot, an aging ex-con turned survival expert, stands between them and one of the most devastating plots ever hatched by the deviated mind of a killer: to blow up the five-mile-long Mackinac Bridge and detonate enough plutonium to contaminate the area for decades. When an encounter with the bomb-toting terrorists occurs deep in the woods of the Upper Peninsula, Eliot finds himself in a dangerous cat-and-mouse game with these murderers. Rod may be the only person who can stop them. But he's in over his head.

Due to Eliot's checkered past, law enforcement officials have him pegged for the crimes that unfold over the next few days. Only one, a seasoned FBI agent who is on his trail, thinks Eliot is innocent and is willing to prove it.

$24.95 Hardcover • ISBN 978-1-62087-632-9

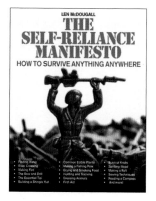

The Self-Reliance Manifesto

Essential Outdoor Survival Skills

by Len McDougall

Storm approaching? Need a fire? Out of water? Lost? Whatever situation you find yourself in, Len McDougall has probably been there himself and can get you out of trouble. He reveals his way of living and teaches readers how to have the same confidence in any scenario. In this comprehensive, fully-illustrated guide, McDougall reveals how to make water safe for drinking, build a fire in any conditions, find and build shelter, use basic medical skills, and more. McDougall has field-tested everything from kayaks, backpacks, and boots to cameras, tents, and water filters, and because of his research and experience, everyone can feel more safe.

$19.95 Paperback • ISBN 978-1-61608-061-7